SECRETS *of the* SOUTHERN TABLE

SECRETS *of the* SOUTHERN TABLE

A Food Lover's Tour of the Global South

Virginia Willis

PHOTOGRAPHS BY ANGIE MOSIER
FOREWORD BY SEAN BROCK

Houghton Mifflin Harcourt
Boston   New York   2018

For information about permission to reproduce selections from this book,
write to trade.permissions@hmhco.com or to Permissions,
Houghton Mifflin Harcourt Publishing Company, 3 Park Avenue, 19th Floor, New York, New York 10016.

hmhco.com

Library of Congress Cataloging-in-Publication Data
Names: Willis, Virginia, 1966– author. | Mosier, Angie, photographer.
Title: Secrets of the southern table a food lover's tour of the global South /
Virginia Willis ; photography by Angie Mosier ; foreword by Sean Brock.
Description: Boston : Houghton Mifflin Harcourt, 2018. | Includes index.
Identifiers: LCCN 2017059031 (print) | LCCN 2017051914 (ebook) | ISBN
9780544931831 (ebook) | ISBN 9780544932548 (paper over board)
Subjects: LCSH: Cooking, American—Southern style. | Cooking—Southern
States. | LCGFT: Cookbooks. Classification: LCC TX715.2.S68 (print) |
LCC TX715.2.S68 W5564 2018 (ebook) |
DDC 641.5975—dc23
LC record available at https://lccn.loc.gov/2017059031

Book design by Rachel Newborn

Printed in China
C&C 10 9 8 7 6 5 4 3 2 1

In hope of a nation where, in the words of
Dr. Martin Luther King Jr., people will
be judged not by the color of their skin,
but by the content of their character.

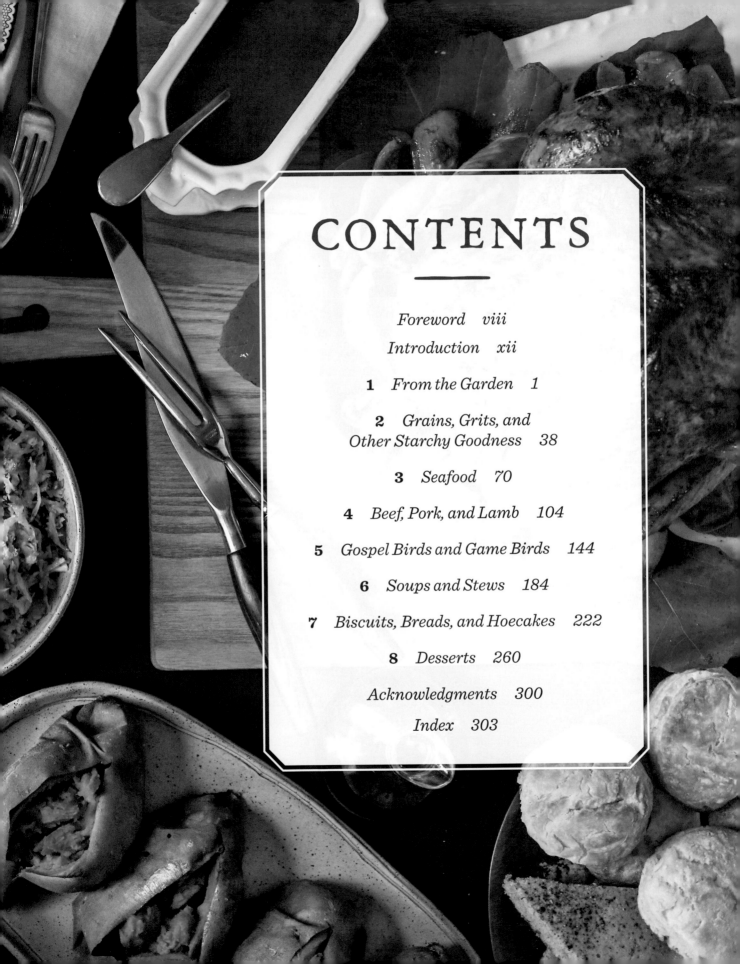

CONTENTS

FOREWORD

In 2011, I sat trembling with fear on a panel in Tokyo with some of the world's best chefs. We were all there to experience Japan and create a meal inspired by our experiences at the week's end. As I stood in front of the sea of Japanese journalists during a press conference, one reporter asked me why I had been chosen to participate since Southern food was merely ketchup on smoked meats and fried chicken. Her question was an earnest one and I sensed no condescension in her voice. KFC and "the Colonel" are often synonymous with Southern food, both outside the United States and within it as well. Regardless of her intention, it felt like I had been punched in the heart. There is a misconception around the world that Southern food is a singular cuisine. In my opinion, it's one of the globe's most misunderstood cuisines. In reality, the South makes up nearly 40 percent of the U.S. population and covers nearly 1 million square miles. If you were to break off the South from the rest of the United States and cut and paste it next to Europe, you would see in relation its size. Then think about how many cuisines make up Europe. People don't use the term "European cuisine," for instance. Europe is known for its multitude of distinct and delicious cuisines. I believe the American South isn't far behind.

Virginia and I both grew up uniquely Southern. We both got our start knee-high to a grasshopper in the kitchen, schooled in the art of biscuit-making by our grandmothers. We also both experienced vastly different cuisines and cultures within the South: Virginia moved from Georgia to the Bayou as a young girl, and I moved from the Appalachian Mountains to the Low Country as a teen. Experiencing micro-regions and micro-cuisines from an early age led to an understanding of the role and value of immigrants in the culinary and cultural diversity of the South. The food that I smelled and tasted in Charleston on my first trip was worlds apart from my gran's table in Appalachia. I was dumbfounded and not much has changed since then—I hope to spend my life experiencing these kinds of discoveries.

Those who sought a new life in the American South brought with them the agricultural practices, flavors, seeds and seasonings, ingredients, and the soul of their homelands. Each region in the South is home to a distinct mix of immigrants, and therefore cultural influences. If you break down each micro-region like we do at Husk, you'll quickly realize that there are micro-cuisines within micro-cuisines.

Despite its short history, the South had one of the first recognizable cuisines in America, and it changed as the country changed—spurred by pivotal events like the abolition of slavery and the great depression. Fast forward to 2018, and it's fascinating to take the same look at the micro-regions and who is living where now. The settlers gave way to the thriving Vietnamese community in Houston and the Kurdish influence in Nashville, while the Creole of Louisiana and the Gullah Geechee traditions in Charleston continue to shine. As immigrants began to combine their flavors with the ingredients of their newfound home, a new multicultural South was born.

I often ask myself what the future of Southern food is. The answer to that question begins in these pages. Virginia examines the individual relationships in each region, and then steps back to showcase the cultural and culinary diversity of the South as a whole. The future of the South is as multicultural as anywhere in the country. *Secrets of the Southern Table* examines the possibilities of a fully realized welcome table where everyone adds some wisdom to the skillet. Food unites us and sparks the dialogues that need to happen, even the difficult ones. The future of Southern foodways is exhilarating, intriguing, and insanely delicious. A hot wedge of cornbread with kimchi sounds good to me. I can't wait for you to dig in to this book and start exploring.

SEAN BROCK
Executive chef and partner, Husk, McCrady's, and Minero
Nashville and Charleston

INTRODUCTION

My full name is Virginia Louise Willis. My mother's name is Virginia and my grandmother's name was Louise. From the moment of my birth, my given name bound me inextricably to two strong Southern women who would shape me into the person I am today.

I was born in Augusta, Georgia and spent the first few years of my life in nearby Evans. My grandmother had a double-sided steel sink and, during my early years, she would settle me in one compartment of the sink while she shelled peas or snapped beans in the other side. Her plain, simple kitchen is at the heart of some of my earliest recollections. It was a small, tightly packed room with Georgia pine walls and a window dressed with starched blue-and-white gingham curtains. A table for two—three with my stool—sat at the center with a cast-iron paper napkin holder, the kind that might be picked up at a touristy mountain store, that read, "Bless this House Oh Lord We Pray, Make It Safe By Night and Day."

Even after the home was air-conditioned, an oscillating fan constantly hummed on the linoleum countertop, providing a soothing background noise that was enhanced by the sizzling sound of chicken frying, the tinny rattle of steam escaping a pot of simmering butterbeans, or the whir of an electric mixer beating batter for buttery pound cake. There are photos of me as a towheaded youngster standing on the kitchen chair making biscuits with my grandmother. She would punch out the biscuits, then we'd roll out the scraps of dough and she'd let me make a handprint. It was my form of modeling clay or Play-Doh. Mama taught me to poke a hole with the stem of a wooden spoon in the steaming hot, tender biscuit and fill it with butter and homemade scuppernong jelly. The warmth of the biscuit would transform the two into a molten concoction that would deliciously seep into the crooks and crannies of the tender crumb. Being in the kitchen with my grandmother and mother comprise some of my favorite childhood memories.

At age three, my father's work took us to Louisiana, where I spent my elementary school years. It was here, on steamy spring weekends at the water's edge of the dark bayou, where I learned to tie a chicken neck to the cotton nets used to catch crawfish and fished with my mother for bass, bream, and catfish in the rivers and lakes. Summer vacations brought fishing off the jetty and crabbing off the dock on the "Redneck Riviera" of Alabama and Florida. In the fall, my father hunted for

*Southern cuisine is a living,
breathing, growing thing.*

game in the sportsman's paradise and brought home wild boar, deer, duck, quail, dove, and wild turkey. Much of our outdoor activity and family fun eventually wound up on a plate. Louisiana is where I learned to love rich, smoky savory gumbo; salty, spicy jambalaya; and the sweet, succulent taste of Gulf seafood.

During the summers and on holidays we returned to Georgia to visit my grandparents. My grandfather grew much of the food that found its way to my grandmother's kitchen. He had a rusty old tractor and he'd hitch a plow to the back that he would guide as my grandmother drove the tractor. It was quite the sight, she in her floppy-brimmed hat with him tagging along, the metal blade cutting furrows in the soil and the dark earth cleanly spilling to either side of the metal blade. To this day, I can't keep a houseplant alive, but I love to dig in the dirt. It's a family tradition. In Louisiana, Mama always had a little patch for growing squash, okra, and tomatoes in the backyard and my grandfather's garden was tremendous. He grew up in the Depression and like many Southerners of that generation, was accustomed to living off the land. He had a cornfield planted in the dark rich soil down by the river. Closer to home, he cultivated a plot nearly the size of a football field! Every few years he'd seed clover and move his garden to let the soil regenerate. He was an amazing gardener; he could put a stick in the ground and it would grow. Growing, harvesting, and preserving from our garden or locally grown food was simply part of life. With nearly a twelve-month growing season in the South—there's something coming out of the ground or off a tree almost every month of the year.

When I entered junior high we returned to Georgia, to a sleepy little town in the Southwest corner of the state tucked alongside the Flint River. The landscape transforms on the drive south from Atlanta as the land flattens out. There, the hardwoods are outnumbered by loblolly pines and the colors become more muted under the blue-gray sky. Off the busy interstate corridor, miles and miles of two-lane blacktop connect sleepy, small towns and communities with names like Unadilla, Musella, Oscilla, and Montezuma—where I grew up. Often lining those highways are peanut fields, cotton fields, and pecan groves as far as the eye can see.

It was there Mama built her dream kitchen in her new home with its large bay window and kitchen island. It was there that fragrant, sweet peaches from local orchards were peeled and transformed into golden, glistening jelly; earthy peanuts were boiled in bracingly salted water and canned; and sweet summer corn, creamy butterbeans, and tender field peas were frozen into quart-size packets for enjoyment and sustenance during the winter months.

Mama loved then and still loves to experiment with different recipes. The Cajun and Creole recipes from my childhood were considered quite foreign in South Georgia. While my family longed for crawfish boils, my Georgia friends only knew "mudbugs" as bait. She began to experiment with more exotic cuisines and would prepare Chinese eggrolls, French crepes, and Mexican tamales. And, while she enjoyed cooking more international fare, she did not ignore the Southern classics. We enjoyed Brown Butter and Thyme Whole-Grain Cornbread; Pimento Cheese Tomato-Herb Pie; Cheesy Broccoli and Rice Bake; and of course, Cathead Biscuits. I no longer needed to stand on the chair to help, and being by my mother's side in the kitchen created different kinds of memories. Food was always at the very center of our lives and it was this exposure to many different foods that truly piqued my interest in the world of food and set me on my path.

Home to peanuts, peaches, and pecans, growing up in the Deep South was for me somewhat idyllic. Yet even as a young teen I could not ignore the economic disparity between the classes and races. The county itself was predominantly black, with whites in the minority. Where I grew up is part of the Black Belt, a crescent-shaped band that extends through the Deep South, about 300 miles, making its way from southwest Tennessee to east-central Mississippi and then east through Alabama and Georgia. The term Black Belt is twofold, referring to a rich swath of soil that arches through the South, as well as the population, a result of the descendants of the enslaved Africans who once toiled on the plantations. The poverty level has been, for as long as I can remember, even as a child, quite significant. While I had attended public school in Louisiana, in Georgia I attended an all-white private school that had been born out of the court-mandated public-school desegregation in the mid-1960s. Apart from African-Americans, in my particular corner of the South the only "others" I ever saw were the Hispanics working in the fields.

This imbalance of money and power is and has been for a long time a simmering pot seemingly ready to boil over. Once, I remember being

in the car driving through town and my friend's mom reaching over to lock the door. The road wasn't dangerous; it was simply a predominantly black neighborhood. A young man walking on the sidewalk, hearing the click of the lock, became outraged and yelled at the car, "I don't want nothing in your damn car." It shook me. I remember feeling embarrassed and conflicted.

The South is a complicated place, especially when it comes to race, and Southern food is a complicated cuisine. Southern foodways are integral to the American culinary tradition. Southern cooking is seen as seen one of the true American cuisines, a cookery that can simmer alongside the elevated and exalted cuisine of France, the cast-iron skillet toe-to-toe against a French black steel sauté pan. Southern cooking is often compared to Italian food, humble, but fresh, flavorful, and delicious. It has always drawn upon the conflux of cultures that at once both conspired and collided to create the South we know today—Native American, European, and African. However, the questions of ownership of Southern cooking are some of the most provocative points in our ongoing struggles over race. There is a historical canon of Southern recipes that are barely, if even, credited to a brigade of nameless, faceless black women called "Mammy." The Creole food of New Orleans is described as a mélange of French and Spanish influences, ignoring the fact that most of the people who cooked it through the centuries were black. And the same holds true for the something as simple as barbecue.

While it is important to acknowledge and appreciate tremendous African influences, it is also true that many Southerners did not own slaves before the Civil War—nor have had black domestic help in the 150-plus years since. There have been many nameless, faceless poor white women, as well. It is a question of both race and class. And, for that matter, the same reality still exists that in the South— as well as much of the United States—currently, the folks fixing the food in many of the kitchens are Hispanic. The lines of ownership of Southern food aren't clearly marked on a map. There is a rich narrative that lies beneath, a tangled and compelling web of race, politics, and social history that is served up alongside our beloved biscuits and gravy.

I've been writing as a professional for more than a decade and have traveled from Maine to California, Florida to Alaska. During this journey I have been front and center in challenging Southern stereotypes. Due to the media portrayal, people assume that all Southern food is fried and unhealthy, that all we eat is fried chicken, biscuits, and butter. (Meaning butter as a food group.) I often say to judge Southern food as only fried chicken and biscuits would be like deeming Mexican food to solely consist of burritos or for Italian food to only be spaghetti and meatballs. The South is very complex. It's thirteen states—nearly a quarter of the continental United States. The food from Appalachia is different from Coastal Carolina is different

from the food from the Gulf. We've got extreme geographical differences and many climates and sub-climates.

I learned years ago that my accent could trigger certain negative assumptions. My Southern drawl was equivalent to dumb, redneck, or worse. Of course, when folks discovered that I was reasonably intelligent and could speak in complete sentences, their assumptions fell away, or at least most of the time.

I don't know what it feels like to grow up as a person of color or someone of the Jewish, Muslim, or Hindu faith in the Deep South. All I know now is that I feel I need to do what I need to do to bridge that gap, make that wrong right, and unlock the barriers that I can. I am not alone. There are many other Southerners like me uncomfortable with the status quo. Division is a truth in the South, like in much of the U.S., but it's not the only truth and it's not my truth.

Several years ago I participated in a book fair in Western Kentucky. A small group of authors were collected by a cheerful volunteer at the airport. As we made our way in the van to our respective hotels small talk broke out and we told one another where we were from and what our genre was. One of the fellow authors was from the Midwest and had never been to the South. She seemed mesmerized that I was from Atlanta.

She asked, "Have you ever met a Jewish person?"

I remember blinking slowly, not certain if I had actually heard her correctly.

Incredulously I responded, "I said I was from Atlanta, not the moon."

Caught a bit off guard, she said, "I didn't mean to offend you, but I didn't think there were any Jewish people in the South."

Believe it or not, I've been asked the ridiculous question about knowing a Jewish person more than once. Although I find it annoying, generally I laugh it off and tease, "Didn't you see *Driving Miss Daisy*? Of course there are Jewish people in the South." The truth? Congregation Beth Elohim in Charleston, South Carolina, was founded in 1749. It is one of the oldest Jewish congregations in the United States and the sanctuary is the second oldest synagogue building in the United States.

While the South is primarily built on a black-white narrative, it is actually not as homogenous as it seems. The largest population of Vietnamese in the United States outside of California lives in Houston, Texas. Six of the ten states with the fastest growing Latino populations are in the South. North Carolina ranks in the top five states as home to the Hmong people from Southeast Asia. And it's not solely new immigration. The Appalachian region has long been thought of by outsiders as a predominantly white section of the United States, particularly in comparison with the rest of the country. Yet since the nation's early origins, nonwhites always have been present in Appalachia. There have been Chinese residents in Mississippi since just after the Civil War. In the mid-1800s New Orleans hosted the largest population of Italian immigrants in the entire country. Greeks began immigrating to the South in the 1800s as well. In reality, the South has long been home to a variety of ethnicities and populations. This range of varied populations have led to a rich diversity of cuisine and multiple influences on Southern foodways, recipes that I showcase in this book.

Several years ago en route to Texas, I texted my dear friend Amy C. Evans, artist and former oral historian for the Southern Foodways Alliance; Amy now lives in Houston. I wanted for us to get together and eat some crawfish. She pinged me back, "Asian or Cajun?" "What?" I pondered. I soon found out. We paid a visit to a cavernous Vietnamese restaurant packed with all different sorts of people. It was a Sunday afternoon and the crowd included African American church ladies in their Sunday finery, frat boys (possibly still inebriated from the night before), Mexican families, Vietnamese teenagers, cowboys in town for a rodeo, and a table of roughnecks in from the oil rig. As we sat at the table eating delicious spicy, garlicky shrimp, butter coating our messy fingers, I smiled deep in my soul and realized, "This is my South, too."

Memory shapes the story of our lives and allows us to interact with the world. It is my sincere hope that *Secrets of the Southern Table: A Food Lover's Tour of the Global South* will expand people's culinary landscape. This assorted collection of recipes and stories features the familiar—as well as the unexpected, looking beyond the stereotypes and misinterpretations of Southern food and cooking. I strongly believe Southern cuisine is a living, breathing, growing thing and have included recipes that reflect the rich diversity. From white linen formal to farm table to well-worn Formica—and with influences from the many diverse people who live here—there's world-class food in the South. The country is embracing Southern food—and learning that what defines Southern food has evolved and changed. The food of the South is biscuits and burritos, catfish and chapatti, and hoecakes and hummus.

Welcome to the global Southern kitchen—pull up a chair. Everyone is welcome at my table.

Bon Appétit y'all!

Virginia Willis

CHAPTER 1

From *the*
Garden

SIX GENERATIONS *at* WHITE OAK PASTURES

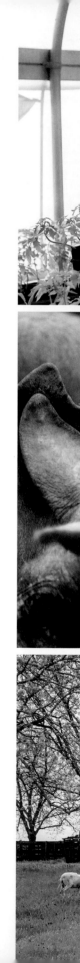

The open-top Jeep bounces down the highway under a royal-blue sky and tufts of billowing white clouds. Loose gravel kicks up under the tires as the steering wheel turns sharply away from the blacktop and we veer off to visit the town of Bluffton, Georgia. The driver quickly downshifts through the gears with a firm grip and the engine hums as we settle into a slower pace. It's midmorning in late spring and the air is already dense, hot, and thick; the sun aggressive. It's going to be a South Georgia scorcher.

My friend and guide, Will Harris III, is a cowboy straight out of central casting. He's tall and rugged with a rich, deep voice and a legendary drawl. His gun lies beneath the seat and his knife rests on his belt. He is a Deep South cattleman from the top of his Stetson hat to the tip of his well-worn leather boots. His family has lived on the outskirts of Bluffton for six generations. An untrained eye might take a look at Will sitting in his truck with the gun rack in the back window and simply see a South Georgia farmer. They might hear his thick accent and assume his thoughts and concerns about the earth were about as deep as the red Georgia clay caked on his leather boots. They might make all the social and educational assumptions that one might make about a South Georgia farmer. They would be wrong.

I know Will Harris. I know that his ancestor, James Edward Harris, founded White Oak Pastures when he returned home from fighting for the Confederacy during the Civil War and that the land has been farmed by his family for 150 years. His daughters are the fifth generation to farm this land. I also know that he has the largest USDA Certified Organic farm in the state of Georgia; he grows vegetables and raises cattle, sheep, goats, hogs, poultry, and rabbits by the same methods his great-grandfather used 150 years ago.

This wasn't always the case. Formerly, he was part of the commodity system as a Cargill executive. But in 1995 he made the conscious decision to return to a production system that would be better for the environment, for the animals, and for the people who eat his meat and produce. There wasn't a single epiphany. He drawls, "There was no lightbulb moment or burning bush." It was just a slow and persistent realization that factory farming wasn't the right thing to do.

We're on a tour to see his farm and view his expanded vegetable operation, but there's more to this trip than the story of one Southwest Georgia family. Our tour

is not solely about White Oak Pastures; it's the story of American agriculture. Will wants to show me what has happened to the family farm, not by what *is* in Bluffton but by what is *not* in Bluffton. The streets are mostly vacant. A handful of folks still live there, but there are no businesses—no stores, no shops, outside of those that are part of White Oak Pastures. We pass a bent, elderly man slumped over the wheel of a riding mower as he motors in an even course across his lawn. We zip past another man ambling out to his worn and dented pickup truck. Will waves his hand to the first, tips his cowboy hat and nods his head to the other. We halt to a dead stop in the center of the former town. As soon as the wheels slow to a stop, gnats begin to buzz incessantly around our eyes and ears. He points out where the motor court had been, the feed store, the movie house, the drugstore, and the juke joint where he used to get a griddle-fried hamburger and an ice-cold Coke—a setting out of a Rockwellian boyhood. What was once a busy little town is now a series of dilapidated buildings.

I grew up two hours northeast of Bluffton and I have seen dried-up Southern towns like this all my life, but I had no idea why they had ceased to be vibrant communities. I was accustomed to seeing boarded-up brick warehouses with faded "For Lease" signs, rusty window frames with the glass shattered by restless teenagers. I had never seen those small country towns busy or thriving. All my life I thought enticing jobs pulled people away to the big cities. The truth was the opposite: Lack of work pushed people to leave the country. There's a huge difference in being pulled and being pushed.

The South was an agrarian-based economy for over 250 years. Changes began with the end of slavery and continued as the industrial revolution introduced cotton mills. However, Georgia remained a primarily agrarian state until after WWII and the advent of industrial agriculture. It used to take one man a full day to plow an acre using a mule and plow. With modern tractors, one man can plow a hundred acres in a day. There's a 10,000-acre farm near White Oak Pastures with only five men running the place. What brought this change? A desire for inexpensive food. We wanted cheaper food, and industrial agriculture delivered with breathtaking efficiency. The drawback? We now have a food system plagued with problems. As Will says, "Food is cheap, but someone else is paying for it somewhere else." More and more, people understand the negative impact that industrial agriculture has on the environment, public health, and rural communities.

Industrial agriculture requires monoculture, the practice of growing single crops on a very large scale. Corn, wheat, soybeans, cotton, and rice are all commonly grown as single crops across the entire United States. Monoculture fields are highly attractive to certain weeds and insect pests. And growing the same plant in the same place year after year robs the nutrients from the soil. Therefore, monoculture farming relies heavily on pesticides and chemical fertilizers.

"Nature abhors a monoculture."
—WILL HARRIS

The truck pulls up to a barren, grassless expanse of red Georgia dirt with cattle at the edge eating a bale of hay. Will had just bought the land, which had previously grown cotton. He explained that the soil was dead, but feeding his cattle on the land would both aerate and enrich the soil. "Nature abhors a monoculture," Will says as he tilts his head toward me. "We didn't mean to turn our soil into a dead mineral medium, but we did. We didn't mean to implement a confinement system that deprived our animals of the ability to express their instinctive behavior, but we did. We didn't mean to contribute to the economic and social decline of our rural village, but we did."

As part of their commitment to full-circle land stewardship, White Oak Pastures started a small-scale organic farm on the property in 2009 and now grows more than forty different kinds of heritage vegetables, fruits, and nuts—all planted and harvested by hand and fertilized with rich compost produced on the farm. They do not use pesticides or synthetic fertilizers. The tractors run on biodiesel made from the recycled cooking grease and tallow from their On-Farm Dining Pavilion. They manage a 200-share Community Supported Agriculture (CSA) program with drops in three states—Georgia, Florida, and Alabama—along with a wholesale boxed-vegetable program with chefs and grocers.

Will Harris and White Oak Pastures are enriching both the soil and the soul of farming in the South.

RETURNING TO ROOTS *at* THE FARMER & THE LARDER

I'm in Southeast Georgia a mere six miles from the intracoastal waterways of the Atlantic. The air is already thick, wet, and steamy. We're at Gilliard Terrace, a one-lane dirt road that defines Gilliard Farms and claims its place on this earth. Just to the right of this road stands an old wooden homestead. To the left of that, a crooked, sandy trail enters the dark, wooded canopy. Shaggy, hairy masses of curly gray Spanish moss hang from the tree branches. Insects dance in the light as my guide, Matthew Raiford, walks ahead, on the lookout for snakes in the low brush as he simultaneously brandishes a walking stick overhead to remove shimmering multitudes of spiderwebs. His broad shoulders and mass of braids form an imposing silhouette and I, for one, am most grateful that he is blazing this trail.

As we walk deeper into the woods, the temperature drops quickly. Scattershot beams of light pierce the forest floor as incandescent sprites seemingly dance in the glow. Mosquitoes and gnats buzz around our eyes, prompting us to blow puffs of self-generated air upward—what passes as gnat deterrent in South Georgia. Occasionally one of us will succumb and fan the air with the wave of a hand—some level of defeat for a Southerner. The aroma is sweet and earthy, intensely herbal and almost spicy. Matthew points out the lack of Spanish moss in this microclimate. It is as if we've entered another world. The sounds are muffled and there's a quietude that is nearly touchable. The birds are chirping and flitting in the trees, and as we move along the path, we can hear small animals in the underbrush. In the forest, the sandy path transforms into dark loamy soil composed of clay, humus, and sand topped with fallen leaves. The woods are thick with brush, palmetto fronds stab their pointy branches upward, and many of the trees are cabled in fat, winding vines. It's seemingly out of the pages of *Where the Wild Things Are.* This verdant, tropical landscape is alive and positively vibrating with life.

We are walking atop a former railroad bed the length of a football field, and we can see the light of an opening at the opposite end. As we walk, Matthew's business and life partner, Jovan Sage, points out various wild herbs she uses for healing tinctures and teas. Jovan is a holistic health coach as well as an avid pickler and fermenter. She spent fifteen years working with local, national, and international nonprofit organizations, and spent the last five years focusing on sustainability, food, and agriculture—including working as a food retail consultant and as director for Slow

*Gilliard Farms is one of the
oldest African American farms
in the entire United States.*

Food USA in New York City. In fact, Matthew and Jovan met while in Turin at Terra Madre Salone del Gusto, the international Slow Food conference. Jovan's radiant smile lights up her face and I know that this lush world is both her pantry and her playground.

We walk and Matthew points out the newly built hog pen. He explains that they are in the process of expanding the livestock operation. As we continue to walk through the forest he tells me the history of the farm and a little bit about his background. Gilliard Farms was founded in 1874 by his great-great-grandfather Jupiter Gilliard. It's one of the oldest African American farms in the state of Georgia; indeed, the entire United States. I knew some of what he was telling me. It was very intentional that I chose to start this book with White Oak Pastures (page 2), a farm founded by a veteran returning home from the Civil War, and Gilliard Farms, founded by a man who was emancipated by the Civil War. So much of what defines the South starts with the complex and entwined story of black and white. I know that the secret of the Southern table was birthed in this story.

After a short lapse of the farm lying fallow, Gilliard Farms is now managed and worked by Matthew and his sister, Althea Raiford. They raise chickens for eggs and grow various fruits and vegetables, including blueberries, plums, tomatoes, peppers, and squash. In its 140-plus-year history, the farm's land and crops have remained completely organic; chemicals have never been used. Matthew also explains that, since the farm has never changed hands, they are able to refer to the farm records about what crops were planted, what crops failed, and what crops succeeded. He believes that their long-dead ancestors are helping them on the farm. Althea writes on the Gilliard Farm website, "The peace I find at Gilliard Terrace is unique and special to me. I see it in my mind's eye, in its glory being what it was once before, and by the grace of God more than it was. Matthew and I are just picking up where our family left off, living off the land, building a stronger community, and taking care of those we love. My passion for Gilliard Farms comes from my love and appreciation for my family's legacy and my family's future." Powerful words appropriate for a powerful vision.

At the end of our long tunnel we exit the darkness at the edge of a dry creek bed. There are crushed ovals in the tall grass where the whitetail deer had been resting in the shade in the heat of the afternoon. It's still quite warm, but also gentle and peaceful. Matthew says it's his favorite time of day, and comments that the birds are settling in for the night. It's serene, and in the same breath he points at the land on the opposite side of the creek. He says, "That's owned by a white man. When I was growing up, if blacks were caught on the main county road in front of the homestead, then his daddy would charge a toll." Now, mind you, this was a completely illegal, self-created, self-policed tax on a road paid for by taxpayer dollars—including the

Raiford family's tax dollars. Matthew finished, "As a result, as a young kid I learned to walk along this creek and in the woods instead."

We turn to walk back to the main part of the farm, and his words weigh heavy on me. Damn. Seriously, damn! I realize all at once that I have no real idea about this South. Matthew's family once toiled on nearby land as slaves. It all seems untenable and irrevocable at the same time. I'm stung by the juxtaposition of the breathtaking beauty of this veritable Georgia jungle against the bigotry and hatred that also can grow in this fertile soil.

I quietly ask him, "Why did you come back?"

He takes a deep breath and answers. After ten years in the army and twenty years in food service, he tells me, he attended the Culinary Institute of America. His successful culinary career took him all over the world and culminated in a position as the executive chef of the U.S. House of Representatives. He said once he reached that point, he realized he wanted to do something different, to make a difference, to return home to his family farm. He told Althea of his dream to return to Gilliard Terrace. She also felt it was the right thing to do. Matthew applied for and received a grant to attend the Center for Agroecology & Sustainable Food Systems (CASFS) at University of California, Santa Cruz. The center is dedicated to increasing ecological sustainability and social justice in the food and agriculture system. Their hopes and dreams were aligned and ready to soar.

After graduation, he returned to the loamy southeastern soil, but the kitchen still beckoned. In 2015 he and Jovan opened The Farmer & The Larder, a café in downtown Brunswick, Georgia. With his certificate in Ecological Horticulture from CASFS, Matthew appropriately calls himself a "CheFarmer." He has a foot on the family land, as well as in his kitchen. He starts his day at five thirty a.m., walking his property to check the crops by first light. After feeding the chickens and ducks, he harvests the eggs and heads to the restaurant to start lunch preparation at nine a.m. I cannot possibly think of more arduous professions than farming and cooking. Both are nonstop, backbreaking work with small profit margins.

The next day, I sit at a long communal table made from reclaimed wood at The Farmer & The Larder, watching Matthew work and nibbling on a Ploughman's Platter of house-cured charcuterie and spicy mustard. On the side is a *lahpet,* an intensely flavored Burmese tea leaf salad with a crunchy mix of peanuts, yellow split peas, toasted sesame seeds, sunflower seeds, and garlic chips. The textures and seasonings are incredible—and let's just say that most of the tea round these parts is sweetened in a pitcher, not fermented and in a salad. His hands are a blur as he works the lunch tickets. I listen to him mentor a potential employee, a young African American man who is helping his mama pay the bills since she's had a stroke. I can hear the strength in Matthew's voice as he coaches the teenager.

I also observe the ebb and flow of lunch at a restaurant. Tables are seated; tables are cleared. The light fixtures are handcrafted and the tables are repurposed from a local resort. Jovan points out the lawyer with his tie flipped over his shoulder who comes in for lunch every single workday to order the Cubano, a hearty sandwich made with bacon-wrapped pork loin and housemade mustard on a baguette, served with a side salad of local greens and freshly made herb goddess dressing. Over the course of a few short hours while the sounds and smells of the kitchen permeate the air, I meet Rachel Bregman, a rabbi transplanted from New York, and her delightful baby daughter, Lilith. A regal elderly white matron whose husband is in a nursing home. A colorful, bejeweled, youthful artist whose work adorns the walls of the café. In the corner at a large table, a group of coworkers—some black, some white—from the local bank. Black, white, young, and old, there is a real and true community at The Farmer & The Larder. It makes my heart full. It makes me realize that the secret of this Southern table is change. The Farmer & The Larder mission statement reads, "We know that good food & community go hand in hand. We bring delicious & fresh food to your table. Let's explore our shared foodways & cultures." This is the real reason Matthew returned to the southeast coast of Georgia. Sharing food at the table bridges religion, culture, race, and creed. I know in my heart and in my head that Matthew is making the difference that he seeks in the world.

Brussels Sprout and Benne Seed Coleslaw

Serves 4 to 6

Benne seeds are an heirloom sesame seed originally from Africa. They were widely home-grown throughout the South in the Colonial and Antebellum periods. Enslaved Africans consumed the plant at every stage: the young leaves, petite seed pods, and flavorful mature dried seeds. They also pressed the seeds for oil. But when modern farming started to breed sesame seeds to maximize oil output rather than flavor—modern American sesame bears no resemblance to heirloom benne—the seeds fell to the wayside, only seen in Chinese restaurants or atop fast-food hamburger buns.

Today, however, sesame seeds are increasingly returning to Southern cooking as a featured ingredient, as seen in this recipe. This salad is best in the fall when Brussels sprouts are in season.

½ cup sesame seeds, plus more for garnish

Zest and juice of 2 lemons

2 tablespoons white wine vinegar

2 garlic cloves, crushed

2 teaspoons honey, or to taste

½ cup extra-virgin olive oil or benne seed oil

Coarse kosher salt and freshly ground black pepper

1 pound Brussels sprouts, stem ends trimmed

1 medium shallot, halved lengthwise and very thinly sliced

¾ cup chopped fresh mint, plus sprigs for garnish

1 In a small skillet, toast the sesame seeds over low heat, stirring often, until fragrant and lightly browned, 3 minutes. Transfer them to a food processor and let cool just slightly. Add the lemon zest and juice, vinegar, garlic, and honey. Pulse until combined and then, with the machine running, add the oil in a slow, steady stream and blend until smooth, 1 to 2 minutes. Season with salt and pepper. Transfer to a small bowl and set aside. Don't bother washing the food processor bowl.

2 Replace the blade with the slicing blade set to very thin, if possible. Working with a handful of Brussels sprouts at a time, process until they are thinly shaved; place the Brussels sprouts and shallot in a large bowl.

3 Pour a little of the dressing over the Brussels sprouts and toss to coat. (I never pour it all at once; instead, I pour a little at a time. You can always add more, but it's hard to take out.) Taste and adjust for seasoning with salt and pepper. This dish can be made ahead and left at room temperature for up to several hours. Just before serving, chop the mint and toss it with the salad. To remind yourself of this step, if you are making ahead, place the whole sprigs on top of the salad. Taste and adjust for seasoning with salt and pepper and garnish with more sesame seeds just before serving.

Southern Stir-Fry with Turnips and Greens

Serves 4 to 6

The Mississippi River Delta, stretching for about one hundred miles along the banks of the mighty Mississippi and extending eastward fifty miles across the state, is one of the richest agricultural regions in the world. After the Emancipation Proclamation was enacted and slaves no longer worked the cotton fields, Chinese men migrated to the Delta in search of work. As is often the case today, many intended not to settle permanently, but to earn money to send home, but when they arrived, they found hard labor and low pay. To achieve economic independence, these new immigrants opened grocery stores, selling to the black freedmen who had formerly used the plantation stores. The first Chinese grocery store in Mississippi likely appeared as early as the 1870s.

Chinese immigrants continued to come to Mississippi over the generations, joining their extended families and incorporating their cooking into the local cuisine, as seen with this recipe for stir-fried turnips and greens.

1 cup homemade chicken stock or reduced-fat low-sodium chicken broth

1 tablespoon sherry

2 tablespoons peanut oil or canola oil

2 ounces country ham, cut into small dice

2 garlic cloves, very finely chopped

6 thin slices ginger, peeled and cut into julienne

1 small sweet onion, thinly sliced crosswise

4 small or 2 medium turnips (about 4 ounces), peeled and thinly sliced into half-moons

Coarse kosher salt and freshly ground black pepper

4 heaping cups chopped turnip greens (about 6 ounces)

2 teaspoons honey (optional)

1 Stir together the stock and sherry. Set aside. Heat a 14-inch flat-bottomed wok or large skillet over very high heat until a drop of water evaporates within a second or two when added to the pan. Add the oil and heat until shimmering. Add the ham and cook until sizzling. Add the garlic and ginger and cook just for 10 seconds. Add the onion and cook, stirring continuously, for 1 minute. Add the turnips and stir-fry for another minute or two, then season with salt and pepper. Add the stock mixture to the pan and toss together quickly with the vegetables. Add the greens and cook, stirring, until the vegetables are crisp-tender—3 to 5 minutes. Taste and adjust for seasoning with salt and pepper. Drizzle with honey, if you choose, and serve immediately.

Pan-Seared Summer Squash with Spiced Lemon Vinaigrette

Serves 4 to 6

Summer squash thrive in the semitropical South. My grandparents always had a garden with many mounded rows of squash, and my grandfather taught me that summer squash bear both male and female flowers. The female flowers are easy to identify by looking for a miniature squash just below each blossom. Male flowers sit directly on the stem and do not produce fruit. Pick these male blossoms for using the flower. If you pick the females, you won't have any squash. Simple biology.

This dish was inspired by chef-owner Rafih Benjelloun of Imperial Fez, a beloved Atlanta institution for more than twenty-five years. At his restaurant, guests are magically transported to Morocco—the tea is mint, not sweet; diners rest on comfortable pillows surrounded by opulent colors; shoes are left at the door; and belly dancers dance and sway to the music.

3 or 4 small yellow squash (about 1 pound)

3 or 4 small green squash (about 1 pound)

Zest of 1 lemon and juice of ½ lemon

2 tablespoons extra-virgin olive oil

3 garlic cloves, mashed to a paste with a pinch of salt (see note, page 22)

1 teaspoon harissa or chile paste, or to taste

¼ teaspoon ground cumin

Coarse kosher salt and freshly ground black pepper

2 tablespoons chopped fresh parsley

1 Trim the stem and flower ends of the squash, and then use a chef's knife to quarter each one lengthwise. Using the tip of your knife, trim away the seeds. (The seeds can make the dish watery.) Cut the squash into 1-inch pieces.

2 Heat a large nonstick skillet over medium-high heat. Without crowding, add the squash to the dry skillet and cook, stirring often, until lightly blistered on both sides and tender to the point of a knife, 5 to 7 minutes.

Recipe continues

Harissa is a spicy, aromatic, and flavorful chile paste used in Middle Eastern and North African cooking. The blend differs from country to country, but it's a puree of hot chile peppers, garlic, olive oil, and spices such as cumin, coriander, and caraway. It can be found at Middle Eastern markets, well-stocked gourmet stores, and natural foods stores.

3   Meanwhile, in a small bowl or jar with a lid, combine the lemon zest, lemon juice, oil, garlic, harissa, and cumin to make the dressing. Stir or shake to combine. Season with salt and pepper.

4   Place the squash in a large bowl and drizzle some of the dressing over the top. Toss to coat and combine, and add more as needed. Sprinkle with the parsley. This dish is excellent served hot or room temperature or cold as a salad. If you serve it cold, make sure to taste and adjust for seasoning with salt and pepper before serving, as chilling dulls the seasoning.

To prepare the garlic paste, place the unpeeled garlic on a cutting board, broad-side down, set the flat side of a chef's knife on top, and give the knife a quick whack with the palm of your hand to crush each clove. Remove the papery skin and trim away the tough basal plane at the end of the clove. Halve the garlic and remove any of the green shoot, if present, as it is bitter. Coarsely chop the garlic, then sprinkle it with a pinch of coarse salt. (The salt acts as an abrasive and helps grind the garlic.) Using the side of the knife like an artist's palette knife, press firmly on the cutting board and crush the garlic a little at a time. Repeat until the garlic is a fine paste.

Roast Beets with Arugula and Feta-Buttermilk Dressing

Serves 4 to 6

My friend and colleague, Chef Steven Satterfield of Miller Union in Atlanta, is a vegetable whisperer. His flavor combinations bring out the absolute best of the vegetable in season. One such dish is his Feta Snack, a super-simple starter that features creamy feta cheese from Georgia-based Decimal Place Farm and crisp crudités for dipping. I've swapped out his fresh vegetables for sweet roast beets and peppery arugula. This combination of the earthy beets with the deliciously salty dressing is positively addictive.

Beets are notorious for staining cutting boards, wooden utensils, and, yes, your hands when working with them. The pigment that gives them their vibrant color, betalain, is water soluble, not oil soluble, meaning that the pigment cannot penetrate oil. The best way to prevent stains is to lightly coat your hands, any utensils, and the cutting board with just a touch of oil, although then, of course, you must be careful handling the knife.

4 medium fresh beets (about 2 pounds)

2 garlic cloves, halved and green shoots removed, if necessary

2½ tablespoons extra-virgin olive oil, plus more for your hands

¼ cup pecans, walnuts, or pistachios, for garnish

1 cup crumbled feta cheese (about 6 ounces)

½ cup buttermilk

1 tablespoon chopped fresh mint

Coarse kosher salt and freshly ground black pepper

6 ounces arugula

1 Heat the oven to 350°F. Lay each beet, along with half a garlic clove, on a sheet of aluminum foil large enough to fully wrap around the beet. Drizzle the beets with 1 tablespoon of the oil and then individually wrap each beet in the foil. Bake the wrapped beets until completely tender when pierced with the point of a knife, 1 to 1½ hours. Let the beets rest in the foil for a few minutes to steam and loosen the skin. When cool enough to handle, slip off the skins and slice the beets ¼ inch thick. Finely chop the roasted garlic and set aside.

2 Meanwhile, while the beets are roasting, toast the nuts on a rimmed baking sheet in the oven until browned, about 10 minutes. Let the nuts cool slightly, then coarsely chop them and transfer to a small bowl.

3 In a medium bowl, whisk together the feta, buttermilk, chopped roasted garlic, mint, and 1 tablespoon of the olive oil. Season heartily with pepper.

Recipe continues

4   To serve, toss the arugula with the remaining ½ tablespoon olive oil and season with just a touch of salt and pepper. Divide among serving plates and top with the warm beets. Sprinkle with the toasted nuts. Serve with the dressing on the side.

True feta is made in Greece, and according to the European Union, you can't call it feta unless it was produced there. Nonetheless, all across the South—and the rest of the United States—there's a tremendous amount of delicious domestic and locally produced feta to seek out at your farmers' market, natural foods store, or specialty market.

Roasted Tomatoes Stuffed with Summer Vegetables

Serves 4 to 6

Fresh tomatoes are *only* ever good in summer. There is nothing as wonderful as the full, rich, almost winelike flavor of a vine-ripened tomato—just as there is nothing as disappointing as the dull, insipid flavor of a cold-storage tomato shipped from halfway around the world. I don't eat those out-of-season tomatoes and strongly suggest that you don't, either. So when it's tomato season, I heartily endorse eating the glorious ripe ones as often as possible.

One of my favorite ways to eat tomatoes is packed with fresh summer vegetables like sweet corn and squash. You could use other cooked and cooled vegetables, as well, such as lady peas, black-eyed peas, butterbeans—even okra or eggplant. Tortilla chips take the place of bread crumbs and add another layer of corn flavor, and are gluten-free as well.

4 to 6 large tomatoes (2 to 3 pounds), each about the size of a tennis ball

1 tablespoon pure olive oil

½ sweet onion, chopped

1 garlic clove, very finely chopped

Kernels from 4 ears fresh sweet corn (about 2 cups)

1 small zucchini, seeded and diced

Coarse kosher salt and freshly ground black pepper

1 (6-ounce) log creamy goat cheese (about 1 scant cup)

1 tablespoon chopped fresh herbs, such as basil, cilantro, or parsley

1 cup coarsely crushed corn tortilla chips (about 3 ounces)

1 Heat the oven to 350°F.

2 To form the tomato shells, with a serrated knife, slice off the tops of the tomatoes and remove their cores. Using your index finger, remove and discard the seeds. Then, using a melon baller or a spoon, scoop out the pulp, transferring the juices and pulp to a small bowl. Using your hands, squish the pulp and seeds until smooth but slightly chunky. Set aside and wash your hands.

3 Meanwhile, heat the oil in a large skillet over medium heat. Add the onion and cook until soft and translucent, 3 to 5 minutes. Add the garlic and cook until fragrant, 45 to 60 seconds. Add the corn and zucchini; season with salt and pepper. Cook, stirring occasionally, until the vegetables are tender, 8 to 10 minutes. Add the tomato mixture and cook, stirring occasionally, until it has been absorbed into the vegetable mixture and the skillet is dry, 3 minutes. Set aside to cool slightly. Place the goat cheese in a bowl. Add the warm vegetable mixture and chopped herbs. Stir until smooth and well-combined. Taste and adjust for seasoning with salt and pepper.

4   Arrange the tomato shells, cut-side up, in a small casserole dish. Spoon some filling (about ⅓ cup, depending on the size of the tomato) into each tomato. Sprinkle the chips over the filling.

5   Bake until the filling is heated through, the tomato shells are tender, and the topping is golden brown, 20 to 25 minutes. Serve immediately.

If you cook or eat a tomato between the months of October and June, there's a high likelihood that tomato came from the Sunshine State. Florida accounts for one-third of all fresh tomatoes produced in the United States, with exceptionally high production during the fall and winter months when the temperature in the furthest points south in the South registers in the mid to upper 70s. These seemingly seasonal abnormalities are bred to be perfectly formed and are shipped around the country and into your local grocery store without bruising, breaking, or cracking. As with much misguided modern agriculture, the emphasis has been on "shipability" and yield, not flavor. There's an even more disturbing side to tomatoes grown in winter than a simple lack of flavor: the tremendous human and environmental costs. The drive for low cost and high yield is achieved by the work of thousands of migrant workers, some of whom are undocumented, and many live and work in nearly slave-like conditions. The tomatoes are picked rock-hard and green, and then gassed with ethylene until their skins obtain a marketable hue. Modern agriculture has tripled yields, but produces fruits with a fraction of the vitamins and minerals. They don't taste good in more ways than one. As my dear friend Will Harris of White Oak Pastures says, "When food is cheap, the cost is paid for somewhere else" (see page 5). I believe that every bite we take is a choice and hope that you will carefully consider your choices when you fill your grocery cart. Vote with your fork.

Smashed Fried Okra with Spicy Yogurt Dipping Sauce

Serves 4 to 6

I love okra. I love it boiled, grilled, steamed, stewed, fried. I am an okra apostle. Several years ago I wrote a book about okra. When I would talk about my okra book, folks would get excited, then ask, "Did you get to meet her?" I realized they thought I was talking about *Oprah*. Now I specify that I wrote a book about "the green vegetable okra."

Okra originated in Africa and was brought to the South during the era of the West African slave trade. India is the largest producer of okra in the world, where it is known as *bhindi*. In this Indian-inspired recipe, it is crisply fried, tossed in warm spices, and served with nicely herbed dipping sauce. Chef Vishwesh Bhatt of Snackbar in Oxford, Mississippi, says about okra, "Okra is my favorite vegetable. It is a great symbol of how interconnected the world we live in is. Okra, along with black-eyed peas and peanuts, are three things that link where I grew up in India to where I am now in the South."

For the dipping sauce

2 tablespoons chickpea flour or chickpea and fava bean flour

1½ teaspoons cumin seeds, crushed

1 cup plain 2% Greek or 0% Icelandic yogurt

1 teaspoon chopped fresh cilantro

1 teaspoon chopped fresh mint

Coarse kosher salt and freshly ground black pepper

For the okra

1 pound okra (about 40 pieces), stem ends trimmed

½ cup canola oil

1 teaspoon garam masala

1 teaspoon ground coriander

½ teaspoon ground turmeric

¼ teaspoon cayenne pepper, or to taste

Coarse kosher salt and freshly ground black pepper

1 *To make the dipping sauce,* heat a small skillet over medium heat. Add the chickpea flour and cumin seeds. Toast, stirring continuously, until aromatic and slightly darkened, 2 minutes. Transfer to a medium bowl. Add the yogurt, cilantro, and mint; stir to combine. Season with salt and pepper and set aside.

2 *To make the okra,* use a meat mallet or the bottom of a cast-iron skillet to smash the okra, starting at the tip of the pod and working toward the stem end. (You can also thinly slice it lengthwise. I like using a mixture of both smashing and slicing.)

3 Line a bowl with paper towels and have it nearby. Heat the oil in a large skillet over medium-high heat until shimmering. When it is hot but not smoking, add the okra. Fry until crisp and browned on both sides, 5 to 8 minutes. Remove with a slotted spoon and drain in the prepared bowl. While the okra is hot, sprinkle it with the garam masala, coriander, turmeric, and cayenne. Season with salt and black pepper. Toss to mix and combine. Serve immediately with the yogurt dipping sauce.

Greek Okra and Tomatoes

Serves 4 to 6

The first Greek immigrants to Birmingham, Alabama, arrived in the late nineteenth century to work in the iron and steel mills. Men came to earn money to bring over to their families and to pay dowries so that female relatives could marry. Some immigrants went into low-overhead ventures such as shoeshine booths, carts for selling candy and cigars, fruit stands, flower stalls, and—most interestingly—hot dog carts and sandwich wagons. Those fledgling food-truck precursors were the seeds that started Birmingham's eventual prosperous Greek restaurant community. Greek immigrants are behind some of Birmingham's most beloved restaurants—from Gus's Hot Dogs to white-tablecloth fine dining establishments like The Bright Star to Jim 'N Nick's BBQ, a barbecue joint with a commitment to sustainable food in multiple locations across the United States.

For this recipe, use fresh tomatoes when in season, but otherwise, I find canned to be perfectly acceptable. I am of the mind that you can chop, but you can't unchop, so I generally keep only whole canned tomatoes in the pantry instead of myriad canned tomato choices. The easiest and least messy way to "chop" whole tomatoes is to insert a pair of kitchen shears into the opened can and snip a few times to cut the tomatoes into chunks.

¼ cup pure olive oil

1 sweet onion, sliced

3 garlic cloves, finely chopped

1 pound fresh okra, stem ends trimmed, cut into ½-inch pieces

3 fresh tomatoes (about 1½ pounds), cored and diced, or 1 (28-ounce) can whole tomatoes, chopped, with juices

Coarse kosher salt and freshly ground black pepper

1 tablespoon chopped fresh oregano or marjoram

¾ cup crumbled feta cheese (about 3 ounces)

1 Heat the oil in a large heavy pot over medium-high heat. Add the onion and cook until soft and translucent, 3 to 5 minutes. Add the garlic and cook until fragrant, 45 to 60 seconds. Add the okra and cook, stirring occasionally, until the okra is bright green, 3 minutes. Add the tomatoes and season with salt and pepper. Bring to a boil, then reduce the heat to maintain a simmer. Cook over low heat, uncovered, stirring occasionally, until the okra is tender, 10 to 12 minutes. Add the oregano and feta and stir to combine. Taste and adjust for seasoning with salt and pepper. Serve immediately.

> The elephant in the room when it comes to okra is its famously mucilaginous texture. My top three tips for minimizing the slime are: add an acid, such as tomato, lemon juice, vinegar, or wine when cooking; don't crowd the pan; and cook it quickly over high heat.

Pimento Cheese Tomato-Herb Pie

Makes 1 (9-inch) pie

Growing up, pimento cheese was served on the following items: celery sticks; sliced bread, most often white; and sometimes, for a fancy luncheon, stuffed into a cherry tomato. Pimento cheese was never slathered on a burger, globbed into cheese grits, or married with BBQ pork for "Southern Nachos." Here's the deal—marrying a bunch of Southern ingredients together doesn't make something "extra" Southern. I would gently suggest that it creates a certified Southern train wreck. (Having said that, mayonnaise and tomatoes are a culinary combination like no other.) This recipe is deliciously mid-century, reeking of a Junior League cookbook.

Savory tomato pies have a long history on the summer Southern table dating back to the 1800s. According to Perre Coleman Magness, author of *Pimento Cheese: The Cookbook*, "There are as many ways to make pimento cheese as there are cooks who make it, and everyone in the South has an opinion. The opinions may divide, but the love of pimento cheese certainly unites." Pimento cheese is a year-round indulgence. Put these two particular Southern favorites together and sometimes, well, less isn't more, but more is indeed more.

4 tomatoes (about 1½ pounds)

1½ teaspoons coarse kosher salt, for sprinkling

2 slices bacon, cut into lardons (see note, page 32)

1 tablespoon pure olive oil (optional)

1 sweet onion, very thinly sliced

1 (9-inch) French Pie Pastry crust (page 282), blind baked

½ cup mixed chopped fresh herbs, such as chives, parsley, and basil

Freshly ground black pepper

1¼ cups grated sharp cheddar (about 5 ounces)

⅓ cup mayonnaise

1 tablespoon diced pimento

1. Line a rimmed baking sheet with paper towels. Core the tomatoes with a paring knife. Using a serrated knife, slice the tomatoes ¼ inch thick. Place a layer of tomato slices on the prepared baking sheet. Sprinkle with some of the salt. Top with additional paper towels. Repeat until all the tomatoes are sliced and salted. Set aside for at least 30 minutes while you prepare the rest of the pie. This is an important step; if you skip it, the tomatoes in your pie will be soggy.

2. Heat a medium skillet over medium heat. Add the bacon and cook until crisp, 5 minutes. Use a slotted spoon to transfer the bacon to a paper towel–lined plate to drain. Pour off all but about 1 tablespoon of the rendered fat from the pan (discard the fat or reserve it for another use). Or, if you don't want to cook with bacon fat, you can pour off all the fat and add the olive oil instead. (Alternatively, you can completely skip the bacon and just start with 1 tablespoon olive oil.)

Recipe continues

3   Heat the fat over medium heat, then add the onion and cook until lightly caramelized and golden brown, 5 to 7 minutes. (Don't skip this step; if you don't cook the onion, you will wind up with a soggy mess!)

4   Working a layer at a time, pat the tomatoes dry with paper towels. Place a layer of the tomato slices in the bottom of the piecrust. Add half the cooked onion, bacon, and herbs. Season with pepper. Repeat to make a second layer. In a small bowl, combine the cheese, mayonnaise, and pimento. Spread the mixture on top of the herbs. Bake for 30 minutes, or until lightly browned. Transfer to a wire rack to cool. Slice with a serrated knife. Serve warm or at room temperature.

There's nothing like the flavor of bacon, and when I eat bacon or suggest bacon in a recipe, I suggest you buy a good-quality bacon with a nice balance of meat, salt, and smoke. *Lardon* is the French term for a matchstick-size piece of bacon. I find cutting the bacon before cooking to be easier than cooking whole pieces and then crumbling the bacon. Lastly, bacon can be hard to cut. To avoid a slippery hazard while cutting, simply pop the bacon into the freezer for a few moments to firm things up for easier slicing.

Braised Collards with Parmesan-Tomato Broth

Serves 6

The word *umami* means "yummy" or "delicious" in Japanese. It's also known as the "fifth taste" and is sometimes described as "savory" to go along with sour, salty, bitter, and sweet.

Think of the meaty flavor of mushrooms, the earthiness of sweet potatoes, the richly vegetal flavor of winter greens, and the natural saltiness of a tomato. Other foods that are intensely savory include cured meats and cheeses. That means there's a scientific reason Southerners love collard greens simmered with a smoky ham hock. This vegetarian recipe replaces the ham hock with a triple punch of umami-rich tomato, Parmesan rind, and freshly grated Parmesan served on top.

1 tablespoon pure olive oil

1 sweet onion, sliced

6 garlic cloves, smashed

3 fresh tomatoes (about 1½ pounds), cored and diced, or 1 (28-ounce) can whole tomatoes, chopped, with their juices

6 cups homemade chicken stock or reduced-fat low-sodium chicken broth, or 4 cups stock and 2 cups water (I offer the alternative because most store-bought stocks come in quart containers)

1 Parmesan cheese rind (about 3 ounces)

1 teaspoon Aleppo pepper, piment d'Espelette, or red pepper flakes, or to taste

1 (16-ounce) bag chopped collard greens, or 1 (1½-pound) bunch collard greens, stems removed, leaves coarsely chopped (about 8 cups)

Coarse kosher salt and freshly ground black pepper

¼ cup freshly grated Parmesan cheese (about 1 ounce), for serving

1. Heat the oil in a pot over medium-high heat. Add the onion and cook, stirring occasionally, until golden brown, 5 to 7 minutes. Add the garlic and cook until fragrant, 45 to 60 seconds. Add the tomatoes with their juices, stock, Parmesan rind, and Aleppo pepper. Bring to a boil, then reduce the heat to maintain a simmer. (If you are using canned whole tomatoes, you can mash them with a spoon or an old-fashioned tomato masher to help break them down, if desired.) Cook, stirring occasionally, until the broth is rich and flavorful, 30 minutes.

2. Return the mixture to a boil. Add the chopped collard greens a handful at time, stirring between each addition. Season with salt and pepper. Cook, stirring occasionally, until the greens are just tender, 15 to 20 minutes. Taste and adjust for seasoning with salt and black pepper. Serve immediately, topped with the grated Parmesan.

Grits and greens are great together. *Grit* and greens? Not so much. The best way to clean greens, leeks, and sandy herbs is to fill a sink or bowl with cold water. Add the greens and swish them around so that any soil falls to the bottom of the sink. Lift the greens out, rinse the sink, and repeat until no grit remains.

Tomato-Ginger Green Beans

Serves 4 to 6

Green beans are also known as string beans or snap beans and are traditionally simmered for a long time with a hunk of some kind of pork—bacon, fat back, or hog jowl. My grandfather could eat a mountain of green beans and planted his garden accordingly. My grandmother would cook them in her pressure cooker, which would transform them from a bright green, crisp vegetable into soft-as-silk, army-green vegetable noodles. I remember the safety valve emitting little bursts of steam and the meaty, vegetal aroma that filled the air. There's always going to be a place in my heart and at my table for those old-fashioned Southern recipes, even as I appreciate the influences on Southern food and cooking from different cuisines and cultures.

Tomatoes are actually a fruit, not a vegetable, and marry particularly well with spicy ginger in this dish. While most ginger is imported, the sandy soil and hot climate of the Southeast is conducive to growing ginger, and a number of farmers are adding both it and turmeric to their crop rotation. And no, it's not a typo. I'm suggesting ¼ cup chopped ginger in this Southeast Asian–inspired side dish.

1 pound string beans (French-style haricots verts work especially well), stem ends trimmed

1 tablespoon canola oil

1 shallot, finely chopped

¼ cup very finely chopped fresh ginger

4 garlic cloves, finely chopped

2 tomatoes, cored, seeded, and chopped

½ jalapeño, or to taste, seeded and chopped

¼ cup chopped fresh cilantro

Coarse kosher salt and freshly ground black pepper

1. Bring a large pot of salted water to a rolling boil over high heat. Fill a large bowl with ice and water and set it nearby. Line a plate with paper towels.

2. Add the beans to the boiling water and cook until crisp-tender, about 3 minutes. Drain well in a colander and then set the colander with the beans in the ice-water bath to set the color and stop the cooking, making sure the beans are submerged. Once chilled, transfer the beans to the prepared plate. Pat dry with paper towels and then transfer to a bowl.

3. Heat the oil in a large skillet over medium-high heat. Add the shallot and cook until tender, about 3 minutes. Add the ginger and garlic and cook until fragrant, 45 to 60 seconds. Add the tomatoes and jalapeño and cook until warmed through, 5 minutes.

4. Add the cooked green beans and toss to coat and combine. Cook, tossing and stirring, until the green beans are heated through, 3 to 5 minutes. Add the cilantro; taste and adjust for seasoning with salt and pepper. This dish is delicious served hot, warm, room temperature, or cold. If served cold, make sure to taste and adjust for seasoning with salt and pepper, as chilling a dish dulls the seasoning.

CHAPTER 2

Grains, Grits, *and* Other Starchy Goodness

LIFE SKILLS, SELF-SUFFICIENCY, *and* SWEET POTATOES

Every holiday season, in anticipation of Thanksgiving cooking, grocery stores construct towering pyramids of canned yams, flanked by bags of marshmallows and boxes of brown sugar. The truth is that the contents of those orderly cans are not yams at all. What is often labeled and sold as yams are actually sweet potatoes. Botanically speaking, yams are tubers and a member of the lily family; sweet potatoes are the root of a member of the morning glory family. Yams originated in Africa, whereas sweet potatoes are New World plants. That sweet, orange-colored vegetable in the produce department is actually a sweet potato. Most people think that long, red-skinned sweet potatoes are yams, but they really are just one of many varieties of sweet potatoes. Compared to sweet potatoes, yams are starchier and drier. True yams can be tough to find. They aren't carried in many local grocery stores, so your best chances of finding them are in international and specialty markets.

I used to think I didn't like sweet potatoes because they were so sweet, and then I realized it wasn't the sweet potatoes I didn't care for—it was the copious amounts of sugar typically heaped upon them. They thrive in the Southern climate, store well over the winter months, and are highly nutritious. Sweet potatoes were a common food for impoverished Southerners, including enslaved Africans, as they could be grown to supplement meager rations. Because they were somewhat similar to the yams native to Africa in shape, color, and texture, African Americans adapted to eating sweet potatoes when they arrived on the American continent, and they became a cornerstone ingredient on the Southern table. Adrian Miller writes in *Soul Food: The Surprising Story of an American Cuisine, One Plate at a Time*, "The fact that sweet potatoes got African Americans through hard times enhanced its culture value, and we see that elevated status in the way sweet potatoes were cooked by African Americans during slavery and after Emancipation."

One man who is inextricably linked to the sweet potato is Dr. George Washington Carver. Born into slavery in Missouri around 1864—the exact year and date of his birth are unknown—he went on to become one of the most prominent scientists and inventors of his time. As head of the Department of Agriculture for the

"By working on an urban farm, residents can learn basic life skills, build community, develop entrepreneurial skills, and lead healthier lives."
—Bobby Wilson

Tuskegee Institute, his areas of research included methods of crop rotation and the development of alternative cash crops instead of cotton for Southern farmers and sharecroppers. This was especially important due to the devastation of the cotton crop by the boll weevil in 1892. In his efforts to teach farmers self-sufficiency and conservation, Dr. Carver created a series of free brochures that included information on various crops, cultivation techniques, and recipes for nutritious meals—including more than one hundred recipes for the sweet potato.

The genesis of the Metro Atlanta Urban Farm was cut from the same cloth as Dr. Carver's desire for self-sufficiency. Headed by CEO and Mississippi native farmer Bobby Wilson, the farm grows vegetables for retail sale, donates produce to organizations that help those in need, offers agriculture training for local citizens, and rents parcels for those interested in chemical-free urban farming. The farm is set on a beautiful five-acre tract of land established in the 1880s on Main Street in the heart of College Park, Georgia, just minutes away from downtown Atlanta. The offices are located in a stunning Victorian-era home with a large wraparound porch surrounded by rose bushes and pomegranate trees. The restored home features ornate woodwork, bay windows, a grand staircase, and tiled fireplaces. The greenhouse is now built atop the footprint of the original barn and the caretaker's cottage is used for classes and storage.

However, the formerly affluent area now has a poverty rate of nearly 40 percent according to the 2015 U.S. census. Equally concerning is that 30 percent of the residents do not have health insurance. On my first visit, I drove past the grand house twice, without a clue of what was hidden on the grounds. It's a veritable urban oasis tucked between a package store and a gas station. Urban gardening is the practice of cultivating, processing, and distributing food in or around a village, town, or city. It happens in backyards, on rooftops and balconies, and through community gardening in vacant lots and parks—or on managed tracts as it is with the Metro Atlanta Urban Farm. Despite their relatively small size, urban farms grow a surprising amount of food.

Birds chirp in the trees and I can hear a dog barking in the distance as Bobby and I walk the farm. I am astonished by the setting. Except for the hum of the cars and the sounds of MARTA, Atlanta's mass transit system, I could have been anywhere in the rural South, not in metro Atlanta with its population of nearly 5.5 million. The farm motto, "sustainability works," is evidenced by the onsite wells in addition to the state-of-the-art solar panels the farm uses to generate power. "We started out about five years ago with the purpose to address some of the needs in food deserts across the metro Atlanta area," Bobby says. "People did not have access to fresh produce, and we wanted to provide opportunities for individuals to be more self-sufficient and grow their own fresh vegetables."

A food desert is an urban area in which it is difficult to buy affordable, good-quality fresh food. Nearly 2 million Georgia residents, including about a half million children, live in food deserts. The USDA has classified more than thirty-five food deserts in metro Atlanta. Through my work with the Atlanta Community Food Bank, I know there is a direct correlation between food deserts and the state's high rates of obesity and chronic diseases such as hypertension, diabetes, and cancer. Stroke and heart disease are among the top three leading causes of death in Georgia, accounting for nearly one-third of all deaths in the state.

On this beautiful fall day, it's hard to conceptualize such tragic facts. Sweet potatoes are harvested in early October in most of the South when much of the summer produce has declined, although I notice a smattering of tomato, chile pepper, and okra plants still producing. One of the community gardeners is preparing his large plot for winter greens—collards, turnips, and kale. Bobby smiles and nods at the older gentleman, who he tells me is in his late seventies but works his vegetable patch nearly every day. The community garden is neat and tidy; someone has planted flowers around the edges of the plot. Bobby believes an agricultural framework is an excellent and cost-efficient tool to building stronger communities. Leaning on his worn shovel, he says, "Agriculture offers a multidisciplinary approach to providing workable solutions to communities. By working on an urban farm, residents and their families can learn basic life skills, build community, experience job creation, develop entrepreneurial skills, and lead healthier lives. In short, agriculture is the instrument for creating economic and health empowerment zones."

I laugh at the CDs hanging in the fruit trees, modern-day scarecrows of sorts. Bobby explains the farm is a certified "naturally grown" farm. This certification means those working on the farm do not use synthetic herbicides, pesticides, fertilizers, antibiotics, or hormones or grow GMO vegetables. He continues, "The 'naturally grown' certification allows them to offer organic-quality produce to customers at a fraction of the price of organic-labeled foods." The farm does a great deal of work with local churches and senior centers. I later learned that in 2015, the farm provided food for more than 5,000 homeless people, taught 1,900 students how to plant vegetables, and provided 2,600 pounds of food to needy families.

In metro Atlanta, food-related problems are complex and far-reaching. They include food insecurity, diet-related diseases, threatened ecosystems, and far too many communities with low access to fresh, healthy foods. The impact of these problems is vast. Conversely, there are more than eighty farms in a ten-county radius of metropolitan Atlanta, including the Metro Atlanta Urban Farm. Proponents of locally grown food know it contributes to community vitality, economic development, health and nutrition, and environmental stewardship. And it can start with something as simple as a bed of sweet potatoes. I'm certain Dr. Carver would agree.

The LANDSCAPE of LOUISIANA RICE CULTURE

Jamba-lye, crawfish pie, filé gumbo . . . My family moved from Georgia to Louisiana when I was three years old. My mother has always been an adventurous cook and immediately upon her arrival purchased several Junior League cookbooks with titles like *First You Make a Roux, Cotton Country, Talk about Good*, and *River Road Recipes*. She explained to me that she didn't know anyone and it was her way of getting to know her new community. Her inquisitiveness set me on a path to understanding and learning about different foods.

When I was young, every spring Saturday, a mixture of friends and family caravanned with coolers and wooden picnic baskets laden with food out to a lake near Alexandria, Louisiana, where I grew up. I remember picnic tables lined with newspaper and veritable bathtub-size pots of crawfish, corn, potatoes, and sausage. My tiny fingers quickly became adept at shucking the crawfish, pulling out the tail meat, and sucking the rich juices from the head. My parents bought nets and early on I learned how to assemble the trap and tie chicken necks to the webbed mesh. I grew up eating savory red beans and rice; thick, comforting gumbo served over rice; tangy tomato, crawfish, and shrimp étouffée with rice; fragrant, spicy jambalaya made with rice; meaty, earthy dirty rice; and boudin, a traditional pork sausage made with ground pork butt, spices, and rice.

We ate a lot of rice. Rice runs through the Louisiana culture like the bayous and rivers lace the landscape.

While it's true that rice cultivation began in the Carolina and Georgia colonies, rice has long been an important crop in the cuisine and history of Louisiana. Between 1865 and 1880, rice production along the East Coast declined rapidly due to the Civil War, the end of slavery, and the lack of available capital. Conversely, in Louisiana, production grew due to the introduction of steam-powered engines allowing for water to be pumped over the levees into rice fields; the mechanization of large-scale plowing, seeding, and harvesting (a good match for the level coastal plain of Louisiana); and the completion of the Southern Pacific Railroad from Houston to New Orleans. Land was cheap and the railroad promoted its availability, bringing a migration of Northern and Midwestern farmers into the Southwestern coastal prairie of Texas and Louisiana. New Orleans rapidly became the center of

*Rice runs through the
Louisiana culture like
the bayous and rivers
lace the landscape.*

rice milling and marketing activities. Rice became an integral part of both Cajun and Creole cooking.

The heart of Louisiana's rice belt is located on the southwest part of the state, where Crowley, the self-proclaimed rice capital of the world, is situated. It's deep in Cajun country. About 25 miles south of that is Kaplan, home to Richard (pronounced *Ree-shard*) Rice Farms, owned by Christian and Julie Richard. Both sides of Christian's and Julie's families have a long tradition in the rice industry. Christian represents the sixth generation as a rice farmer in south Louisiana. His father's family worked for Riviana Foods, when it was located in nearby Abbeville. (Riviana Foods has been processing, marketing, and distributing rice throughout the United States and around the world for over a century.) His grandmother was a bookkeeper for the Godchauxs, the family who spearheaded the establishment of the Louisiana State Rice Company, a consolidating entity created to increase efficiency in rice production. His grandfather and uncle were rice buyers and his father is a rice farmer. On his mother's side, his grandfather and his uncle were also both rice farmers. Julie is the daughter, granddaughter, and great-granddaughter of rice farmers. Before she started working for their farm—and raising her three children—she was the assistant director of field services for the Louisiana Farm Bureau. She and Christian met at a Louisiana Farm Bureau meeting about—yes, you guessed it—rice farming.

The Richards have a large metal shed adjacent to their rice silos fitted with a small apartment containing a homey kitchen and sitting area. A parish map hangs on the wall and a collection of ancient family farm journals rests on the shelf. We sit down at the table to a heaping plate of steaming-hot jambalaya with chicken and sausage dropped off earlier by a neighbor. The rice dish is hearty, filling, and delicious. With the jambalaya's zippy kick of Cajun spice, I immediately am taken back to my childhood. I comment on how good it is. Julie laughs and replies, "Our jambalaya is brown, not red like in New Orleans," implying this is not a chef's version of the dish; this is down-home country cooking. The Richards' three kids are in the nearby room playing with miniature tractors and trucks. It's a family business and it feels like one. However, this is not "small town" by any stretch of the imagination. While I've included smaller farms and artisan purveyors in this book, it's also important to consider that one of the secrets of the Southern table is that the agriculture is big business in the South. Half the rice grown in the United States is exported to over 120 countries. According to the USDA, Louisiana rice production was a $342 million business in 2014.

We hop in Christian's pickup to head out to the fields. Julie and the boys, Saul and Pauley, follow in a second truck, while young Katherine stays home with Grandma. As we rattle along the dusty road, Christian describes how he rotates his fields to optimize soil quality. "We farm 4,000 acres—2,000 acres of rice, 1,500 acres of soybeans, and 500 acres of crawfish." The rice is planted in early March and the fields are flooded. Then, by late July, he drains them to let them mature for harvest. In August, there's a primary harvest, and then the fields are flooded and the rice sprouts again for a second smaller crop known as a ratoon. After all the rice is harvested in the cooler month of September, he floods the crawfish ponds. Crawfish season runs from November until June. Christian says, "Water is the key to everything we do." His particular focus is on water conservation. "We take surface water, put it back on a rice field, and let the rice field filter out some of the sediments and nutrients." He points out that his fields are "flatter than a pancake." They are measured and leveled using GPS, which allows for greater water control and less water usage. Christian serves as president of the local soil and water conservation district. He operates on the philosophy that water conservation and farming go hand in hand.

We pull up to the field and stark-white egrets gracefully fly above the golden expanse. It instantly brings to mind the patriotic song "America the Beautiful" and its mention of amber waves of grain. A mammoth John Deere combine rumbles to where we are standing. We scale the ladder to the air-conditioned cab and Keith Whitley is playing on the radio. A bank of screens monitors the activity. Christian explains that everything is coordinated and monitored by GPS. With the technology, he's able to fertilize only the areas that require attention. He even has an app on his cell phone that's part of the process. It's all very high tech and precise. We run the length of the field and the massive machine veritably turns on a dime—not a blade of grass is missed. As we trundle along, a sensor sounds to indicate that the combine hopper is full. Christian radios for a transfer and a second tractor with a container attachment pulls up even with the combine. I smile as I see his two young sons in the tractor cab. A large unloader arm shoots the harvested rice into the transfer bin. This bin will be in turn transferred to an 18-wheeler container and taken to the silos where its moisture is measured and calculated. The process appears seamless.

But this is farming, and no amount of GPS and monitors can control the weather. A week after my visit, Vermilion Parish of Louisiana was devastated with a record-breaking twenty inches of rain, what was referred to in the news as a hundred-year flood. The rainfall tally shattered records and pushed rivers to their limits across parts of southern Louisiana and Mississippi. Two weeks into the harvest, Christian and Julie lost two-thirds of their soybeans, almost a quarter of their initial rice crop, and their entire second ratoon crop. Yet somehow, thinking of the family and their long history, I still believe that one day there will be a seventh generation of Richard rice farmers putting rice on the Southern table.

Savory Sweet Potato and Greens Gratin

Serves 8 to 10

Thanksgiving makes for a complicated Southern table. One family member insists on mashed potatoes, another requests sweet potatoes. Macaroni and cheese must make an obligatory appearance. For me, it's simply not Thanksgiving without cornbread dressing. We've not even really gotten started on the feast, and we already have four dishes of starchy goodness. I'm going to complicate things even further with this recipe for Savory Sweet Potato and Greens Gratin.

The holiday can also be a nightmare for gluten-free folks. I have found that chickpea flour, or chickpea–fava bean flour, can be used successfully to thicken the gravy in this gratin, and it's just as delicious as gravy made with all-purpose flour.

3 tablespoons pure olive oil, plus more for the baking dish

Coarse kosher salt

1 (16-ounce) bag chopped collard greens, or
1 (1½-pound) bunch collard greens, stems removed, leaves coarsely chopped (about 8 cups)

6 garlic cloves, very finely chopped

Freshly ground black pepper

2 tablespoons all-purpose flour, chickpea flour, or chickpea–fava bean flour

1½ cups homemade chicken stock or reduced-fat low-sodium chicken broth

½ teaspoon freshly grated nutmeg

Pinch of ground allspice

Leaves from 4 sprigs thyme, chopped

6 medium sweet potatoes, peeled and sliced ¼ inch thick (about 3 pounds)

1 Heat the oven to 400°F. Grease a large gratin dish with olive oil.

2 Bring a large pot of salted water to a rolling boil. Add the collard greens to the boiling water and cook until bright green, 3 to 5 minutes. Drain well in a colander and then squeeze out any excess water.

3 Heat 1 tablespoon of the oil in a large skillet over medium-high heat. Add the well-drained greens, and then the garlic. (You add the garlic after the greens so the garlic won't burn.) Cook until the greens are slightly wilted, 3 to 4 minutes. Taste and adjust for seasoning with salt and pepper. Transfer to a bowl and set aside.

4 Wipe out the skillet and set it over low heat. Add the remaining 2 tablespoons oil and heat until shimmering. Add the flour and cook, stirring, until foaming, about 1 minute. Add the stock and whisk until thickened, 2 to 3 minutes. Add the nutmeg, allspice, and thyme. Taste the gravy and adjust for seasoning with salt and pepper.

3 tablespoons fresh plain or whole-wheat, panko, or gluten-free bread crumbs

⅔ cup freshly grated Parmesan cheese (about 2½ ounces)

1 tablespoon unsalted butter, for the topping

½ teaspoon paprika

5   Place half the sliced sweet potatoes in the prepared gratin dish and season with salt and pepper. Spoon the seasoned collards over the potatoes and then top with the remaining potatoes.

6   Pour the gravy over the gratin and spread to cover and coat. Cover the entire dish with aluminum foil. Bake until the sweet potatoes are soft when pierced with the tip of a knife, about 40 minutes.

7   Meanwhile, combine the bread crumbs and cheese in a small bowl. Season with salt and pepper. Decrease the oven temperature to 375°F. Remove the foil from the gratin dish and sprinkle the bread crumb mixture over the sweet potatoes. Dot with the butter and sprinkle with the paprika; bake, uncovered, until golden brown, about 10 minutes more. Transfer to a wire rack to cool for about 10 minutes before serving.

Spicy Macaroni and Cheese

Serves 8 to 10

Farmer's Daughter is a farm-driven artisan food business celebrating the flavors of the Southern table and the *terroir* of the North Carolina Piedmont while gaining inspiration from food cultures worldwide. It was founded in 2007 by April McGreger, who learned the art of preserving at the elbows of her mother and grandmother in rural Mississippi. Her Sweet Potato Habanero hot sauce is a potent and delicious blend of sweet heat; the sweet potatoes add body and also tame the heat of the chile. Farmer's Daughter products are available online, in specialty markets, and in Southeastern Whole Foods Markets. I prefer using penne so that the creamy sauce can seep into all the nooks and crannies. If I have it handy, I always use Farmer's Daughter hot sauce in this recipe, but any hot sauce will be delicious.

4 tablespoons (¼ cup) unsalted butter, plus more for the baking dish

Coarse kosher salt

1 pound penne pasta

1 sweet onion, chopped

Freshly ground black pepper

2 garlic cloves, very finely chopped

2 jalapeños, or to taste, seeded and chopped

¼ cup all-purpose flour

2 cups 2% or whole milk, warmed

2 cups grated Gruyère cheese (8 ounces)

1 tablespoon dry mustard powder

1 teaspoon hot sauce, or to taste

½ teaspoon red pepper flakes, or to taste

1 cup fresh plain, whole wheat, or panko bread crumbs

1 teaspoon cayenne pepper, or to taste

1 Heat the oven to 350°F. Butter a large ovenproof casserole or baking dish.

2 Bring a large pot of water to a boil. Salt the water, add the penne, and cook according to the package directions. Drain well and return to the pot.

3 Melt the butter in a saucepan over medium heat. Add the onion and cook until soft and translucent, 3 to 5 minutes. Season with salt and black pepper. Add the garlic and jalapeños and cook until fragrant, 45 to 60 seconds. Add the flour and cook, stirring often, for 1 to 2 minutes. (This helps remove the raw taste of the flour.)

4 Whisk in the milk and increase the heat to medium-high. Bring to a gentle boil, stirring continuously, until the mixture thickens enough to coat the back of a spoon. Remove from the heat. Add 1 cup of the cheese, the mustard powder, hot sauce, and red pepper flakes. Taste and adjust for seasoning with salt and pepper. Pour the sauce over the drained pasta and stir to combine. Transfer the mixture to the prepared casserole.

5 In a small bowl, combine the bread crumbs, cayenne, and remaining 1 cup cheese. Season with salt and pepper and stir to combine. Sprinkle the topping evenly over the cheesy pasta. Bake until bubbling and golden brown, about 30 minutes.

Meme's Cornbread and Oyster Dressing

Serves 8 to 10

November and December are the perfect time of year for oysters, as tradition dictates to primarily consume them in the months that end in R. The R-month dictum isn't, or at least didn't used to be, a mere superstition. The summer months, all without an R, is when oysters spawn, making them flabbier and far less palatable.

My grandmother, whom I called Meme, would occasionally make this seafood stuffing as a celebration for the holidays, a holdover, I believe, from the days before consistent shipping and refrigeration, when enjoying oysters was a special treat. It seems most Southerners "dress" instead of "stuff," meaning we cook the dish outside the turkey instead of stuffing the bready mixture inside the bird. If you buy cornbread as a timesaver instead of making it from scratch, make sure the cornbread you purchase is made without sugar.

6 tablespoons unsalted butter

1 pint shucked oysters, cleaned of shells and debris

2 cups homemade chicken stock or reduced-fat low-sodium chicken broth, plus more if needed

4 cups day-old Brown Butter and Thyme Whole-Grain Cornbread (page 242)

1 pound country white bread, cut or torn into 1-inch cubes

3 celery stalks, finely chopped

1 sweet onion, finely chopped

2 large eggs, lightly beaten

1 tablespoon chopped fresh sage

1 teaspoon chopped fresh thyme

Coarse kosher salt and freshly ground black pepper

1 Heat the oven to 350°F. Using 1 tablespoon of the butter, grease an ovenproof gratin or casserole dish.

2 Drain the oysters in a fine-mesh sieve set over a bowl, reserving the oyster liquor. Measure the liquid and add stock to make at least 2½ cups liquid.

3 Coarsely chop the oysters into ½-inch pieces. Set aside. Combine the cornbread and cubed bread in a large bowl.

4 Melt 4 tablespoons of the butter in a large skillet over medium heat. Add the celery and onion and cook until soft, 5 to 7 minutes. Transfer the cooked vegetables to the bowl with the bread mixture. Pour the stock mixture over the bread and add the chopped oysters, eggs, sage, and thyme. The mixture should be fairly soupy. Season with salt and pepper. (If you want to taste and adjust for seasoning, simply zap a teaspoon or so of the mixture in a bowl in the microwave to cook the eggs and season as needed.)

5 Transfer the mixture to the prepared baking dish. Cut the remaining 1 tablespoon butter into bits and dot them over the dressing. Bake until heated through, puffed, and golden brown, about 45 minutes. Let cool slightly before serving.

Greek Crispy Lemon-Herb Potatoes

Serves 6

Tarpon Springs, Florida, has the highest percentage of Greek Americans of any city in the United States—more than New York, Chicago, or Boston. Located 30 minutes north of Tampa on the Gulf of Mexico, it is known as the "sponge capital of the world." Sponge diving—to collect natural sea sponges for household use—was a traditional business in the Mediterranean. At the turn of the twentieth century, a sponge-harvesting entrepreneur in Tarpon Springs named John K. Cheney partnered with a Greek diver, John Cocoris, to incorporate Greek techniques. Cocoris then recruited divers from Greece, the genesis of Tarpon Springs' robust Greek population.

Today, there are many Greek restaurants in the area, and some offer this tasty side dish on their menu. Perfectly cooked Greek potatoes are crispy on the outside, creamy on the inside, and zesty with mouthwatering lemon flavor and spicy oregano. The secret to these potatoes is twofold: baking them in a single layer so they roast, and cooking them in stages. The key is using a bare minimum of chicken stock. I don't bother peeling the potatoes, but do suggest at least halving them so the flesh can soak up some of the delicious juice.

1½ pounds Yukon Gold potatoes, halved, if small, or cut into 1-inch cubes

3 tablespoons pure olive oil

4 garlic cloves, mashed to a paste with salt (see page 22)

½ teaspoon chopped fresh oregano or marjoram

¼ teaspoon cayenne pepper, or to taste

Coarse kosher salt and freshly ground black pepper

3 tablespoons homemade chicken stock or reduced-fat low-sodium chicken broth

Zest and juice of 1 lemon

1   Heat the oven to 400°F.

2   Combine the potatoes, oil, garlic, oregano, and cayenne in a shallow baking dish. Season with salt and pepper and then spread the potatoes around so they are in a single layer. Bake for 20 minutes.

3   Remove the potatoes from the oven. Add the stock, lemon zest, and lemon juice to the baking dish and stir to combine, making sure to loosen any pieces of potato stuck to the bottom of the pan. Return the potatoes to the oven and bake until crispy and tender to the point of a knife, 25 to 30 minutes more. Taste and adjust for seasoning with salt and pepper. Serve immediately.

Yukon Gold and Butternut Squash Colcannon

Serves 4 to 6

I couldn't possibly have a book about the global South without mentioning the deep Scots-Irish roots. The Scots-Irish first immigrated to New England, and then found their way down the spine of the Appalachian mountains, settling into Virginia, Tennessee, Kentucky, North Carolina, Georgia, Mississippi, Alabama, and parts of South Carolina. Many no longer identify as an ethnic group, but their influences permeate Southern culture. Country music is the direct descendant of Scots-Irish folk music. Most Scots-Irish now identify as Baptists, the largest Protestant denomination in the United States and most definitely the largest religious group in the South.

Colcannon is a traditional Irish dish made with potatoes and cabbage—and lots of butter. I like mixing up my mash, so here, I add butternut squash. You can also try turnips or rutabaga. While many recipes call for sautéing the greens separately, this step isn't necessary if you use baby greens; you can simply wilt the greens in the simmering water at the end of the potatoes' cooking time.

1 pound Yukon Gold potatoes, cut into 1-inch cubes

1 pound butternut squash, peeled and cut into 1-inch cubes

2 garlic cloves, halved

Coarse kosher salt

5 ounces baby kale

½ cup 2% milk, warmed

2 tablespoons unsalted butter

Freshly ground black pepper

1 Place the potatoes, squash, and garlic in a large saucepan. Add cold water to cover. Season with 1 teaspoon salt. Bring to a boil over high heat. Reduce the heat to maintain a simmer and cook until tender, about 25 minutes. Add the kale and then immediately drain in a colander. Return the vegetables to the pot. Add the milk and butter and season with salt and pepper. Using an old-fashioned potato masher, mash until smooth. Taste and adjust for seasoning with salt and pepper. Serve immediately.

Baked Farro and Mushrooms

Serves 6

The South is well-known for its love of casseroles. One of the most adored is wild rice made with the familiar red-and-white can of cream of mushroom soup, the modern era's ultimate kitchen shortcut: instant béchamel. This dish evokes those same flavors. I've subbed out the wild rice blend for farro. When you want the earthiness of the farro and mushrooms to be more forward, go ahead and opt for the stock-only option. If you want it to be more indulgent, like the classic casserole, use the combination of stock and heavy cream.

Whole-grain farro is hulled using a process that leaves the germ and bran intact and requires overnight soaking before cooking. Look instead for semi-pearled, as it is quick-cooking and has the nutritional germ and bran mostly intact. If your container isn't labeled, just consider that if your package says it will cook in less than 15 minutes, it's probably pearled; if it takes around 30 minutes, it's probably semi-pearled. And if it takes 60 to 80 minutes or suggests overnight soaking, it is whole or unpearled.

1 tablespoon unsalted butter

1 sweet onion, chopped

1 pound mixed mushrooms (such as white button, cremini, chanterelle, morel, and shiitake), sliced (about 8 loosely packed cups)

Coarse kosher salt and freshly ground black pepper

2 garlic cloves, very finely chopped

2 tablespoons sherry

1½ cups semi-pearled farro

4 cups homemade chicken stock or reduced-fat low-sodium chicken broth; for a creamier casserole, use 3 cups homemade chicken stock or reduced-fat low-sodium chicken broth and 1 cup of heavy cream or half-and-half

1 bay leaf, preferably fresh

¼ cup chopped pecans

½ cup freshly grated Parmesan cheese (2 ounces)

¼ cup chopped fresh parsley

1. Heat the oven to 350°F.

2. Melt the butter in a large ovenproof skillet over medium-high heat. Add the onion and cook until soft and translucent, 3 to 5 minutes. Add the mushrooms and season with salt and pepper. Cook, stirring occasionally, until all the liquid has cooked away and the mushrooms are tender and no longer "squeaky," 5 to 7 minutes. Add the garlic and cook until fragrant, 45 to 60 seconds. Add the sherry and cook until the pan looks dry, about 1 minute.

3. Add the farro, stock (or stock and heavy cream), and bay leaf; bring to a boil. Cover and transfer to the oven.

4. Bake until the farro is tender and the liquid has been absorbed, 40 to 45 minutes. Remove from the oven, remove and discard the bay leaf, and stir in the pecans, Parmesan, and parsley. Taste and adjust for seasoning with salt and pepper. Serve immediately.

Stovetop Winter Squash and Herb Rice Pilaf

Serves 8 to 10

Folks often forget that Florida is the South, too! The Sunshine State has become increasingly more diverse, with immigrants coming from the Caribbean, Mexico, Central America, and South America. This classic Cuban pilaf is most often made with a hard winter squash called calabaza that can be found in Latin American markets. Annatto seeds add a distinctive red color. They are available at Latin American markets and in the Latin section of many supermarkets.

2 cups long-grain rice

2 tablespoons Annatto Oil (recipe follows) or pure olive oil

1 sweet onion, finely chopped

1 poblano pepper, seeded and finely chopped

3 garlic cloves, finely chopped

1 winter squash, such as calabaza, butternut, or acorn, seeded, peeled, and cut into ½-inch cubes (about 2 pounds)

3 sprigs cilantro, plus chopped fresh cilantro for garnish

3 cups homemade chicken stock or reduced-fat low-sodium chicken broth

Coarse kosher salt and freshly ground black pepper

1. Place the rice in a sieve set in a bowl, cover with cold water, and swish the rice around with your hand until the water clouds. Drain and repeat the process until the water remains clear, three or four times more. Drain again and set aside.

2. Heat the oil in a medium pot over medium heat until shimmering. Add the onion and poblano and cook until the onion is soft and translucent, 3 to 5 minutes. Add the garlic and cook until fragrant, 45 to 60 seconds. Add the rice and cook, stirring continuously, until lightly toasted, 1 to 2 minutes.

3. Add the squash, cilantro, and stock. Season with 1 teaspoon salt. Increase the heat to medium-high and boil until the stock has reduced, 8 to 10 minutes. Reduce the heat to low, cover, and cook until the rice is tender, about 20 minutes. Taste and season with salt and pepper. Discard the cilantro sprigs. Garnish with chopped cilantro and serve immediately.

ANNATTO OIL Makes 1 cup

¼ cup annatto seeds

1 cup pure olive oil

Combine the annatto and oil in a small saucepan over medium heat. Bring just to a simmer, adjusting the heat as needed so that the oil never boils. Cook until bright red, *about 20 minutes. Strain through a fine-mesh sieve and discard the seeds. Store the oil in an airtight container in the refrigerator for up to 4 weeks.*

Sweet Potatoes with Soy-Citrus Glaze

Serves 4 to 6

Housed in one half of a building that is shared with a convenience store, Heirloom BBQ in Atlanta meets the criteria of a classic Southern BBQ joint. From the cars jamming the overflowing parking lot to the neatly stacked piles of wood to the smoke lingering in the air, it's clear that this must-visit stop is the real deal. It's also not what you might expect. Kimchi coleslaw? Gochujang-rubbed pulled pork? Miso-injected smoked brisket? Chef-owners Jiyeon Lee and Cody Taylor met working in Atlanta restaurants; their pedigree includes some of the finest white-tablecloth dining establishments in the South. Taylor grew up in Texas and Tennessee. Lee recorded hit pop songs in late-eighties Korea. Their East-West mash-up is a welcome addition to the Southern table.

One of my favorite dishes on their menu is a Korean classic, deep-fried sweet potatoes with soy-citrus glaze. I've adapted the glaze and keep it on hand to drizzle over baked sweet potatoes. Topped with a pat of butter and a sprinkling of spicy red pepper, it's perfect as a side dish or even solo for supper.

1 cup water

¾ cup sugar

¼ cup low-sodium soy sauce or tamari

¼ orange, halved

1 teaspoon black peppercorns

1 (1½-inch) piece fresh ginger, thickly sliced

2 garlic cloves

1 whole clove

4 sweet potatoes, about 8 ounces each

1 tablespoon unsalted butter, or to taste

Coarse kosher salt

1 teaspoon Aleppo pepper, piment d'Espelette, or red pepper flakes, or to taste

1 Combine the water, the sugar, soy sauce, orange, peppercorns, ginger, garlic, and clove in a medium pot. Bring to a boil over medium-high heat. Reduce the heat to maintain a simmer and cook until the sauce has reduced and become syrupy, about 40 minutes.

2 Meanwhile, heat the oven to 400°F. Line a rimmed baking sheet with a silicone baking mat or parchment paper. (This will help with cleanup, because sometimes when sweet potatoes cook, they exude sweet juice that will burn in the heat of the oven.) Place the sweet potatoes on the prepared baking sheet and bake until tender to the point of a knife, about 1 hour.

3 Using a knife, split the potatoes open lengthwise. Top with butter and drizzle over some of the soy-citrus glaze. Sprinkle with salt and Aleppo pepper. Serve immediately. Store any remaining glaze in an airtight container in the refrigerator for up to 2 months.

Whole-Grain Parmesan Cheese Grits with Spinach and Shrimp

Serves 4 to 6

My first job cooking was on a TV-cooking show hosted by the grande dame of Southern cooking, Nathalie Dupree. I stayed on after the series taping ended and apprenticed with her for another year before she sent me off to culinary school. While I come from a strong culinary background—my mother is an excellent cook, as was her mother before her—I often say that "Nathalie took me out of my mother's kitchen." She exposed me to things I had never seen or heard of, and most certainly had never tasted or cooked. She's helped me and guided me my entire career. While she's always going to be my mentor, she's now become a very dear friend, and I love her very much.

Nathalie uses vast quantities of heavy cream to cook grits, and I tease her that the result is more akin to heavy cream thickened with ground corn than grits—delicious, but very, very rich. This recipe, inspired by hers, is a bit cleaner and simpler. Once upon a time, shrimp and grits was solely a food of the less fortunate—corn was cheap or farmed at home, and shrimp harvested from the creek or ocean was free for the taking, as long as you had a net. Now it has become a ubiquitous Southern dish seen from white-tablecloth restaurants to fast-casual diners.

2 tablespoons pure olive oil

1 sweet onion, grated

1 garlic clove, very finely chopped

2 cups 2% milk

2 cups water

¼ cup heavy cream (optional)

Coarse kosher salt

1 cup whole-grain stone-ground or coarse-ground grits

3 cups spinach, stems removed and coarsely chopped

½ pound large (21/25-count) shrimp, peeled and deveined, cut into ½-inch pieces

Pinch of cayenne pepper

¼ cup grated Parmesan cheese (1 ounce)

Freshly ground black pepper

1 Heat the oil in a heavy-bottomed medium saucepan over medium heat. Add the onion and cook until soft and transparent, about 3 minutes. Add the garlic and cook until fragrant, 45 to 60 seconds. Add the milk, water, cream (if using), and 1 teaspoon salt. Bring the mixture to a boil over high heat. Whisk in the grits, decrease the heat to low, and simmer, whisking occasionally, until the grits are creamy and thick, 45 to 60 minutes.

2 Stir in the spinach and shrimp. Cook until the shrimp are firm and white, about 2 minutes. Add the cayenne and cheese; taste and adjust for seasoning with salt and pepper. Ladle into warmed bowls and serve immediately.

Cheesy Broccoli and Rice Bake

Serves 8 to 10

There are many variations of this Southern-comfort staple: church-lady recipes that use cans of soup, Junior League mayonnaise–cream cheese combinations, and "cheffed-up" versions with heavy cream and toasted fresh bread crumbs. I've lightened it up by preparing a béchamel sauce with low-fat milk, to which I add a combination of reduced-fat and regular cheddar cheese. It's far less fatty and rich than the traditional version—and still tastes delicious.

1 cup freshly grated extra-sharp cheddar cheese (4 ounces)

1 cup freshly grated reduced-fat cheddar cheese (4 ounces)

1 cup fresh plain or whole wheat or panko bread crumbs

2 cups homemade chicken stock or reduced-fat low-sodium chicken broth

2 cups 2% or whole milk

2 tablespoons unsalted butter

2 tablespoons canola oil

1 sweet onion, chopped

1 celery stalk, diced

8 ounces white button mushrooms, ends trimmed, thinly sliced (about 4 loosely packed cups)

Coarse kosher salt and freshly ground black pepper

2 garlic cloves, very finely chopped

¼ cup all-purpose flour

2 cups long-grain rice

1 cup baby spinach, very finely chopped

¾ cup sour cream

Pinch of cayenne pepper

¼ teaspoon freshly grated nutmeg

1 pound broccoli florets

1. Heat the oven to 350°F.

2. Combine both of the cheeses in a small bowl. In a separate bowl, combine half the mixed cheeses with the bread crumbs. Heat the stock and milk in a medium saucepan over low heat until steaming. Keep warm.

3. Melt the butter with the oil in a large ovenproof casserole or skillet over medium heat. Add the onion and celery. Cook until the onion is soft and translucent, 3 to 5 minutes. Add the mushrooms and season with salt and pepper; cook, stirring occasionally, until tender, 5 to 7 minutes. Add the garlic and cook until fragrant, 45 to 60 seconds. Add the flour and stir to combine. (The mixture will be dry.)

4. Whisk the warmed stock mixture into the vegetable mixture. Add the remaining cheeses and rice; stir to combine. Add the spinach, sour cream, cayenne, and nutmeg; stir until smooth. Cover with a tight-fitting lid and bake until the rice is tender, about 40 minutes.

5. Meanwhile, place the broccoli in a microwave-safe bowl with ¼ cup water. Cover and microwave on high until just tender and bright green, about 2 minutes, depending on the strength of your microwave. Drain the broccoli and keep warm.

6. Once the rice is tender, remove from the oven and stir in the broccoli. Sprinkle with the reserved bread crumb–cheese mixture. Bake until the topping is golden brown, about 15 minutes. Let cool slightly.

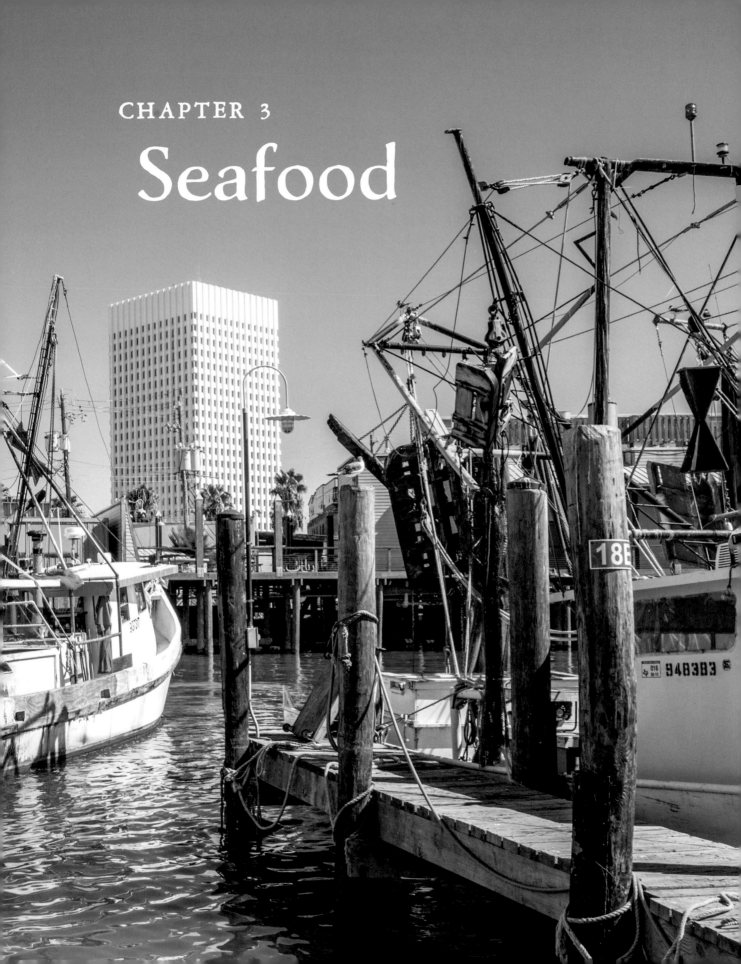

CHAPTER 3

Seafood

FLORIDA SEAFOOD

From its string of tropical keys trailing off into the divide between the Gulf of Mexico and the Atlantic Ocean to slender barrier islands on the Emerald Coast, from tiny fishing villages along the Panhandle to one of the most international cities in the United States, the state of Florida is swimming with incredible seafood sources. Seafood markets offer freshly caught Florida seafood right off the dock, and fisherman the state over deliver their fresh catch to seafood counters even before their fishing lines have had time to dry. High-end restaurants feature pristine fillets dusted with exotic spices, garnished with glistening foam, and bathed in fine French butter, as chilled white wines flow into crystal stemware. Countless laid-back dives pepper the state, where chalkboard menus hang on the wall, beers chill on crushed ice, and platters of seafood come piled high—fried, grilled, blackened, and steamed. Surrounded by salt water on three sides and hosting an intricate lacelike maze of freshwater lakes, rivers, streams, and springs, Florida has a fishing culture unlike any other state.

Florida boasts many iconic images: Disney World, acres of citrus groves, retirement communities for golfing grandparents, and sandy beaches. And right off those sandy beaches, underneath those crashing waves and inextricably tied to the booming tourism industry, is Florida seafood. Tourism in Florida has a long history; snowbirds have gravitated to Florida since the industrial revolution; in fact, those early wealthy pioneers developed South Florida. Florida has drawn people to it for many years and many reasons. There's "New Florida," with towering high-rises and slick developments, an influx of South Americans, Europeans on holiday, and endless tracts of mini malls and chain restaurants. There's also "Old Florida," made of small communities of rustic bungalows, mermaids and bottomless boats, and kitschy tourist traps where Native Americans fight alligators. One classic dish of Old Florida is smoked mullet. My mother has told me of seeing smoked mullet shacks alongside the St. Johns River in Jacksonville, Florida, when her family vacationed there as a child. The dish, for which a mullet is filleted, brined, and smoked for several hours over low heat, is a particular delicacy of North Florida. Once, you could find smoked mullet in every coastal restaurant and market in North Florida, but now it's more likely to be found at a chef-driven restaurant than a seafood shack.

An example of Old Florida that has evolved with the times is Joe Patti's Seafood on Pensacola Bay at the intersection of South A and Main Street. The business began in the early 1930s with native Sicilians Anna and Joe Patti selling fish and

"Having lived and cooked in Florida all of my adult life, I both cherish our bounty and want to see it protected and sustained for future generations."

—NORMAN VAN AKEN

shrimp from their front porch. Today, it's a sprawling warehouse facility with a large selection of seafood including shrimp, oysters, clams, and crabs, plus a nearby seafood restaurant with sushi as well as an in-house bakery and deli. Joe Patti's rose to prominence during WWII when it became a seafood supplier to the U.S. government. When Joe Patti's was primarily a shrimp business, the shellfish were not eaten as widely as they are today and most shrimp were used as bait; due to limits on refrigeration, only fresh product could be sold. Patti began freezing his catch in a new process called IQF (individually quick frozen). When the war started, another Italian shrimper out of Savannah, Joe Circone, was called on to use his shrimp trawlers to help patrol the East Coast for German U-boats. He also lent his fuel barge to the war effort—on the stipulation that the government buy his shrimp, creating a guaranteed customer. Circone's mother lived in Pensacola, and soon Joe Patti became the supplier of Gulf shrimp. The military began feeding shrimp to the soldiers, and on their return home, they wanted shrimp. That's how the Patti seafood dynasty was born, and the surprising way Americans began eating shrimp!

Floridians eat more than twice the national average of seafood when compared to other Americans. More than eighty types of seafood are harvested off Florida's coast, and the state of Florida ranked seventh among U.S. states in 2014 for fresh seafood production, with 99.2 million pounds harvested and a whopping dockside value of $257.7 million. Florida seafood is big business. Perhaps too big: Several Florida species are considered overfished by NGOs (non-governmental organizations) like Seafood Watch and Oceana. Overzealousness for those famous Florida grouper sandwiches and stuffed snapper entrées has taken its toll on wild populations. Fortunately, there are responsible fishers who want to save and preserve Florida seafood, not simply fish the fish into extinction. James Beard Award–winning chef Norman Van Aken, one of the more famous faces of Florida cuisine, says, "Having lived and cooked in Florida all of my adult life, I both cherish our bounty and want to see it protected and sustained for future generations. In my restaurants we purposely feature less well-known but prized seafood like wreckfish, barrelfish, lion fish, cobia, wahoo, and more from small-business fishing enterprises."

One troubling fact in this overfishing landscape is that a not inconsequential amount of Florida seafood is mislabeled—as much as 30 percent in recent studies have proven to bear incorrect labeling. The secret of some Florida tables is that the seafood isn't what it's supposed to be, with less-desirable species of fish labeled as a more expensive species. As quotas are tightened and seasons are limited, there's tremendous pressure to always have certain fish on the menu or in the refrigerated case. The fish passes through so many hands that its actual species can be nearly impossible to trace. A white fillet looks like every other white fillet, and can be mislabeled relatively easily. The fraud leaves consumers with little ability to know what they are eating or feeding their families and less ability to make informed choices that promote sustainable fishing practices. State leaders now recognize it is in their best interest to speak to the issue to protect wild seafood and for the greater good of the industry.

Aquaculture is one alternative to harvesting wild seafood and the inherent issues associated with it. Aquaculture refers to the breeding, rearing, and harvesting of plants and animals, such as fish and shellfish, in all types of water environments including ponds, rivers, lakes, and oceans. Shellfish aquaculture in Florida consists primarily of clam farming. Florida hard clams are harvested year-round and are always available in steady supply. Though some clams are still wild-caught, clam farming is a growing industry.

The Panhandle is a strip of land in Northwest Florida that is positioned between the Gulf of Mexico and the state of Alabama. Locals call this part of the Florida Panhandle "the Forgotten Coast," but once you see the tremendous snow-white dunes and taste the oysters in Apalachicola, you'll never forget it. Along the Panhandle and primarily in Apalachicola, however, several operations culture the Eastern oyster, which is found from the Yucatán Peninsula in the Gulf of Mexico to the St. Lawrence River in Canada.

For many Southerners—especially those who spend their summers vacationing in the Sunshine State—Apalachicola means oysters. These oyster fanatics are not alone—Native Americans left oyster and clam middens dating back to 2000 BCE, and oysters were Apalachicola's first seafood industry. Oysters were sold locally as early as 1836, harvested much the same as they are today with scissor-shaped tongs hoisted aboard shallow-draft skiffs. By 1850, oysters had begun to be packed in barrels and shipped aboard steamers headed north or to other neighboring states. Oysters have long been a Florida seafood mainstay, but due to water resource limitations, native oyster production is becoming increasingly challenging. However, according to chef Irv Miller, a pioneer of "New Florida Cooking" and author of *Panhandle to Pan: Recipes and Stories from Florida's New Redneck Riviera*, established oyster farms in Gulf communities such as Panacea and Cedar Key have been producing oysters for several years. Says Miller, "Off-bottom farm-raised Gulf oysters are the future for the oyster industry, provide jobs, and assist in sustainable oyster harvests as we rebuild our bay beds. They rival the finest cold-water farmed oysters, and they are shaking up the oyster market in raw bars and restaurants all around the country."

Old to new, wild to farmed, shack to chef-driven, Florida seafood is shaking things up all over the Southern table.

VIETNAMESE SHRIMPERS *in* TEXAS

When folks think of Texas, they likely most often think of open prairies, rugged cowboys, and branded longhorn steers, not Southeast Asians, altars of smoldering incense, and steaming bowls of spicy seafood. Yet there are more Vietnamese in the southeast corner area of Texas than in any other part of the United States outside of California, and Houston hosts the third-largest Vietnamese community in the country. How did this part of the South come to be a population center for Vietnamese immigrants? The migration started with the end of the Vietnam War, which devastated the country and left millions dead. Many of the South Vietnamese who had fought alongside the Americans were forced to leave the war-torn country. There were two waves of immigration, the first in the mid-1970s, which primarily consisted of educated professionals, and a second wave a few years later of thousands of refugees who came to be known as the "boat people." So many in the latter migration died in their attempts to escape that the United Nations intervened in what had become a humanitarian crisis. A large number of the refugees were settled in such ports as Houston, Galveston, Port Arthur, and other coastal cities across the Gulf of Mexico, as well as in San Antonio and Dallas.

Penniless and knowing little English, the refugees with fishing backgrounds gravitated toward the seafood industry. These fishermen and their families pooled their savings and began to buy their own boats. They worked hard, long hours and found a degree of success—except they had escaped one war to find themselves in another. Angry at the competition, a group of white fisherman invited members of the Ku Klux Klan to Seabrook, Texas, near Galveston. In 1981, the KKK waged a terror campaign against Vietnamese fishermen in Galveston Bay. Armed Klansmen patrolled the waters; crosses were burned, effigies were hung, shots were fired, and boats were destroyed. Eventually, a lawsuit filed by the Southern Poverty Law Center put a stop to the violence, and the KKK retreated. It was a significant victory for the Vietnamese immigrants pursuing the American dream and making the region their home.

Nonetheless, making a home in a new country with limited language skills and opportunities is challenging, to say the least. I know that when I lived abroad—and even when I lived in New York City—and felt particularly untethered from my kith and kin, I would make a batch of homemade buttery biscuits, a skillet of tangy

WILD CAUGHT
GULF HEAD ON
JUMBO SHRIMP
Tôm Lớn Có Đầu
$5.99 LB.

HEAD ON LARGE SHRIMP
Tôm Có Đầu
40-50
$5.69 LB.

SALE
HEAD ON SMALL SHRIMP
Tôm Nhỏ Có Đầu
91-110
$3.99 LB.

HEAD LESS SMALL SHRIMP
Tôm Nhỏ Không Đầu
91-110
$4.79 LB.

HEAD LESS SHRIMP
Tôm Không Đầu
41-50
$5.79 LB.

HEADLESS
Tôm Khô
36-40
$6.

ABALONE
BAO NGƯ TƯƠI
$19.99

FRESH FISH   LIVE CRABS

415

Traditional Vietnamese cuisine is a sophisticated mix of French and Asian—with an emphasis on fresh seafood, hot chile peppers, and cilantro—that is easily adapted to the coastal region of Texas.

buttermilk cornbread, or a platter of golden fried chicken. Nothing, absolutely nothing, soothes those sharp pangs of homesickness more than food. Faced with hostile neighbors and a sense of displacement, the refugees acclimated to making Vietnamese food in Texas.

Traditional Vietnamese cuisine is a sophisticated mix of French and Asian—with an emphasis on fresh seafood, hot chile peppers, and cilantro—that is easily adapted to the coastal region of Texas. One adaptation that has infiltrated local Southern foodways is a style called Viet-Tex. The other style is called Viet-Cajun and is primarily a response to the crawfish culture found in East Texas. After all, Houston is located almost as close to New Orleans as it is to Dallas—and Louisiana doesn't have a lock on bayous. Vietnamese Houstonians are particularly well-known for crawfish and pho, a beef broth–based soup, influenced by the plentiful supply from crawfish farms in Louisiana and prime quality beef from the cattle ranches on the Texas prairie. Historically, culinary evolutions such as Viet-Tex and Viet-Cajun start in port cities, where folks who recently arrived start to make their new home.

To delve into this food landscape I made it my mission to visit Vietnamese restaurants firsthand. Mapping out my game plan, I consulted with Robb Walsh, an award-winning food writer, cookbook author, and restaurant owner based in Galveston, Texas. He's a cofounder of Galveston Eats, a nonprofit dedicated to preserving Galveston food culture, associated with The Gulf Coast Food Project at the University of Houston's Public History Center. Robb also cofounded Foodways Texas, a nonprofit dedicated to preserving Texas food history. I also reached out to my friend, artist and former Southern Foodways Alliance oral historian Amy C. Evans. Amy's not technically a native, moving from California at age 2, but I pretty much think that's a technicality. Last, I paid a visit to Underbelly, where James Beard Award–winning Chef Chris Shepherd features locally sourced food inspired by the ethnic diversity of Houston. Chris is so enamored of Vietnamese cuisine, he actually traveled to Vietnam to gain a better understanding of the Vietnamese food in his hometown.

I knew better than to think that one restaurant would exemplify the best Vietnamese food in the entire city. That's rarely a question that can easily be satisfied with one answer in any cuisine, much less a complex cuisine that had experienced shifts and changes in its adopted home. It's very unusual that one place executes every dish better than any other place in the city. More often, restaurants become known for a specific, particular dish. I set out on my Houston tour wanting to focus on the Houston specialties and gain a greater understanding of the Viet-Tex culture. Having grown up in Louisiana and gifted with a love of crawfish, for purely selfish reasons I put Viet-Cajun crawfish at the top of my list. Amy and I visit Crawfish Café, located in the enormous Hong Kong City Mall—also home to numerous telephone-card stores and a cavernous Asian market with a veritable wall of rice—which is one of the more popular Vietnamese crawfish houses in the city. Viet-Cajun crawfish is made with myriad ingredients—spicy garlic, sweet citrus, and other aromatics—that are added to the boil to enhance the flavor of the crawfish, and is finished with a slippery toss of garlic butter. Crawfish Café offers six different flavors including Original Cajun, Kickin' Cajun, Garlic Butter, Lemon Pepper, Thai Basil, and "The Mix," a potent blend of garlic butter and lemon pepper. Amy and I gleefully eat our fill of boiled crawfish while a basketball game blares on the television. My Houston food tour is off to a stellar beginning.

For pho, Robb suggests we visit Pho Binh Trailer, a Southside institution founded in the early 1980s. Located in a ramshackle trailer backed up against a drainage ditch, it is consistently rated in the top one hundred Houston restaurants. The tiny room is tightly packed with Vietnamese families and a handful of Anglos. Watching the dragonflies flit along the water out the window and listening to Vietnamese pop music, I enjoy a steaming bowl of pho, the nourishing soup served with a side plate of culantro, cilantro, basil, bean sprouts, and lime wedges for garnish. The broth is umami rich, meaty, and evenly spiced with fragrant star anise. I contemplate the influence of French colonization on Vietnam and perhaps the classic French dish pot au feu—a beef stew—on the Vietnamese soup.

The Vietnamese influence is not remotely relegated to the suburbs or outskirts of town. Amy tells me of Beck's Prime, an upscale local burger joint that features banh mi burgers with thinly sliced prime pork sirloin, Asian spread, Sriracha, fresh jalapeños, cilantro, red onion, and cucumber. I also visit upscale restaurant Mai's in midtown—a more cross-cultural experience than I could have imagined. Mai's was founded in the late '70s and three generations later, after rebuilding in 2010 after a terrible fire, the restaurant is still a popular destination for Houstonians. During my lunch, the restaurant is filled with a veritable United Nations of ethnicities, teens getting takeout, a working-class security guard on her lunch break, and medical professionals. The menu offers perhaps the ultimate modern Southern–East Texas–global mix: Vietnamese fajitas. They are made with sweet Texas shrimp; crisp romaine lettuce; zesty shiso, pungent cilantro, and mint; bean sprouts, crunchy julienned carrots, and cucumber; and fried shallots with crunchy toasted peanuts. This fresh and flavorful take on a Tex-Mex classic is served with rice paper rather than corn tortillas.

Houston is the fourth most populous city in the nation—trailing only New York, Los Angeles, and Chicago. It is the largest city in the entire South, as well as the largest city in Texas, a state known for being big. As a port city, Houston has officially become the most culturally diverse city in the United States. Chef Chris Shepherd calls Houston "the new American Creole city." He says that while there are preconceived notions regarding the term *Creole,* that at its roots, "Creole cuisine is simply the merging of diverse cultures with local ingredients." Houston's eventual embrace of Vietnamese immigrants is the delicious secret to their Creole Southern table.

Shrimp Burgers with Jalapeño Comeback Sauce

Serves 6

Instead of using egg as a binder in this recipe, I puree some of the shrimp in the food processor to bind the burger. A couple of helpful cooking hints to make a great shrimp burger: Don't be tempted to not sauté the vegetables; if you skip this step, the vegetables will release moisture when the burgers are cooking. Also, if you don't want to cook the burgers in the skillet, bake them at 350°F on a baking sheet lined with a silicone baking mat or parchment paper for five minutes per side, although the burgers won't be as pretty and golden brown with this method. These patties work great as a burger or as a cake; they're also great topped with an egg for a brunch rather than sandwiched between a bun.

Originating in Mississippi, comeback sauce is the kissing cousin of rémoulade and is a traditional condiment for fried foods.

For the jalapeño comeback sauce

½ cup mayonnaise

½ jalapeño, or to taste, seeded and chopped

½ sweet onion, grated

3 tablespoons chili sauce

Juice of ½ lemon

2 teaspoons Worcestershire sauce

1 teaspoon paprika

1 teaspoon hot sauce, or to taste

½ teaspoon dry mustard powder

Coarse kosher salt and freshly ground black pepper

1 *To make the comeback sauce,* combine the mayonnaise, jalapeño, onion, chili sauce, lemon juice, Worcestershire sauce, paprika, hot sauce, and dry mustard in a bowl. Season with salt and pepper; set aside.

2 *For the burgers,* heat the oven to 200°F.

3 Heat 1 tablespoon of the oil in a large nonstick skillet over medium-high heat. Add the celery, onion, and jalapeño; cook until light golden, about 5 minutes. Season with salt and pepper; add the garlic and cook until fragrant, 45 to 60 seconds. Remove from the heat and transfer to a bowl to cool.

4 Place 8 ounces (about 1 cup) of the shrimp in a food processor fitted with the blade attachment. Puree until very smooth. Add the remaining 1½ pounds shrimp and pulse until coarsely chopped. Transfer the shrimp to the bowl of cooled vegetables. Add the bread crumbs, parsley, lemon zest, and Old Bay. Season with salt and pepper. (To test for seasoning, zap a tablespoon or so in the microwave to cook it through first.)

For the burgers

3 tablespoons canola oil

1 celery stalk, diced

½ sweet onion, diced

½ jalapeño, or to taste, seeded and chopped

Coarse kosher salt and freshly ground black pepper

1 garlic clove, very finely chopped

2 pounds medium (31/40-count) shrimp, peeled and deveined

1 cup fresh plain or whole wheat or panko bread crumbs

2 tablespoons chopped fresh parsley

Zest of 1 lemon

1½ teaspoons Old Bay seasoning

1 tablespoon unsalted butter

6 buns, for serving (optional)

Lettuce and tomato, for serving (optional)

5   Heat 1 tablespoon of the oil with half the butter in the same large nonstick skillet over medium heat until shimmering. Using a ⅔-cup measure, shape the mixture into 6 burgers. Working with 3 burgers at a time, add the burgers to the skillet and cover. Cook until the bottom is golden brown, about 3 minutes. Flip and cook for 3 minutes more. Transfer to a rimmed baking sheet and place in the oven. Repeat with remaining 1 tablespoon oil, ½ tablespoon butter, and 3 burgers. Place on the warmed buns with lettuce and tomato, if desired. Serve immediately with the comeback sauce on the side.

Slow-Roasted Snapper with Olives and Tomato Vierge

Serves 6

My friend Jason Stanhope is the executive chef at FIG restaurant in Charleston, South Carolina. He and chef-owner Mike Lata have been leaders in the farm-to-table movement since opening more than a decade ago. FIG stands for "Food Is Good" and pays homage to the bounty of the Low Country region by offering a daily changing menu that is honest and straightforward, much like this simple fish dish. *Sauce vierge* (which translates from French to "virgin sauce") is a modern classic French sauce made from olive oil, lemon juice, chopped tomato, chopped herbs, and spices such as coriander seed. This elegant recipe, inspired by one of Jason's menu items, might be more typical of the South of France than the Southern United States, but it's Southern just the same.

1 tablespoon coriander seeds

1 cup extra-virgin olive oil

4 garlic cloves, smashed

6 basil leaves and stems (about ½ ounce), coarsely chopped

3 tomatoes (about 1½ pounds), cored, seeded, and diced

1 shallot, finely chopped

1 tablespoon sherry vinegar

Coarse kosher salt and freshly ground black pepper

1 firm white fish fillet, such as snapper, grouper, or salmon, cut 1½ inches thick (about 2 pounds)

1 lemon, very thinly sliced

8 sprigs thyme

2 bay leaves

½ cup green olives, preferably Castelvetrano, smashed and pitted

1 For the Tomato Vierge: Place the coriander seeds in a dry saucepan and cook, stirring occasionally, over medium heat until the seeds are lightly toasted and fragrant, about 3 minutes. Transfer to a mortar and pestle and lightly crush, or place on a clean cutting board and crush with the bottom of a skillet or a second saucepan. (You don't need to crush them into a fine powder, just make sure most of the seeds are opened.) Transfer the crushed seeds back to the saucepan. Add ¾ cup of the olive oil, the garlic, and the basil and heat over medium heat until you see a slight bubble in the oil. Remove the saucepan from the heat and let steep for 1 hour. Strain through a fine-mesh sieve. Add the tomatoes, shallot, and vinegar. Season with salt and pepper and set aside.

2 Heat the oven to 250°F.

3 Place the fish in a shallow baking dish and coat it with some of the remaining olive oil. Season with salt and pepper. Scatter the lemon slices, thyme, bay leaves, and olives around the fish. Bake until the fish is very tender and slightly opaque, 40 to 60 minutes. (The lower temperature means the fish will take much more time than the standard 10 minutes per inch of thickness, and will not dry out in the process.)

Recipe continues

Because a side of salmon typically isn't as thick as a side of snapper or grouper, I have found that the salmon will take about 40 minutes and a thicker fillet like grouper requires closer to 60 minutes.

4   Leave the fillet in the baking dish or use a spatula to carefully transfer the fish and olives to a platter. Discard the thyme stems and bay leaves and spoon the Tomato Vierge over the fish. Serve immediately.

This recipe features Sicilian Castelvetrano olives, which are best for eating instead of pressing into oil. These olives are known for their rich, buttery texture and meaty, green flavor. They are less briny and sweeter than many other olives and can often be found at Costco, Whole Foods, and gourmet specialty stores and online.

Oven-Roasted Trout with Apple-Fennel Slaw

Serves 4

Frank Stitt is the chef-owner of three award-winning restaurants in Birmingham, Alabama. Frank is a culinary hero of mine and has been recognized with a Lifetime Achievement Award by the Southern Foodways Alliance for his elevation of Southern cuisine. His culinary journey started when he left his native Alabama to move to San Francisco, where as a philosophy student he read essays on food and developed an interest in cooking, soon working his way into Alice Waters' kitchen at Chez Panisse. He also worked in France, where he met other notable chefs and food writers such as Julia Child, Jeremiah Tower, and Simone Beck.

One of my favorite meals of the past few years was at his restaurant Highlands Bar and Grill. It was a lovely, quiet evening with good service, good wine, and good food—the trifecta of what successful dining out should be. One highlight was a simple salad perfectly dressed in vinaigrette. Sometimes the most challenging dishes are those with the fewest ingredients: the fewer the ingredients, the better each individual ingredient has to be, and the better the techniques must be executed. The real secret to world-class cooking is that a simple salad merits the same attention to detail as the most complex dish. Frank understands this concept and has imbued his Southern table with the same thoughtfulness and care. This simple fish recipe was inspired by one of the recipes in his award-winning book *Frank Stitt's Southern Table*.

1 apple, such as Granny Smith or Honeycrisp, cored and thinly sliced

1 small fennel bulb, tough outer layer removed, cored, and thinly sliced

½ cup fresh mint leaves

4 ounces baby kale (4 cups)

Coarse kosher salt and freshly ground black pepper

1 tablespoon unsalted butter, at room temperature

2 headless butterflied trout (about 10 ounces each), or 4 trout, arctic char, or catfish fillets

1 tablespoon sherry vinegar

1 tablespoon best-quality extra-virgin olive oil, plus more for serving

1   Combine the apple, fennel, mint, and kale in a bowl. Season with salt and pepper. Set aside.

2   Heat the oven to 500°F. Brush a baking sheet with the butter. Season the trout with salt and pepper. Place the trout skin-side up on the buttered baking sheet. Bake until the trout is almost firm and cooked through, about 6 minutes. Set the oven to broil to crisp the skin and finish cooking the trout, about 2 minutes.

3   Drizzle the vinegar and oil over the salad and divide evenly among four plates. If using the butterflied trout, halve them into 4 fillets. Top the salad with the fish, skin-side down. Season with salt and pepper. Drizzle with additional olive oil and serve immediately.

Catfish Tacos with Avocado Crema

Serves 4

Wild catfish are bottom-feeders and can taste very muddy. Farm-raised catfish, on the other hand, are fed a diet of corn, and the taste of their flesh is mild and clean. My grandfather's pond had never been stocked with catfish, but occasionally we'd catch one anyway! He explained to me that it was possible that the eggs had traveled on the feet of waterbirds traveling from pond to pond. That, along with many other things about the pond, was a source of wonderment to me. We were taught to heed the water, respect nature, watch out for snakes, and throw back the fish that were too small and the bass that were clearly full and heavy with eggs. Those early lessons eventually led me to the advocacy work that I do for sustainable seafood—including suggesting sustainable farm-raised catfish for this recipe.

For the crema

1 avocado

¼ jalapeño, or to taste, seeded and chopped

¼ cup chopped fresh cilantro with stems

1 cup water

Juice of ½ lime

Coarse kosher salt and freshly ground black pepper

For the pickled onions

½ red onion, very thinly sliced

½ cup white vinegar

1 teaspoon chopped fresh oregano, or ½ teaspoon dried

Coarse kosher salt and freshly ground black pepper

For the slaw

¼ cabbage, cored and thinly shaved

¼ cup carrot matchsticks, or 2 carrots, grated

2 or 3 medium radishes, grated

Coarse kosher salt and freshly ground black pepper

For the fish

1 poblano pepper, seeded and cut into thin strips

1 pound catfish fillets, cut on an angle into 1-inch-wide strips

Juice of 1 lime

2 green onions, thinly sliced

1 small jalapeño, or to taste, seeded and chopped

2 garlic cloves, very finely chopped

Coarse kosher salt and freshly ground black pepper

12 (6-inch) corn tortillas, for serving

3 tablespoons fresh cilantro leaves, for garnish

1 cup grated queso fresco (4 ounces), for serving

Recipe continues

1 *To make the avocado crema,* place the avocado, jalapeño, cilantro, the water, and lime juice in a blender. Puree until smooth. Season with salt and pepper. Set aside.

2 *To make the pickled onions,* place the red onion, vinegar, and oregano in a bowl or mason jar. Season with salt and pepper. Stir or shake to combine. Set aside.

3 *To make the slaw,* combine the cabbage, carrot, and radish in a small bowl. Season with salt and pepper. Set aside.

4 *To make the fish,* heat the oven to 350°F. Line a rimmed baking sheet with a silicone baking mat or parchment paper. Scatter the sliced poblano over the prepared baking sheet. Bake until just tender, about 10 minutes.

5 Meanwhile, combine the catfish strips, lime juice, green onion, jalapeño, and garlic in a large bowl. Season with salt and pepper; stir to combine. Once the peppers have cooked for 10 minutes, place the catfish mixture directly on top of the peppers and return to the oven. Cook until the fish is firm and white, about 8 minutes.

6 *To serve,* spread a dollop of avocado crema on a warmed tortilla. Top with fish and peppers, slaw, pickled onions, cilantro, and queso fresco. Serve immediately.

Fish Steaks with Lemon-Caper Butter

Serves 4

A version of this timeless fish recipe is found at seafood restaurants all along both Southern coasts. It's my favorite way to serve fish for an easy supper. The crispy, buttery croutons soak up the pungent, lemony sauce, and while the arugula is optional, it provides a bit of color for the plate as well as a nice peppery bite. To shop responsibly, look for swordfish caught in the Gulf and Atlantic, which are rated as a "Best Choice" or "Good Alternative" by the Monterey Bay Aquarium's Seafood Watch.

1 lemon

2 tablespoons unsalted butter

2 slices firm white or whole wheat bread, crusts removed, torn into ½-inch pieces

Coarse kosher salt and freshly ground black pepper

4 (4- to 6-ounce) swordfish, halibut, or salmon steaks, cut 1 inch thick

2 tablespoons canola oil

2 garlic cloves, very thinly sliced

1 tablespoon capers, drained and rinsed

¼ cup coarsely chopped fresh parsley

Pinch of Aleppo pepper, piment d'Espelette, or red pepper flakes, or to taste

Several handfuls of arugula, for serving

1 Zest the lemon and set aside the zest for the fish. Using a small sharp knife, slice off the top and bottom of the lemon so it will stand upright on a cutting board. Stand the lemon on one end and, working from top to bottom, slice off the peel, white pith, and outer membranes to expose the segments. Over a bowl, cut each segment from its membranes, letting the segment and any juice fall into the bowl. Squeeze any remaining juice from the membranes into the bowl.

2 Heat the oven to 350°F. Line a plate with paper towels.

3 Melt 1 tablespoon of the butter in a large skillet over medium heat. Add the bread to the pan and cook, stirring and tossing almost continuously, until the cubes are golden brown and crisp, 3 to 5 minutes. Drain on the prepared plate and season with salt and pepper. Wipe out the skillet.

4 Season the fish with salt and pepper. (Go easy on the salt because the capers are salty.) Heat the oil in the same skillet over high heat. Cook the fish on both sides until nicely seared, about 1 minute per side. When you flip the fish, add the garlic, then the lemon zest, lemon juice, lemon segments, capers, parsley, and Aleppo pepper to the skillet. Add the remaining 1 tablespoon butter and transfer the skillet to the oven. Cook until the fish is firm and cooked through, about 7 minutes. Meanwhile, place a handful of arugula on each of four serving plates. Place the fish steak on the arugula and spoon the pan juices on top. Top with the croutons and serve immediately.

Gulf Coast Cioppino

Serves 4 to 6

Once abundant in East Coast bays and waterways, natural populations of clams and oysters are now less viable and cannot support market demand on their own. Hard clam aquaculture is the largest and most valuable of the shellfish aquaculture industries on the East Coast. In most Southern states, farm-raised clams may be harvested year-round. The quahog (pronounced *coe-hog*) is a species of hard-shelled clam and the one we most commonly enjoy in cioppino and chowder, in pasta, atop pizza, and raw on the half shell. The larger the clam, the tougher and chewier the meat. Choose smaller sizes when quickly steaming, grilling, or eating raw. Littlenecks are the smallest size, amounting to 7 to 10 clams per pound. Cherrystone clams are a little larger, with 6 to 10 clams per pound. Top Neck clams are roughly 4 clams per pound. Somewhat confusingly, the only quahog clam actually called Quahogs are quite hefty, weighing in at 2 or 3 clams per pound.

2 tablespoons unsalted butter

1 sweet onion, chopped

4 garlic cloves, finely chopped

1 cup dry white wine

4 cups store-bought seafood stock or homemade shrimp stock

1 (28-ounce) can whole tomatoes, with their juices

Pinch of cayenne pepper

Bouquet garni: 2 bay leaves (preferably fresh), 5 sprigs thyme, 4 sprigs flat-leaf parsley, and 10 black peppercorns tied together in cheesecloth

16 small red potatoes (1½ pounds), halved

2 pounds littleneck clams (16 clams)

1 pound jumbo (16/20-count) shrimp, peeled and deveined

2 pounds mussels

¼ cup chopped fresh parsley

Coarse kosher salt and freshly ground black pepper

1 lemon, cut into wedges, for serving

1   Melt the butter in a large stockpot or deep saucepan over medium-high heat. (It's important to use a taller pot rather than a wider one so the liquid covers the potatoes and doesn't spread too thinly.) Add the onion and cook until soft and translucent, 3 to 5 minutes. Add the garlic and cook until fragrant, 45 to 60 seconds. Add the wine, stock, tomatoes, cayenne, bouquet garni, and potatoes. Stir to combine. Bring to a boil and then reduce the heat to maintain a simmer. Cook until the potatoes are just tender, about 15 minutes.

2   Add the clams and cover; cook until just barely open, about 5 minutes. Add the shrimp and mussels; cook until the shrimp are firm and pink and the mussels open, 5 to 6 minutes. Discard any clams or mussels that fail to open. Add the parsley and stir to combine. Use a slotted spoon to scoop the seafood into large warmed bowls. Taste the broth and adjust for seasoning with salt and black pepper. Ladle the broth over the seafood. Serve immediately with a wedge of lemon.

Steamed Mussels with Apple Cider Broth

Serves 4 to 6

Wild saltwater and freshwater mussels are found from Maine to Miami. The majority of mussel aquaculture is found in the cold, icy waters of the Northeast, but freshwater mussels were once a major food for Native Americans and early settlers of the South. Muscle Shoals, Alabama, is thought to be named for the proliferation of mussels that once populated the nearby Tennessee River.

Always start with fresh mussels. Mussels that do not close before cooking, do not open during cooking, or have chips or cracks in the shell may be dead. The meat of dead mussels deteriorates, increasing your risk of microorganism contamination, food poisoning, infectious disease, and other health problems. These bivalve mollusks are inexpensive, easy to prepare, and an absolutely scrumptious one-pot meal that can be on your table in twenty minutes. Served with a loaf of crusty bread and a green salad, it's the very definition of elegant simplicity.

2 pounds mussels

1 tablespoon unsalted butter

1 sweet onion, chopped

2 garlic cloves, very finely chopped

2 (12-ounce) bottles hard apple cider

2 tablespoons apple cider vinegar

3 sprigs thyme

1 bay leaf, preferably fresh

½ teaspoon Aleppo pepper, piment d'Espelette, or red pepper flakes, or to taste

Freshly ground black pepper

2 tablespoons chopped fresh tarragon

¼ cup heavy cream (optional)

Coarse kosher salt

1 baguette or other crusty bread, for serving

1 Scrub the mussels and remove the beards. Wash them under cold running water, agitating them with your hands. Discard any mussels that do not close to the touch or when gently tapped against the counter.

2 Melt the butter in a large Dutch oven over medium-high heat. Add the onion and cook until golden brown, 5 to 7 minutes. Add the garlic and cook until fragrant, 45 to 60 seconds. Add the hard cider, vinegar, thyme, bay leaf, and Aleppo pepper. Season with black pepper. (Do not season with salt at this point, as the mussels may be naturally salty.) Bring to a boil and simmer for 2 minutes.

3 Add the mussels. Cover tightly and cook over high heat until all the mussels have opened, 5 to 6 minutes. Discard any that fail to open. Use a slotted spoon to scoop the mussels into a large warmed bowl and place the pan back over the heat. Bring the juices to a boil and stir in the tarragon and cream (if using). Taste and adjust for seasoning with salt and black pepper. Pour the sauce over the mussels. Serve immediately with the bread for sopping up the juices.

Spicy Asian Cajun BBQ Shrimp with Grilled Baguette

Serves 6

Barbecue shrimp in New Orleans has nothing to do with a grill, a pit, or even barbecue sauce. Barbecue shrimp in New Orleans is a dish of butter-poached shrimp flavored with dried spices and herbs. It's what happened to shrimp scampi as it traversed the Atlantic and crossed the levies of the mighty Mississippi. In the nineteenth century, trade routes opened between Sicily and New Orleans and thousands of Italians migrated to New Orleans. By 1870, New Orleans claimed the largest Italian-born population in the United States—even greater than the New York City area! A more recent immigration trend in the region has been the Vietnamese (as referenced on page 78), leading to the introduction of new flavors into this Southern dish.

1 baguette, cut into thirds and halved lengthwise

1½ pounds extra-large (16/20-count) shrimp

1 tablespoon Homemade Creole Seasoning (page 219), or to taste

8 tablespoons (½ cup) unsalted butter, cut into cubes

6 garlic cloves, finely chopped

½ jalapeño, or to taste, seeded and chopped

1 tablespoon finely chopped fresh ginger

1 tablespoon finely chopped lemongrass

Juice of 1 lemon

1 tablespoon hot sauce, or to taste

1 teaspoon fish sauce

Coarse kosher salt and freshly ground black pepper

1. Heat a grill pan or skillet over medium-high heat. Working with a few pieces at a time, cook the bread until browned and toasted, 2 to 3 minutes. (Alternatively, heat the oven to broil and broil the bread until toasted, about 2 minutes, depending on the strength of your broiler.) Set aside and keep warm.

2. Place the shrimp in a bowl. Add the Creole seasoning and toss to coat. Melt the butter in a large skillet over medium-low heat. Add the garlic, jalapeño, ginger, and lemongrass. Cook until fragrant, 45 to 60 seconds. Add the shrimp and increase the heat to medium-high. Add the lemon juice, hot sauce, and fish sauce. Cook, turning once or twice, until the shrimp are firm and pink, 1 to 2 minutes per side. Taste and adjust for seasoning with salt and pepper.

3. Spoon the shrimp and juices atop the grilled bread. Serve immediately, with lots of napkins!

Seared Scallops with Radish and Candied Jalapeño

Serves 2 to 4

Both bay and sea scallops are found in the Gulf of Mexico and off the Atlantic coast, and they are most commonly harvested using bottom trawls. Sea scallops are large, with a circumference about the size of a silver dollar, and bay scallops are small, closer to the size of a dime or nickel. Bay scallops are harvested along the northwest coast of Florida and sea scallops are harvested in the South off the coasts of Virginia and North Carolina. Diver scallops are hand-harvested sea scallops. In contrast to most scallops captured by a dredge across the sea floor, diver scallops tend to be less gritty. They are also more ecologically friendly, as the harvesting method does not cause damage to the ocean floor. Look for scallops labeled "dry-packed" for the best scallops with the freshest flavor.

I love the sweetness of scallops seared over high heat until they are dark brown. Paired with the sweet heat of the candied jalapeño and the peppery bite of the radish, these scallops make a simple but "cheffy" starter—and believe me, these candied jalapeños are good on just about everything!

¼ cup sugar

¼ cup water

4 medium jalapeños (about 3 ounces), very thinly sliced

12 large sea scallops (about 1 pound)

Coarse kosher salt and freshly ground white pepper

1 tablespoon unsalted butter, melted

1 tablespoon canola oil

4 radishes, very thinly sliced

Juice of 1 grapefruit

¼ cup freshly picked cilantro leaves

1. Combine the sugar and water in a small saucepan. Add the jalapeños and stir to combine. Bring to a boil over medium-high heat. Reduce the heat to maintain a simmer and cook until the jalapeños are candied, about 10 minutes.

2. Place the scallops in a large bowl and season with salt and white pepper. Drizzle the butter and oil over the scallops and toss to coat. Heat a large skillet until smoking hot. Add the scallops to the pan and sear on one side until deeply golden, 1½ to 2 minutes (depending on size). Turn over and sear other side, about 2 minutes for rare. (If you want to cook the scallops all the way through, reduce the heat to medium and cook until the scallops are warm in the center, about 8 minutes total.)

3. *To serve,* divide the radish slices among four plates. Top with 3 seared scallops each. Spoon the grapefruit juice over the scallops and scatter over a spoonful of the candied jalapeño. (Store remaining jalapeños in a jar in the refrigerator for up to 6 weeks.) Top with the cilantro leaves. Serve immediately.

Mexican Shrimp Cocktail

Makes 4 cups, to serve 4 to 6

I first had this refreshing Mexican-style shrimp cocktail, known as *campechana de mariscos*, in Houston, Texas, at Goode Company, a family-owned restaurant group that features Texas cuisine. Of course, the restaurant makes their own pico de gallo from scratch, but I'm taking a shortcut and suggesting best-quality store-bought—you can often find it in the produce department of better grocery stores and markets. At Goode Company, they serve it with freshly made tortilla chips, and it's also wonderful served on a bed of salad greens or in lettuce cups.

Often when people poach or boil shrimp, they will drain the hot, freshly cooked shrimp in a colander and then run cold running water over it to cool it down quickly and stop the cooking, essentially watering down any flavor from the shrimp boil. Don't wash away the flavor; try amping it up instead! First, make a flavorful cooking liquid; here I suggest lemon, onion, and bay leaves. You can also use your favorite spice combination. Then quick chill some of the cooking liquid with bags of ice. Once you've drained the shrimp, plunge it into the cooled liquid to chill and stop the cooking. Kinda genius, don't you think? For better flavor and a bit more protection against overcooking, cook shrimp in the shell. I do understand that peeling small and medium shrimp can be very tedious, so if you choose to cook shelled shrimp instead, that's fine.

1 lemon, halved

½ sweet onion, peeled

2 bay leaves, preferably fresh

Coarse kosher salt

1 pound shell-on medium (31/40-count) shrimp

1 cup best-quality fresh pico de gallo or tomato salsa

¼ cup tomato juice or Clamato

Juice of ½ lime

2 tablespoons ketchup

2 tablespoons chili sauce

1 teaspoon hot sauce, or to taste

1 garlic clove, very finely chopped

2 tablespoons chopped fresh cilantro

1. To poach the shrimp, combine 12 cups water, the lemon, onion, bay leaves, and 1 tablespoon salt in a large pot. Bring to a boil over high heat and then decrease the heat to low. Simmer gently for about 10 minutes to make a flavorful court bouillon.

2. Have ready a frozen freezer pack sealed in a heavy-duty plastic bag or a large heavy-duty sealable plastic bag filled with ice cubes. Transfer several cups of the broth to a large heatproof bowl. Place the ice pack in the bowl of broth; move the pack around until the broth is well chilled. Drain and add more ice to the bag as needed.

3. Return the heat to high and bring the remaining mixture to a rolling boil. Add the shrimp and boil until the shells are pink and the meat is white, 1 to 2 minutes for shell-on shrimp and about 1 minute for peeled shrimp. Do not overcook.

2 serrano peppers, seeded
and chopped

Freshly ground black pepper

½ pound lump crabmeat

1 avocado, diced (see sidebar)

Tortilla chips or Little Gem lettuce
leaves, for serving

4 Drain the shrimp in a colander or remove with a slotted
spoon and then immediately transfer to the chilled cooking
liquid to stop the cooking process. Set aside.

5 Combine the pico de gallo, tomato juice, lime juice, ketchup,
chili sauce, hot sauce, garlic, cilantro, and serranos in a large
bowl. Season with salt and pepper. Drain the chilled shrimp
in a colander, shaking to remove as much liquid as possible.
Fold the shrimp and crabmeat into the pico de gallo mixture.
Add the avocado; taste and adjust for seasoning with salt
and black pepper. Serve immediately with tortilla chips or
lettuce cups.

To achieve perfect cubes of avocado without the mess, cut the avocado in half lengthwise (around the pit) and twist to separate.
After removing the pit, cut the flesh on each
half, still in the skin, in a crosshatch fashion,
not cutting through the skin, and gently scoop
out the cubes with a large spoon.

CHAPTER 4
Beef, Pork, and Lamb

BLUEGRASS *and* BARBACOA

The rich, meaty aroma of simmering beef combines with the warm, earthy smell of toasted corn. A petite woman in a tank top is standing at a table rapidly bagging steaming-hot tortillas as an absolute beast of a machine noisily rattles and grinds behind her. I watch incredulously as a man loads a mountain of fresh masa into an opening at the top. Below, continuously rotating circular plates cut the tortillas and carefully place them onto a moving chain-link metal conveyor belt. The gentleness is as astonishing as the lightning speed. Periodically, the man grabs a misshapen uncooked tortilla and tosses it back into the chute for a second chance. He's constantly monitoring the action, circling the machine, adding dough, and adjusting levers. The rhythm of the couple and the machine is mesmerizing. The tortillas orderly stream into a metal firebox of blue flame that surrounds, toasts, and delivers them to the woman. Double-handed, her motions a blur, she grabs four at a time for bagging and stacking. Row after row of freshly made and cooked tortillas pour out. It's loud, hot, and fantastical. My stomach rumbles loudly in anticipation.

I have come to Lexington to get to know some of the city's "Appalachicanos"—Mexican Americans living in Appalachia. Lexington is the "Horse Capital of the World," surrounded by rolling hills of well-manicured bluegrass pastures. Church-like steeples pierce the sky, yet these structures are elaborate barns and ornate stables, not temples of worship. This wealthy enclave in Eastern Kentucky is not technically part of Appalachia, but the next county over is officially part of the Appalachian Regional Commission. Although Appalachia has abundant natural resources, such as coal and timber, the people of Appalachia have long struggled with poverty and have not enjoyed long-term benefits from these industries, which were developed during the industrial revolution. Frankly, some places over the county line may as well be in another country. In recent years, Appalachia has diversified its industries and has largely joined the economy of the rest of the country, but it still lags behind in most economic indicators. The region struggles with access to healthcare and quality education. However, Appalachia is far more than what is exhibited in "poverty porn"—media that exploits the poor's condition in order to sell newspapers, increase charitable donations, or generate web traffic as click-bait. In contrast, Appalachia has a widely diverse population, including a

DELICIOSAS Paletas De HIELO

PANADERIA
AGUASCALIEN
RESTAURAN
AGUASCALIEN

*This demographic shift has added
a toasty flame-licked tortilla to
the Southern breadbasket.*

thriving Latino population, and not all people face poverty to the same degree. Not everyone in Appalachia who is facing hard times lives in a dilapidated trailer or a rundown shack.

Many Hispanic immigrants in the region find work in the horse industry and the adjacent service industries that build, support, and maintain the palatial stables. In 2017 I was the featured chef at the Mansion at Churchill Downs for the Kentucky Derby. On the morning the day before the big race, we toured the stables, and I learned that an overwhelming number of the jockeys, grooms, and attendants were Latinos. The Hispanic population is growing faster in much of the South than anywhere else in the United States. Across a broad swath of the region stretching westward from North Carolina on the Atlantic seaboard to Arkansas across the Mississippi River and south to Alabama on the Gulf of Mexico, sizable Hispanic populations have emerged suddenly in communities where Latinos were a sparse presence merely a decade or two ago. Over 34 percent of Mexican Americans live in the South, second only to California and Texas, and have tremendously influenced local foodways. The South has absorbed the largest increase of Latinos of any region in the country over the past twenty years, and this demographic shift has added a toasty flame-licked tortilla to the Old South breadbasket of flaky buttermilk biscuits.

My friend chef Jeremy Ashby, a Kentucky native, and I are on a tour of Lexington, nicknamed "Mexington" for the thousands of Mexican immigrants living in the area. Migrants from across Mexico have brought their cultures, traditions, and renowned cuisine to the community established in the neighborhoods on Lexington's East Side. As we turn onto Alexandria Drive, Jeremy smiles and points out the house his grandmother lived in during the 1950s. The neighborhood is immaculate. The yards are tidy, brightly colored flower beds are manicured, and the vegetable gardens in the backyards are well kept. There are crucifixes on the doors of a handful of houses and many are proudly flying the Stars and Stripes. It's the middle-class American dream: Work hard and buy a piece of land.

Surrounding Eisenhower-era strip malls are now a series of Hispanic stores, part of the local Aguascalientes supermarket chain. There's a seafood restaurant, several bakeries, an ice cream shop, and a large grocery store. The parking lot is full at Tortillería y Taquería Ramírez. This simple restaurant is framed by a small kitchen; a wall of coolers hosts Mexican Coke made with cane sugar, ice-cold fruity Jarritos, tamarind-flavored sodas, and water. The twenty-year-old tortilla-making equipment commands a prominent place in the restaurant. A bank of juice machines bubble and froth near brightly colored tables. Benches line the linoleum-tiled room, and perched above them are a couple of TVs featuring *fútbol* and breathy telenovelas. Bold laminated photos feature posole, *caldo*, and *mariscos*, and the menu board boasts winning a national burrito competition. Yet the homemade tortillas are the real draw. Our list of taco choices is lengthy—*asado*, *pastor*, *lengua*, *carnitas*, barbacoa, chorizo, *cesos*, *tripa*, *pollo*, and *cabeza*—and are all cradled in the fresh tortillas made from local corn prepared by owners Laura Patricia Ramírez and her husband, Alberto.

Jeremy's other suggestion is across town, away from the core Latino neighborhood. We pull up to Maria's Kitchen with a sign that boasts "Happy Hour All Day" and "burbon" and Coke; I expect these attempts may be a play for the partying college students from the nearby University of Kentucky. Don't expect nachos bathed in neon orange cheese to go along with the bargain beers and misspelled libations. Maria's Kitchen, formerly a walk-up consisting of little more than an enclosed kitchen with tables and chairs, has become a sit-down restaurant offering authentic Mexican cuisine. Menu items include *gorditos*, pastry made with masa and stuffed with cheese, meat, or other fillings; beef tongue tacos; and even *tripas fritas*, described as fried chitlins, but I know this is a bit lost in translation. There is also a slew of other equally authentic, tasty, and more familiar dishes for American palates like *coctel de camarones* and burritos or meats in various traditional salsas.

My trip to Appalachia is authentic, but the secret to these Southern tables isn't shuck beans and stack cakes; it's tacos and tortillas. And this Southerner thinks it's *muy bien*.

maria's
kitchen
la cocina de maria

mexican restaurant

LOVE WHAT YOU MAKE

Florence is tucked in the northwest corner of Alabama, adjacent to the broad and picturesque Tennessee River. Native Americans of the region thought the river was magic and called it Singing River, because they believed a mystical woman dwelled in its flowing waters, guiding them with her melodies. The area is certainly no stranger to the music scene. On the other side of the riverbank is Muscle Shoals, home to Fame Studios, which recorded some of the most powerful R&B music in history. The "Father of Rock and Roll," Sam Phillips, who had the first recording contract with Elvis, was born in Florence, as was W. C. Handy, the "Father of the Blues." Hits produced in the region include "When a Man Loves a Woman," "I'll Take You There," "Mustang Sally," and "Freebird." The list of artists that recorded at Muscle Shoals reads like a veritable Who's Who of music: Etta James, Aretha Franklin, Otis Redding, The Rolling Stones, Paul Simon, and Cher.

Ranked as one of the top five safest communities to live in in the United States, it does seem to be one of the epicenters of the universe where creativity flows. Florence, Alabama, population roughly 39,000, is also home to two successful internationally known fashion designers: Natalie Chanin and Billy Reid. Even though I've tasked myself with sharing the lesser-known side of the South, I have to admit that I find this fact somewhat surprising—sartorial sophistication in a small town in the Deep South seems unlikely, at first glance. Of course, Dixie is long known for King Cotton and the dark years of slavery that put it on its throne. After the Civil War, a lack of unions and cheap labor encouraged the proliferation of textile mills, and before the passage of NAFTA in the mid-nineties, Florence was known as the T-shirt capital of the world. So, perhaps I should instead consider that the fertile ground for these two innovative, creative artists was there all along, simply covered in obscuring vines.

I walk into Natalie's office and she smiles broadly, her long white tresses piled atop her head. She's dressed in one of her own flowing ankle-length skirts, a tank top, and tennis shoes. She is the artist and designer behind Alabama Chanin, a lifestyle company that produces well-designed, thoughtfully made goods. The company uses 100 percent organic cotton jersey fabric, which is sustainably sourced from seed to shelf, in its designs. The textiles are not made by cheap labor overseas or in a factory sweatshop; they are stitched by a team of local Alabama seamstresses who are paid a viable, living wage. Natalie cares very deeply about advancing what she

"I'd suggest taking it one step, one garment, one organic tomato at a time."
—NATALIE CHANIN

calls the "living arts"—those skills necessary to sustain life and advance culture. Similar to the Slow Food movement, Natalie advocates for slow fashion.

The results are not inexpensive and indeed, what might appear to be a simple tank top may cost hundreds of dollars. In an effort to level the elitism of her designer goods, she espouses an "open source" philosophy: All the patterns and techniques for her garments are openly available through her books and workshops. Her hope is that people who cannot afford to buy her products will make them for themselves. She considers herself an educator and a maker. She says, "Once you start to purchase investment pieces that last for years versus a handful of wears, it becomes sensible. I'd suggest taking it one step, one garment, one organic tomato, as it were, at a time." She's a steward of the environment, the land, and her community.

We're at The Factory, a former T-shirt manufacturing facility from the 1980s and home to the entire Alabama Chanin operation, which includes a retail shop, café, design studio, manufacturing facility, and workshop space. The décor is sleek and minimal. Long cotton panels hang from the ceiling to divide the cavernous space. Simple metal racks host hangers of cotton clothing, and tables are laden with beautifully crafted Heath ceramic bowls and dishes, leather goods, and wooden cutting boards. The entire experience is thoughtfully created and curated. It's one of those artsy places where you feel like a rock star or celebrity might walk through the door at any given moment, and indeed, one might. An old-fashioned portable outdoor sign with a flashing arrow rests against a wall and reads "LOVE WHAT YOU MAKE" in capital block letters. The expression seems to perfectly define Natalie and the work she does.

But there's no pretention, and rows of rough-hewn tabletops atop painted white sawhorses form the seating area of the café. Natalie's an avid cook and it's clear the restaurant is her pet project. The menu consists of a delightful selection of house-made pickles, salads, soups, sandwiches, breads, baked goods, and quiches. We enjoy a creamy bowl of turnip vichyssoise topped with a dollop of herb pesto, tomato pie, and crisp lettuces, and finish our luncheon with lemon-blueberry crepes. Each bite is full-flavored and delicious. Ingredients are thoughtfully sourced in similar fashion to Natalie's fabric. The fruits, vegetables, pastured poultry, grass-fed beef, and eggs for the café come exclusively from local farms in the community.

One of the farms is Bluewater Creek Farm, named for the crystal clear spring-fed Bluewater Creek that feeds into the magical Tennessee River. Bluewater Creek is a family-owned sustainable farm near Killen, Alabama, not far from The Factory. Liz and Collins Davis manage it in partnership with Liz's parents, Donna and Doug Woodford. Liz is a registered nurse and nutritional therapist. Collins is an Environmental Sciences major who managed farms in Georgia and California before returning home to Alabama. Liz's father, Doug, is a physician and advocate of holistic medicine.

BLUEWATER CREEK FARM
· June 2016 ·

WE HAVE THE BEEF!

CHUCK   RIB   SIRLOIN   RUMP   ...AND PORK AND PRODUCE!

BRISKET   FLANK   ROUND

SHANK   SHANK

Early the next morning, Natalie and I visit the farm for a tour. Under powder blue skies, we drive around in an open four-wheel-drive cart and Collins shows us the containers with candylike SunGold tomatoes, herbs, buckwheat, and peppers. We drive past rusty-colored cattle, and Collins shares that one of the most successful animals they raise is the American Guinea Hog, a small, black breed of swine unique to the United States. The American Guinea Hog is a heritage breed that fell out of fashion, but was reintroduced due to its visual similarities to small pot-belly pigs kept as pets. Short in stature and only about 125 pounds, the breed is also known as the Pineywoods Guinea, Guinea Forest Hog, Acorn Eater, and Yard Pig. Collins explains that the Guinea Hog was once the most numerous pig breed found in the Southeast and currently is listed in the Slow Food Ark of Taste. The reason the Guinea Hog was so popular is because it was primarily raised for the lard, a key ingredient in traditional Southern cooking. Collins explains that on the farm, all the animals are hormone- and antibiotic-free, and it's clear that they have plenty of room to roam, graze, root, and forage. They feast on a diet of hickory, acorn, and black walnut, and we laugh as he refers to the pen as "Pigtopia."

The Bluewater Creek Farm mission statement is "to produce nutrient-dense, clean food in a sustainable way. This increases the nutritional value of the food produced, shows respect for the living beings in our care, and makes a positive impact on our local environment. Bluewater Creek Farm is a platform to educate our community about the importance of real food free of harmful chemicals and additives, sustainable farming methods, and a clean environment to achieve and maintain optimal health." Sounds a whole lot like "love what you make," doesn't it?

Garlic-Rubbed Skirt Steak and Vidalia Onions with Peanut Romesco

Serves 4 to 6

In this age of seasonless grocery stores, where strawberries and squash are always available, Vidalia onions remain a spring treat, with a harvest from late April through mid-June. Every spring, without fail, many Southerners buy a big mesh sack of these sweet onions and store them knotted in panty hose in a cool, dry place for as long as they'll last. Here their unique sweetness provides a great complement to rich steak and tangy romesco sauce. The sauce makes about 2 cups and can be easily doubled for a crowd.

Skirt steak is a thin, long cut of beef from the diaphragm muscles of the cow (when purchasing, you may need more than one steak, as they are generally sold in pieces). It is very lean and fibrous with an intense beefy flavor, and is often used in fajitas (the Spanish word *fajita* means "belt" or "cummerbund," referring to the long beltlike shape of the steak). Skirt steak is best cooked over very high heat and should only be cooked to rare or medium-rare for the tenderest texture; when you serve, cut across the grain of the meat. You may use other steaks such as flank or hanger in this recipe with equally delicious results.

For the steak

2 pounds skirt, hanger, or flank steak

6 garlic cloves, mashed to a paste with salt (see page 22)

2 tablespoons pure olive oil

2 or 3 large sweet onions, preferably Vidalia, sliced

For the romesco sauce

½ cup roasted peanuts

1 (12-ounce) jar roasted red bell peppers

½ cup tomato puree

2 garlic cloves, plus more for garnish

1 slice country white bread, toasted and crumbled

1   **To prepare the steak,** using paper towels, pat the steak dry and place in a large bowl; slather the garlic paste and olive oil all over meat, turning to coat. Add the onions. Cover and refrigerate for at least 30 minutes or up to overnight.

2   **To make the romesco sauce,** grind the peanuts in a food processor. Add the roasted peppers, tomato puree, garlic, bread, and paprika. Process into a paste. Add the vinegar and pulse to blend. With the motor running, gradually pour the oil through the feed tube in a steady stream until the mixture thickens like mayonnaise. Taste and adjust for seasoning with salt and pepper and then transfer to a serving bowl.

3   When ready to grill the steak, scrape any excess garlic off the beef and discard. If using a charcoal grill, prepare the fire using about 6 pounds of charcoal and burn until the coals are

Ingredients and recipe continue

1 tablespoon smoked paprika

⅓ cup sherry vinegar

⅔ cup extra-virgin olive oil, plus more for garnish

Coarse kosher salt and freshly ground black pepper

completely covered with a thin coating of light gray ash, 20 to 30 minutes. Spread the coals evenly over the grill bottom, position the grill rack above the coals, and heat until medium-hot (when you can hold your hand 5 inches above the grill surface for no longer than 3 or 4 seconds). If using a gas grill, turn all the burners to High, close the lid, and heat until about 500°F, 10 to 15 minutes. If using a grill pan, heat the pan over medium-high heat.

4 Grill the meat and onions over direct heat until char lines appear, the meat is done to taste, and the onions are tender and charred, 3 to 5 minutes per side. Let rest for 5 minutes before slicing the meat across the grain. Serve the steak and onions with the romesco sauce on the side.

CHOOSING OILS

All oil has what's called a smoke point, which is just what it sounds like: the point at which oil starts smoking and breaking down when heated. Canola oil is flavorless and has a high smoke point, so I use it a lot in recipes where I want the flavor of the food to shine through and when I need to cook at a high temperature. Olive oil has a lower smoke point and imparts its own flavor, so I use it on lower-temperature recipes where I want the flavor of the oil to add to the flavor of the dish. When choosing an olive oil for a recipe, I often look at the country in which the oil was produced; generally speaking, the hotter the country where the olives were grown, the more robust the flavor of the oil. (For example, olive oil from Italy tastes different from olive oil produced in Greece.) Of olive oils, extra virgin is the highest-quality oil, and you'll note many recipes in this book specifically call for it. Extra virgin is cold pressed, using pressure only, without heat or chemicals. It's fairly unrefined and has a moderately low smoke point; it is best used for dipping, drizzling, and dressings. Pure olive oil is more refined, has a higher smoke point, and is better for cooking.

Greek-Style Beef Tenderloin Medallions with Oregano Butter

Serves 4

With all four-legged mammals, the parts that get the most exercise are the toughest. They also have the most flavor, but need long, slow cooking to become tender. Conversely, the muscles that get the least exercise are the most tender and respond well to quick cooking. There are two muscles called the loin—one on either side of the backbone of all four-legged mammals including cows, pigs, and sheep—that stretch from the shoulder blades to the hip. The loin muscle in the rib area is known as the rib-eye and the loin muscle closer to the hip is the sirloin. The tenderloin is the muscle that rests below the loin. This prized steak goes by a number of fancy names: chateaubriand, tournedos, and filet mignon. It runs from the short loin section—near the waist of a cow, if a cow had a waist—into the sirloin section near the hip. Sometimes you will find a partial piece labeled "butt tenderloin" from the area nearest the sirloin. The tenderloin is blissfully tender, but actually has little flavor. That is why it is often served with flavorful horseradish sauce, wrapped in bacon, or—as with this recipe—marinated in lemon and topped with compound butter.

This recipe was inspired by a classic Greek restaurant called The Bright Star that was founded in 1907 in Bessemer, Alabama. The restaurant draws patrons from throughout the Southeast, as well as nearby Birmingham. Famous for steaks and seafood, The Bright Star was designated by the James Beard Foundation as an American classic in 2010.

For the steak and marinade

¼ cup pure olive oil

¼ cup freshly squeezed lemon juice

4 garlic cloves, mashed to a paste with salt (see page 22)

2 teaspoons chopped fresh oregano

4 (8-ounce) beef tenderloin steaks, about 2 inches thick

1 **To marinate the steak,** combine the oil, lemon juice, garlic, and oregano in a resealable container. Add the steaks to the marinade and turn to coat. Refrigerate for at least 2 hours.

2 **Meanwhile, to make the oregano butter,** use a rubber spatula to combine the butter, garlic, lemon juice, oregano, and parsley in a small bowl. Season with salt and pepper. Cover and keep at room temperature until ready to serve.

3 When ready to cook, heat the oven to 400°F.

Ingredients and recipe continue

Shown with Greek Crispy
Lemon-Herb Potatoes (page 58)

4 tablespoons (¼ cup) unsalted butter, at room temperature

1 garlic clove, mashed to a paste with salt (see page 22)

1 tablespoon freshly squeezed lemon juice

1 tablespoon chopped fresh oregano

1 tablespoon chopped fresh parsley

Coarse kosher salt and freshly ground black pepper

4   Remove the tenderloins from the marinade, discarding the marinade. Pat the steaks dry with paper towels. Season the steaks on both sides with salt—but not pepper, as pepper will burn in the skillet. You can add pepper after the steaks have cooked.

5   Heat a large cast-iron skillet over high heat until very hot. Add the steaks to the pan and sear for 3 minutes on each side. Transfer to the oven and cook for 5 to 7 minutes for very rare (120°F) or 7 to 9 minutes for rare (130°F).

6   Remove the steaks from the oven and loosely cover the skillet with aluminum foil. Set aside to rest and let the juices redistribute, 2 to 3 minutes. Transfer the steaks to warmed plates and top each steak with 1 tablespoon of the oregano butter. Serve immediately.

Shredded Beef Arepas

Serves 6

Arepas, which are prominent in the cuisine of Venezuela, are corncakes made of precooked corn flour known as masa harina. Arepas are eaten across the country, across all socioeconomic groups, at all times of day. Masarepa, a type of harina, is widely available in the United States (check the Latin aisle of your supermarket: Goya, PAN, and Areparina are popular brands). It comes in both yellow and white varieties.

Native Venezuelan Lis Hernandez is a first-generation American and the chef-owner of Arepa Mia located in Sweet Auburn Market, a traditional African American market in downtown Atlanta. She prepares a mouthwatering recipe known as *arepa pelua* ("hairy arepa"), named for the long strands of shredded meat inside; at her restaurants, she uses grass-fed beef from local farms including White Oak Pastures (see page 2). Lis's food, made with locally grown ingredients and sold at the market where Martin Luther King Jr.'s family once shopped, represents so much of what I consider the modern Southern table to be.

If you choose not to prepare the arepas, the filling would make one mean South American sloppy joe on a toasted hamburger bun. You could also serve it between two Summer Hoecakes (page 241) for a real multicultural treat.

For the flank steak

2 tablespoons pure olive oil

1 (2-pound) flank steak

Coarse kosher salt and freshly ground black pepper

1 sweet onion, chopped

1 red bell pepper, cored, seeded, and chopped

3 garlic cloves, very finely chopped

2 Roma (plum) tomatoes, cored, seeded, and chopped (about 1 cup)

2 cups water, divided

¼ cup Worcestershire sauce

3 tablespoons ground cumin

2 tablespoons smoked paprika

1 tablespoon chopped fresh cilantro

1 cinnamon stick

1   Heat the oven to 350°F.

2   ***To make the flank steak,*** heat the oil in a large Dutch oven over medium-high heat until shimmering. Pat the steak dry with paper towels and season on both sides with salt and pepper. Add the steak to the pan and sear until browned on both sides, 5 to 7 minutes. Transfer the steak to a plate.

3   Reduce the heat to medium. Add the onion and bell pepper to the oil and drippings in the pan. Cook, stirring to loosen the brown bits from the bottom of the pan, until the onion is soft and translucent, 3 to 5 minutes. Add the garlic and cook until fragrant, 45 to 60 seconds. Add the tomatoes and cook until softened, 60 seconds. Add 1 cup water, the Worcestershire sauce, cumin, paprika, cilantro, and cinnamon stick. Season with salt and pepper; stir to combine. Return the steak, along with any accumulated juices, to the pan and nestle it into the vegetables and sauce. Cover and

Ingredients and recipe continue

For the arepas

2½ cups warm water

1 teaspoon coarse kosher salt

2 cups masa harina

¼ cup pure olive oil, for frying and handling the dough

2 cups grated cheddar cheese (8 ounces), for serving

Avocado Crema (see page 91), for serving

transfer to the oven to cook for 1 hour. Remove from the oven and turn the flank steak over, bathing the meat in some of the liquid. Add the remaining 1 cup water. Return to the oven and cook until the steak is falling apart and the temperature registers 205°F when measured with an instant-read thermometer, 60 to 90 minutes more. Using two forks, pull the meat apart into shreds.

4 *Meanwhile, to make the arepas,* combine the warm water and salt in a bowl. Add the masa harina in a slow, steady stream, stirring with a stiff rubber spatula to combine. Oil your fingers and hands and knead in the bowl until there are no dry spots or lumps. Set aside to rest and rehydrate, allowing the corn flour to fully absorb the water, for 5 minutes. Divide the dough into 6 even pieces and shape them into balls a little bigger than a golf ball and weighing about 4 ounces each.

5 Oil your hands and pat one of the balls into a disk about 4 inches in diameter and ½ inch thick. Heat a film of oil in the bottom of a large nonstick skillet or large griddle over medium heat. Cook the arepas on both sides, 8 to 10 minutes per side. Reduce the heat as needed; a few nicely charred spots are delicious, but burned is not. Also, if cooking a few at a time, the pan will continue to absorb heat, so the last few will most likely need to be cooked on very low heat. Transfer the arepas to a plate to rest and finish cooking at least 5 minutes before serving.

6 *To serve,* using a serrated knife, split an arepa and fill it with a heaping spoonful of the shredded beef. Stuff with cheese and serve immediately with the avocado crema.

Glazed BBQ Beef Ribs

Serves 4 to 6

Georgia is home to the fastest-growing Korean community in the United States, increasing at a rate of nearly 90 percent in the last decade of the twentieth century. Duluth, about twenty-five miles northeast of Atlanta, has become Georgia's Koreatown. Increasingly, successful Korean Americans are moving from larger cities such as Los Angeles, New York, and Chicago to the sunny South for a better quality of life at a cheaper cost of living. Excellent Korean restaurants proliferate in the Atlanta suburb, some serving these sweet, sticky, and mouthwatering glazed beef ribs.

There are two basic kinds of short ribs: English and flanken. The English style slices between the ribs to separate them, resulting in a thick piece of meat sitting on top of one piece of bone. These ribs can be left as is in one long piece or cut into smaller pieces approximately two inches long. In the flanken style of short rib, the meat and bone are cut horizontally across the bones so that each slice is about a half inch thick and contains a few pieces of bone. This is the style required for these Korean *kalbi* barbecue beef ribs.

1 sweet onion, coarsely chopped

1 pear, cored and coarsely chopped

5 garlic cloves

¾ cup firmly packed dark brown sugar

¾ cup tamari or soy sauce

½ cup water

¼ cup mirin (sweet rice wine)

2 tablespoons dark sesame oil

Freshly ground black pepper

3 pounds flanken-style beef ribs

3 green onions, thinly sliced on an angle

1 In a food processor, puree the onion, pear, and garlic until smooth. (You can also grate the onion and pear on a box grater and finely chop the garlic, but the food processor makes pretty quick work of it.) Transfer to a resealable container. Add the brown sugar, the water, tamari, mirin, and sesame oil; stir to combine. Season the ribs on both sides with pepper and then add them to the container with the sauce. Turn to coat. Cover and refrigerate for at least 4 hours, turning the ribs periodically in the marinade.

2 Drain any excess marinade off the ribs and discard the marinade. If using a charcoal grill, prepare a charcoal fire using about 6 pounds of charcoal and burn until the coals are completely covered with a thin coating of light gray ash, 20 to 30 minutes. Spread the coals evenly over the grill bottom, position the grill rack above the coals, and heat until medium-hot (when you can hold your hand 5 inches above the grill surface for no longer than 3 or 4 seconds). If using a gas grill, turn all the burners to High, close the lid, and heat until about 500°F, 10 to 15 minutes. If using a grill pan,

heat the pan over medium-high heat. (Just know that if you use a grill pan, the marinade will definitely char, but these ribs are still delicious.) You can also cook these ribs under the broiler: Preheat the broiler to high.

3   Grill the short ribs, turning once, until nicely charred and cooked through, 3 to 4 minutes per side. Or, if under the broiler, 5 to 7 minutes per side, depending on the strength of your broiler. Garnish with thinly sliced green onions. Serve whole pieces as a main course or cut into smaller pieces, using kitchen shears, for a beefy nibble.

Mississippi-Style Char Siu Pork Tenderloin

Serves 4 to 6

Char siu refers to a style of Chinese barbecue that is sweet, savory, salty, and sticky all at the same time. It's what you've seen hanging in the window of urban Chinese restaurants, takeout shops, and grocery stores. This recipe was inspired by the Chinese grocery stores in Mississippi. Delta native and cookbook author Martha Foose says, "Though Cantonese, the flavors of *char sui* have always reminded me of the flavors of the Mississippi Delta. Located at the home of the 'Fighting Okra' at Delta State University, the Mississippi Delta Chinese Heritage Museum recounts the stories of tenacious settlers in the flatlands. As exotic as five-spice powder may seem, when ketchup gets stirred into the mix, it reminds me of how down-home ingenuity keeps tradition alive."

1 (1½-pound) pork tenderloin

¼ cup firmly packed light brown sugar

¼ cup soy sauce or tamari

½ teaspoon Chinese five-spice powder

2 teaspoons toasted sesame oil

1 tablespoon grated fresh ginger

1 garlic clove, very finely chopped

Nonstick cooking spray

2 tablespoons ketchup

2 tablespoons honey

Coarse kosher salt and freshly ground white pepper

1 Place the pork in a large plastic zip-top bag. Combine the brown sugar, soy sauce, five-spice powder, sesame oil, ginger, and garlic in a medium bowl. Pour the marinade into the bag with the pork. Press out as much air as possible and seal the bag. Refrigerate for at least 30 minutes or up to 4 hours.

2 Adjust the oven rack to the middle position and heat the oven to 300°F. Line a rimmed baking sheet with aluminum foil and set a wire rack on the sheet. Spray the rack with nonstick spray.

3 Remove the pork from marinade, letting any excess drip off, and transfer the marinade to a small saucepan. Add the ketchup and honey. Bring to a boil over medium heat and then reduce the heat to maintain a simmer. (It is important to boil the marinade to kill any possible bacteria from the raw pork.) Place the pork on the wire rack. Season on all sides with salt and pepper. Roast the pork for 20 minutes.

Recipe continues

4   Remove the pan from the oven and turn the oven to broil. Brush the pork with half the warm glaze; broil the pork until a deep mahogany color, 2 to 3 minutes. Using tongs, flip the meat over and broil until the other side caramelizes, 2 to 3 minutes more. The temperature of the pork should register 145°F when measured with an instant-read thermometer. Cover loosely with aluminum foil and let rest for 5 to 7 minutes to allow the juices to redistribute. Slice into ¼-inch-thick slices and serve immediately.

Pork tenderloins have an area of connective tissue referred to as silver skin for its silvery-white appearance. Also known as fascia or fell, the tissue doesn't dissolve when the tenderloin is cooked, so it needs to be trimmed away. To remove the tissue, position the tip of a chef's or boning knife about 1 inch from one end of the visible silver skin. Push the knife tip under a strip of silver skin about ½ inch wide. Angle the knife up toward the silver skin as you slide the knife down the tenderloin. Use your free hand to hold the silver skin taut as you cut. Once you've cut all the way through the end of the strip, turn the knife around and cut off the end that's still attached. Repeat until all the silver skin has been removed.

Carnitas Nachos

Carnitas are essentially pork confit. Confit is most often meat, such as duck or pork, that has been cooked and preserved in its own fat. Carnitas are typically cooked in water and lard until the fat renders and the water evaporates. The meat is then browned in the rendered fat. I've turned this recipe around a bit to make it a bit more user-friendly and not as greasy. First, the meat is seared and the fat is drained away. Then it's combined with water and spices and cooked until completely tender and falling apart.

Here I serve it atop nachos, and it would be equally good nested in corn tortillas for tacos or even doused in barbecue sauce on white bread. There's also the marriage of Hispanic and Country Boy in a dish known as "Redneck Nachos"—an incredible alliance that opts for grated cheddar instead of queso fresco and barbecue sauce instead of salsa. It's one of those dishes found at the Southern table that's a real example of cross-cultural pollination.

1 tablespoon pure olive oil

3 pounds boneless pork shoulder, cut into 3-inch cubes

Coarse kosher salt and freshly ground black pepper

1 sweet onion, halved

8 garlic cloves, smashed

2 bay leaves, preferably fresh

1 tablespoon ground cumin

2 teaspoons dried oregano

2 cups water

To serve

Tortilla chips

1 cup queso fresco (4 ounces)

1 avocado, chopped (see sidebar, page 103)

Lime wedges

6 green onions, chopped

1 cup fresh cilantro leaves

Store-bought fresh salsa or pico de gallo

1 Heat the oil in a large Dutch oven over medium-high heat. Season the pork with salt and pepper. Add the pork cubes without crowding, in batches if necessary, and brown on all sides, 5 to 7 minutes. Transfer to a plate. Pour off and discard the rendered fat. Return the pork to the Dutch oven and add the onion, garlic, bay leaves, cumin, oregano, and the water. Bring to a boil, skimming any scum that collects on the surface. Reduce the heat to medium-low and simmer, stirring occasionally, until the pork is fork-tender and the liquid has completely evaporated, 2 hours. (Alternatively, combine all the ingredients in a slow cooker, cover, and cook on Low for 8 hours or on High for 4 hours.)

2 Serve the carnitas with bowls of chips, queso fresco, avocado, lime, green onions, cilantro, and salsa alongside, allowing each person to build individual plates of nachos and toppings.

Rainy-Day Ribs

When it comes to deciding what type of ribs to cook, you have basically two choices: spareribs and baby back ribs. Spareribs are cut from the ribs closest to the belly and are meaty, bony, and thick. Baby back ribs are cut from where the rib meets the spine. They're only called "baby" because they are shorter and thinner than spareribs; they don't refer to the age of the pig. Each baby back rib rack averages ten or so curved ribs that are 4 to 6 inches long and weighs about 1½ pounds, which easily feeds two people as a main course. Baby back ribs also usually have a slightly higher price tag, but I think they are well worth the cost, as they are generally leaner, more tender, and quicker cooking.

Discovering low-temperature oven roasting was a serious revelation. Yes, of course ribs taste amazing slowly smoked, but long cook times on a grill isn't the only option for succulent ribs. Rainy-Day Ribs and ribs with little to no effort also sound good to me. Lifting the ribs above the baking sheet on a rack lets the heat circulate on all sides. After a few hours, the meat is tender, nearly falling off the bone, and you'll have finger-licking-good ribs.

Nonstick cooking spray

2 racks baby back ribs (about 3½ pounds total)

1 cup Sweet Heat Rub (see page 138)

Tangy Barbecue Sauce (recipe follows), for serving

1 Adjust the oven rack to the middle position and heat the oven to 300°F. Line a rimmed baking sheet with aluminum foil and set a wire rack on the sheet. Spray the rack with nonstick spray.

2 Rub each set of baby back ribs with ½ cup of the sweet heat rub. Set aside to come to room temperature, 30 minutes. (This step can be done a day ahead for deeper flavor: Rub the ribs with the rub and place in a resealable plastic container, or wrap in plastic wrap. If you use plastic wrap, make sure to place the wrapped ribs on a rimmed baking sheet to catch any seeping liquid due to the salt in the rub. Refrigerate to marinate overnight.)

3 Place the rubbed ribs side by side on the prepared baking sheet. Transfer to the oven and roast until the ribs are done and a knife slides easily into the thickest part of the rib meat, 2 hours.

4 Remove from the oven and let the ribs rest, covered loosely in aluminum foil, for about 10 minutes, and then cut between the bones to separate the individual ribs. Serve immediately with the barbecue sauce for dipping.

TANGY BARBECUE SAUCE Makes about 6 cups

2 tablespoons canola oil

1 sweet onion, very finely chopped

1 (24-ounce) bottle ketchup (2½ cups)

2 cups apple cider vinegar or distilled white vinegar

½ cup Worcestershire sauce

¼ cup Dijon mustard

2 tablespoons firmly packed brown sugar

Juice of 2 lemons

Hot sauce

2 tablespoons freshly ground black pepper, or to taste

Coarse kosher salt

1 *Heat the oil in a saucepan over medium heat. Add the onion and simmer until soft, 5 to 7 minutes. Add the ketchup. Pour the vinegar into the ketchup bottle and shake to loosen all the ketchup from the sides. Pour the vinegar from the bottle into the saucepan and add the Worcestershire sauce, mustard, brown sugar, lemon juice, hot sauce, and pepper.*

2 *Bring to a boil, decrease the heat to low, and simmer until the flavors have smoothed and mellowed, at least 10 minutes and up to 30 minutes. Taste and adjust the seasoning with salt and pepper. Store in an airtight container in the refrigerator. The sauce will last for months.*

Spicy North Carolina Pork Shoulder

Serves 6 to 8

North Carolina native Elizabeth Karmel, also known as the "Grill Girl," is a nationally respected authority on grilling, barbecue, and Southern food. Elizabeth hails from Greensboro, where she grew up on pulled pork barbecue. She says, "Pulled pork is my barbecue touchpoint. No matter how much I love Texas-style brisket or Memphis ribs, there is nothing like a red slaw–topped North Carolina pulled pork sandwich to bring me back home." She says the real secret to pulled pork is cooking it longer and to a higher internal temperature than many will tell you. (This also happens to be the secret to succulent melt-in-your mouth brisket.) Slow roast or smoke your bone-in pork butt or shoulder until an instant-read meat thermometer registers between 190°F and 195°F. This temperature is higher than is recommended by most books but is necessary for the pork to separate easily into the fine, moist, tender shreds characteristic of true pulled pork. You can prepare this butt in the oven or on the grill. Undoubtedly, the oven is easier—less fuss and more regulation—but the grill, while it needs a bit more babysitting, imparts a smoky, traditional flavor.

The rub included here makes about ¾ cup. You may not need all of it, depending on how well you rub it into the meat. The extra will keep in an airtight container for a few weeks. My rub recipe calls for one of my favorite spices—piment d'Espelette, a red chile pepper from France. It is a more delicate alternative to cayenne powder, but cayenne is certainly a fine substitute.

4 cups wood chips, for smoking (see Note)

For the pork and sweet heat rub

10 pounds bone-in pork butt

¼ cup brown sugar

¼ cup paprika

2 tablespoons coarse kosher salt

1 tablespoon garlic powder

1 tablespoon freshly ground black pepper

1 tablespoon piment d'Espelette, Aleppo pepper, or red pepper flakes, or to taste

2 tablespoons canola oil

1 Put the wood chips in a roasting pan and add water to cover. Set aside to soak for 1 hour. Remove the meat from the refrigerator. To make the rub, combine the brown sugar, paprika, salt, garlic powder, black pepper, and piment d'Espelette in a small bowl. Rub the meat with the oil and then rub liberally with the rub. Leave at room temperature for 45 minutes.

2 *Meanwhile, to make the sauce,* combine the vinegar, the water, the onion, Aleppo pepper, and mustard in a small bowl or a resealable jar. Set aside.

3 When ready to grill, set up the grill for indirect cooking at 275°F. Drain the wood chips and wrap them in a double layer of heavy-duty aluminum foil. Place the foil-wrapped chips on the coals.

1 cup apple cider vinegar

½ cup water

1 sweet onion, finely chopped

1 teaspoon Aleppo pepper, piment d'Espelette, or red pepper flakes, or to taste

1 tablespoon dry mustard powder

I use Jack Daniels bourbon barrel stave wood chips. Apple, cherry, and hickory chips would be good, but stay away from mesquite. Soaked hunks of wood are better for a full butt, which requires long cooking, but soaked chips wrapped in foil work just fine for the half butt.

4 Place the pork on the grill, not directly over the flame, and cook until the internal temperature of the meat is 165°F; this should take about 5 hours. Check the meat and grill often; you want to keep the grill temperature somewhere between 200°F and 275°F, preferably 250°F. The goal is to cook the meat low and slow. When the meat has reached the right internal temperature, remove it from the grill and wrap it in a double layer of foil. Return it to the grill and cook until the desired doneness: For sliced pork, cook until the internal temperature reaches 180°F, and for pulled pork, at least 195°F. This will take another 3 hours.

5 To cook the butt in the oven instead of on the grill, heat the oven to 275°F. Transfer the meat to the oven and cook until the meat reaches an internal temperature of 195°F, 8 to 9 hours.

6 Transfer the meat to a cutting board with a moat (an indented area around the board to catch juices). Cover the meat with foil and let rest for 20 to 30 minutes to allow the juices to redistribute and let it cool enough to handle. (The internal temperature will also continue to rise as the outer layer cools, allowing it to pull more easily.)

7 Chop with a chef's knife or shred the meat using a pair of tongs, discarding the fat and bones. Serve with the sauce on the side.

Roasted Leg of Lamb with Mediterranean Spices

Serves 10

Lamb is not typically thought of as a Deep South meat, but sheep and lamb are found in the mountains of Appalachia and are also increasingly available due to the immigration of Middle Easterners to the South. Craig Rogers is the owner of Border Springs Farm, which is nestled at the base of the Blue Ridge Mountains in Patrick County, only 10 miles north of the North Carolina border and 20 minutes from the picturesque Blue Ridge Parkway in Virginia. His lamb is sought after by chefs all across the South. To ensure the best possible flavor, this passionate shepherd emphasizes the importance of the grass first and foremost—how it affects flavor, the sweetness of fat, and growth rate of the sheep. It's exciting to see new kinds of farming being embraced in the South and these quality meats delivered to the Southern table.

Butterflying the leg of lamb results in one piece of meat that is rare, medium-rare, and well-done, all at once, depending on the thickness of the roast. Boneless leg of lamb is often available in better meat markets. To butterfly a boneless leg of lamb, unroll the meat and trim any visible sinew, but don't trim anything that's holding together sections of the leg. Holding a chef's knife parallel to the cutting board, make cuts midway through thicker sections of the meat. Don't cut quite all the way through, but do slice in a direction that will let you open the section like a book. Lamb is typically thought of as a more formal meat entrée, and it certainly can be an elegant roast. But I also like to serve it in a more casual setting; this particular recipe is delicious stuffed into pita bread.

For the lamb

Nonstick cooking spray

1 (5- to 7-pound) boneless leg of lamb, butterflied

10 garlic cloves, sliced

Coarse kosher salt and freshly ground black pepper

2 tablespoons pure olive oil

2 tablespoons ground coriander

1 tablespoon ground cumin

1 tablespoon paprika

½ teaspoon ground cinnamon

¼ teaspoon cayenne pepper

1 **To make the lamb,** line a rimmed baking sheet with a double layer of aluminum foil. Place a rack over the foil and spray with nonstick cooking spray. Trim excess fat from the lamb leg. Make several slits in the meat on both sides. Stuff the garlic slices into the slits.

2 Season the lamb with salt and pepper. Make a paste of the oil, coriander, cumin, paprika, cinnamon, and cayenne in a small bowl. Rub the paste over the entire lamb leg. Place the lamb on the prepared rack and set aside to come to room temperature, 1 hour.

Ingredients and recipe continue

1½ cups 2% Greek or
0% Icelandic yogurt

1 English cucumber, peeled,
seeded, and shredded

Zest and juice of 1 lemon

¼ cup mixed chopped fresh
herbs, such as mint, cilantro,
parsley, or chives

3 garlic cloves, mashed to a paste
with salt (see page 22)

2 tablespoons pure or extra-virgin
olive oil (see Note)

Coarse kosher salt and freshly
ground black pepper

3   While the lamb marinates, heat the oven to 400°F. When the lamb is ready, roast until the exterior browns, 30 minutes. Reduce the oven temperature to 350°F and roast until the meat reaches your desired doneness: 125°F for medium-rare or 130°F for medium, 30 to 35 minutes. Cover loosely with foil and let rest for about 10 minutes to allow the juices to redistribute.

4   While the lamb is roasting, to make the tzatziki sauce, combine the yogurt, cucumber, lemon zest, lemon juice, herbs, garlic, and olive oil in a medium bowl. Season with salt and pepper. Set aside.

5   *To serve,* slice the lamb and serve with the tzatziki on the side.

> You can use pure olive oil in the tzatziki sauce, but it's also a great opportunity to use more full-flavored extra-virgin olive oil. See page 120 for information on Choosing Oils.

Cuban-Style Pork Chops with Mojo Sauce

Serves 4

Mojo sauce is a traditional Cuban sauce made with sour oranges, olive oil, and garlic. If you live in an area with a large Cuban population, such as Florida, you might find premixed bottled *mojo*, but making your own is easy and tastes so fresh, I recommend you skip the store-bought. The produce department in your grocery store or a Latin market might carry the bumpy, bitter, thick-skinned sour Seville oranges that grow throughout Cuba. In this recipe, I use a more readily available combination of lime and orange juice. This recipe would be equally delicious grilled outdoors in the summertime.

4 center-cut bone-in pork chops (2½ to 2¾ pounds), about 1 inch thick

¼ cup freshly squeezed lime juice

¼ cup freshly squeezed orange juice

4 garlic cloves, mashed to a paste with salt (see page 22)

3 tablespoons pure olive oil

1 teaspoon chopped fresh oregano

½ teaspoon ground cumin

Coarse kosher salt and freshly ground black pepper

1 Place the pork chops in a bowl. Add the lime juice, orange juice, garlic paste, 2 tablespoons of the oil, the oregano, and the cumin. Cover and marinate for 30 minutes at room temperature or up to 1 hour in the refrigerator.

2 Heat the oven to 400°F.

3 Heat the remaining 1 tablespoon oil in a large ovenproof skillet over medium-high heat until shimmering. Remove the pork chops from the marinade, saving the marinade to use as a sauce. Season both sides of the chops with salt and pepper. Place the chops in the skillet and sear without moving until browned on both sides, 2 minutes per side. Meanwhile, pour the remaining marinade into a small saucepan and bring to a boil over medium-high heat. Reduce the heat to maintain a simmer and keep warm.

4 Transfer the skillet and pork chops to the oven and cook until an instant-read thermometer inserted into the center of a chop registers 145°F, about 10 minutes. Let rest for 3 minutes to let the juices redistribute. Serve with the warm sauce on the side.

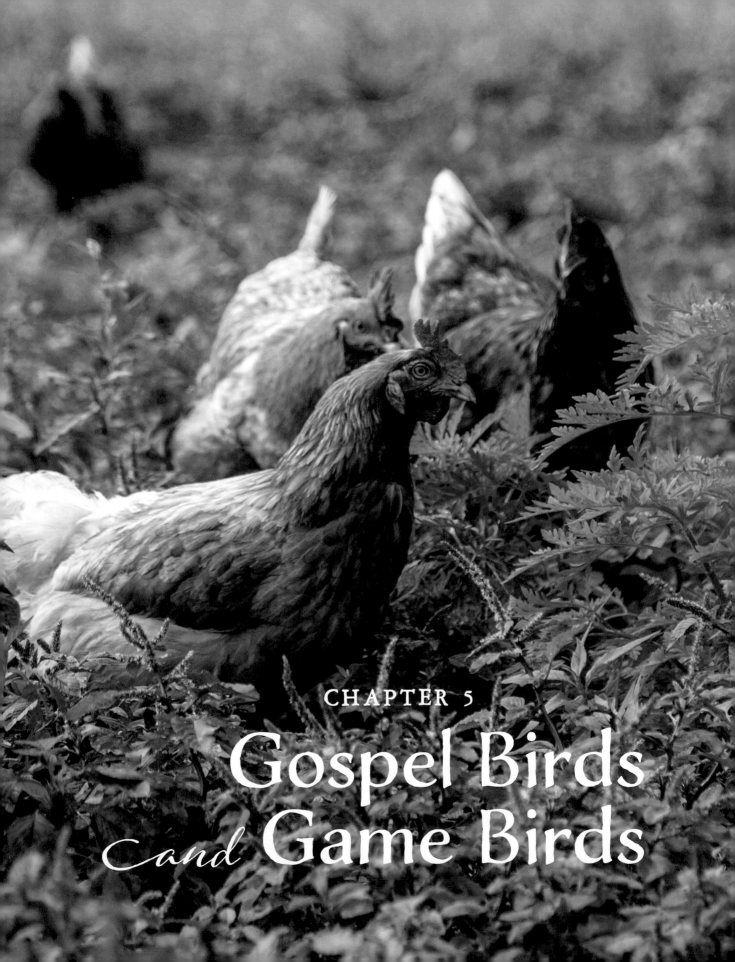

CHAPTER 5

Gospel Birds *and* Game Birds

A BIRD *in the* HAND *at* MANCHESTER FARMS QUAIL

The forceful sound of "bobwhite, bobwhite" ringing from a golden, grassy meadow or the edge of piney woods has long been a characteristic sound of summer in the Southern countryside. I remember the distinctive call of bob-white quail from my childhood, sitting on the screened-in porch with my grandfather as he taught me to mimic their sharp, emphatic whistle. The men in my family were avid hunters of many animals, quail included. There's a long history of hunting in the South. For some families, this was due to need. A morning hunt could put essential food on the table. On the opposite end of the economic spectrum, hunting has long been big business; majestic hunting plantations, with lofty names promising the flush of a wild covey from the underbrush, can be found across the region. Some, not all, enable city slickers to leave their desk jobs, purchase never-to-be used again oilcloth English shooting apparel, and get in touch with their inner woodsman, the winged equivalent of shooting fish in a barrel. In my family, while not necessary to feed the family, the meat was always eaten and the clothing was camouflage, not made by clothiers with "By appointment to Her Majesty the Queen" royal warrants. Quail hunts were always busy endeavors, the men and boys rising early in the morning, layering their long johns and coats to protect them from the chilly fall weather, and anxious, excited bird dogs bounding in the back of muddy pickup trucks.

Once the birds were home and dressed, my grandmother would lightly coat them in seasoned flour and fry them to deep golden brown in her cast-iron skillet. She always required a heaping platter of the crispy birds to satisfy her hungry brood. My sister and I would snatch them up as soon as our tiny hands could hold the sizzling-hot treats. My mother, a more adventurous and less traditional cook, would sometimes sear them and prepare a sumptuous red wine sauce or wrap them in bacon and roast them in a very hot oven. Whether the quail were prepared down-home or uptown, there was always a bit of pointed commentary in regard to the cleaning. The dull sound of birdshot hitting the plate was not an uncommon one at our table in the fall. Certain family members were regarded as more diligent about searching out the metal pellets than others. Sadly, as a result of habitat loss, the wild bobwhite quail that my family hunted on our land have been in sharp decline throughout the past half century, and their haunting calls are far less common. Wild

Wild quail are a priority for conservation; now farm-raised quail are increasingly found on the Southern table.

quail are still hunted, but they are a priority for conservation, and the restrictions and quotas are far stricter. Now farm-raised quail are increasingly found on the Southern table. In large part, their acceptance has been a result of the longstanding hunting tradition.

Hunting tradition was partially the reason for the establishment of Manchester Farms in Columbia, South Carolina, the oldest quail farm in the United States. Founder Bill Odom graduated from Clemson University with a degree in Poultry Science and became a chicken supplier for Campbell's. He raised a few quail on the side, to use for training his hunting dogs, then began selling his excess birds to friends and neighbors in the off-season. Eventually, he realized there was a market; he left Campbell's in the early 1970s and his business was born. There are more than 130 different varieties of quail, including the bobwhite from my childhood, yet quail raised for the kitchen is a different variety. (Bobwhite quail are too prone to disease for farming.) Manchester Farms, named after the nearby state forest where Bill trained his dogs, raise what are known as Pharaoh or Coturnix quail. These birds have been domesticated in Japan since the eleventh century. They are less susceptible to disease, can lay up to three hundred eggs a year, and grow from chick to full-size adult in just five weeks.

Bill Odom may have identified a market, but undeniably it was a small one. Quail eggs are popular in both Asia and Mexico and quail has long been a delicacy on European menus. But in the United States, especially outside the South, quail is pretty much only found on the tables of fine dining establishments. One of my foodie friends derisively refers to them as "little bony birds." Yet in the last forty years, Manchester Farms, which started by solely selling quail by mail order, grew to distribute to food-service clients and restaurants, and now sells to major grocery store chains. Today, their quail can be found in supermarkets such as Publix, Harris Teeter, Bi-Lo, Piggly Wiggly, and Ingles. Appreciated by both top chefs and home cooks, these days Manchester Farms quail is seen on menus from Santa Barbara, California, to Charleston, South Carolina. Manchester Farms is now owned and operated by Odom's daughter, Brittney Miller, and her husband, Matt. Brittney has been a part of the farm since she was a young girl and is affectionately nicknamed "Mother Hen." As we walk, she shows me the operation, and I can see that this multimillion-dollar business is still a family-focused operation. Manchester Farms employs 120 people, some of whom have been with the company for more than two decades. Employees include multiple members from the same family, even multiple generations. That's not just "warm and fuzzy" information. To underscore what that says about Manchester Farms, consider that much of U.S. poultry production is located in the South and can be dirty, dangerous, and demanding work, with workers leaving factories almost as quickly as they are hired on. According to the National Center for Farmworker Health, poultry processing typically has a 100 percent turnover rate.

We pull up to the processing plant and Brittney explains that what started as a one-man operation now occupies nearly 400 acres. The farm produces 80,000 quail per week as well as 250,000 eggs. The plant is spotlessly clean. A group of female employees wearing white coats and hairnets works a line deboning the birds at lightning-fast speed. The workers' finesse is extraordinary. For the European-style semiboneless quail, all bones but the wingbones and drummette of the leg are removed from the small bird. Workers also prepare whole quail; quail knots, a half breast with an attached drumstick; quail halves; spatchcocked quail; bacon-wrapped quail breasts; and quail eggs. So much for "little bony birds . . ."

So which comes first: the hen or the egg? I am soon to find out. "We're completely vertically integrated," Brittney Miller explains. "We own our own hatchery, our own breeder farm, and our own grow-out farm." The quail eggs are gathered from the farms and delivered to the setting room once a week, where workers incubate up to one hundred thousand eggs at a time. Row after row of speckled pale brown eggs are carefully nestled on incubation trays that tilt every thirty minutes, simulating the hen moving the eggs in the nest. The eggs are carefully maintained and monitored by computer control at a constant temperature and humidity before being transferred to the hatching rooms. Every Thursday is hatchlings day. The sight of thousands of quail hatching nearly at once is astonishing. Workers gather the chicks by hand and sort by sight, culling any hatchling that cannot stand and walk on its own. The chicks are then loaded into crates and a climate-controlled van for the ride to the quail house.

We pull up to the quail house and the first thing I notice is what is not present: odor. I've been to chicken farms where the harsh stench of ammonia is enough to make your eyes water. Here at Manchester Farms, the air smells virtually no different from my own backyard. Now, mind you, the sight of tens of thousands of quail is somewhere between an absolute cute overload and, oddly, a bit terrifying, depending on how you feel about birds. Inside the quail house, Brittney explains that there are water and feed stations situated throughout the house to stimulate the birds' movement. As we walk the floor of the quail house, Brittney offers, "I say, 'if it looks dirty, it eats dirty.' We want to have the safest, cleanest, most wholesome environment." I find out that in its forty years in business, Manchester has only used antibiotics once. There are no vets on staff, no medicine in the feed, and absolutely no antibiotics onsite. The farm is the only SQF (Safe Quality Food)—a program globally recognized as the most trusted source for global food safety and quality certification—level 2 Certified Quail Processor in the United States.

Hunting wild quail may be the secret of Southern tables of the past, but forward-thinking poultry farming rooted in the good food movement clearly seems to be the key to the future.

THE NEW FACE *of* FARMING *at* MANY FOLD FARM

I t's no secret that the Southern table is filled with many products grown in the South. Agriculture is a multibillion-dollar business and many states have, or nearly have, a year-round growing season. It is also, however, an industry somewhat in crisis. The average farmer in the United States is a fifty-eight-year-old white male. Barriers to entry include skyrocketing land prices and the cost of equipment such as tractors and combines, which can run into hundreds of thousands of dollars. Located about thirty minutes away from the world's busiest airport, Many Fold Farm is deliberately working to reverse that trend. Owners Ross and Rebecca Williams, both in their thirties, are the new face of farming—or trying to be. Their challenge is economic sustainability.

I knew that Many Fold Farm had a devoted flock of folks who love the farm's chicken eggs, and I was a fan of its sheep's-milk cheeses. Those cheeses include four different varieties, seen as often on New York City cheeseboards as right down the road in Atlanta. Straight out of the gate, they were winning national and international cheese competitions. Shortly after I scheduled my visit, I heard that Ross and Rebecca were reassessing their situation, scaling back their egg output, and shuttering the creamery. It rocked the local food community. The couple are Atlanta natives and middle school sweethearts with two adorable daughters. It was a story straight out of a movie script. Their farm was a success story. What happened? Instead of changing my plans, I felt that their changing story would be equally important to consider.

I head out early one cold November morning to meet Rebecca and get the scoop on why their eggs have such a devoted following, and to find out what was happening with the farm. The hustle and bustle of the city fall away once I get outside the Atlanta perimeter. Driving south from the city, billboards soon give way to rolling hills, and twelve lanes of traffic narrow to two. Many Fold Farm is located on 280 acres in Chattahoochee Hills, a 56-square-mile city with fewer than 2,500 residents—and that's not a typo. The city is part of a burgeoning agricultural economy that seeks to preserve rural Southern heritage and act as an antidote to urban

"*We're trying to feed people good food and be environmentally responsible.*"

—REBECCA WILLIAMS

MANY FOLD FARM
Organically-fed, Posture-Raised Eggs
Keep Refrigerated – Best by DEC 2 5 2016

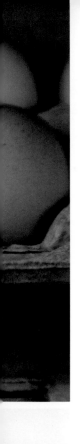

sprawl. The area is largely undeveloped and most of its rural character remains unchanged. It was founded in 2007 to control growth and prevent the miles of traffic that afflict much of metropolitan Atlanta. It has some of the most progressive zoning restrictions in the state in order to keep the area rural.

Founding "empty cities" may appear like a radical move, but it's important to consider that urban sprawl in Georgia is among the most significant and widespread in the nation. According to the U.S. census, between 2000 and 2010, Georgia's population increased 18.3 percent, nearly twice the national average. Metro Atlanta's population increased by 24 percent in the same decade, and the three fastest-growing counties in the state are all either in the metro Atlanta region or immediately adjacent. Each of those counties experienced population increases of more than 70 percent. That's tremendous change in only a decade. Farmland is being lost, family-owned businesses are closing due to competition with big-box stores, and sleepy country towns are losing their character as they transform into suburbia. Ross and Rebecca had seen this pattern in other areas near Atlanta and intentionally chose Chattahoochee Hills to build their farm.

Followed by two English shepherd pups, Rebecca walks down the gravel driveway to meet me. Stylishly dressed and wrapped in a woolen cape, she does not look like a typical farmer. As we walk to the back pasture where the chickens are roosting, I learn Rebecca is a graduate of Sarah Lawrence College with a major in English, a minor in Theology, and a master's degree in Education. Ross attended NYU before transferring to Warren Wilson College in Asheville, North Carolina, where, as Rebecca says, "He fell into farming."

While in college, they started thinking about what they wanted to do with their lives. Both had grown up with gardens and home-cooked food. Rebecca commented that she would take the train to shop at the Union Square Greenmarket in New York City while she was in college. Local food has always been important to her. According to the farm's website, "They didn't know what they wanted to do with their lives except that they wanted to do something real, meaningful, and together. Farming seemed to fit the bill. Together they love to take care of the land, animals, and people and believe that these three things work together to serve and nourish each other."

As we walk, two Mexican female farm hands herd sheep nearby. I ask Rebecca about the decision to stop making cheese. She explains it was economically driven: "We wanted to scale up from a small production to medium, but we would have had to import frozen milk from Nebraska or New York. It was antithetical to our mission. We could keep the business and lose our values or lose our business and keep our values." Thoughtfully, she says, "Small-scale farms are not the answer. We're trying to feed people good food and be environmentally responsible."

We reach the chickens. Massive creamy-colored Italian sheepdogs guard the flock. Chickens are roosting in the trees and all along the edge of the field. Rebecca observes that much of their farm is forested. "Woods are important for farms. They create a climate barrier and provide something for the coyotes other than my chickens!" There are about seven hundred birds milling about, mostly Rhode Island Reds and Ameraucanas, known for their distinctive blue eggs. She explains that the hens produce less in the winter, but at peak they will harvest around 4,800 eggs per week.

She comments about the die-hard fans willing to pay eight dollars for a dozen eggs and says, "Once you've tried pastured eggs, you'll never go back." Many Fold Farm eggs are the product of Ross and Rebecca's belief that "healthy land makes healthy animals makes healthy people." They sell their eggs at various farmers' markets in Atlanta and have standing orders with the popular restaurant Bocado, which uses the eggs in housemade pasta. The eggs are also favorites of James Beard Award–winning chef Linton Hopkins's flagship fine dining establishment, Restaurant Eugene. Scanning the brown pasture, she says, "The grass has less beta-carotene because of the drought, so the yolks aren't as yellow. The greener the grass, the darker the yolk." She continues, "The stiffness of the egg white and the creaminess of the yolk are directly related to how much protein the chickens eat."

We talk about the business of farming and how the United States spends so much less on food than many other countries. We both acknowledge the reality that many people simply cannot afford such expensive eggs, as well as the choices consumers make about what they're willing to spend. She said early on at a farmers' market a potential customer walked up and balked at the price, telling Rebecca that the eggs were far too expensive. Then Rebecca said she watched the same customer pay $2.50 for an ice pop. She says that people often think small farms are elitist, but many of her farmer friends are living in poverty.

At the time of this writing, Rebecca and Ross were planning to maintain a limited egg production and take a year off to "research, think, and rest." Clearly, as the interest and enthusiasm for local foods increases, the challenges of producing small-scale and local food do not decrease. The problems of scale, consumer access, and education can impede the movement toward better food for all. It is Rebecca and Ross's hope that in time they might provide insight and resources toward developing new agrarian economies going forward. I, for one, believe they will succeed.

Chicken Larb with Georgia Peanuts

Serves 4 to 6

Several years ago I visited my cousins in South Georgia, the heart of peanut country. It was in the early fall and I had my car windows rolled down to enjoy the evening breeze. Suddenly, the fragrant scent of soil filled the night air. I instantly realized I was traveling next to a freshly dug field of peanuts. It was one of the most powerful moments, my senses being flooded by the aroma of rich earth. Peanuts grow below the ground, not on a tree like pecans or walnuts. They are very high in moisture when harvested, so they are tilled and allowed to stay in the field for several days to dry out. Georgia is the number one peanut-producing state in the United States, accounting for approximately 49 percent of the crop's national acreage and production.

Larb is a Southeast Asian salad from Laos and Thailand and is most often made with ground pork and traditionally garnished with peanuts. The South isn't exactly known for its Thai food, but one Atlanta family is developing an outsize reputation for this cuisine. Charlie and Nan Niyomkul own Nan Thai Fine Dining and Tamarind Seed Thai Bistro; their daughter Dee Dee and her husband opened Tuk Tuk, rated as one of the top Thai restaurants in the United States. This recipe was inspired by Tuk Tuk's *larb kai* prepared with minced chicken and cabbage.

1 pound ground chicken or turkey

2 cups cold water, more if needed

2 cups fresh mint leaves, washed and dried

1 cup fresh cilantro leaves, washed and dried

¾ cup unsalted roasted peanuts

Juice of 2 limes

3 tablespoons fish sauce

4 Thai red chiles, or to taste, seeded and finely chopped

2 shallots, very thinly sliced (about ½ cup)

3 green onions, chopped

1 cup carrot matchsticks, or 3 carrots, grated

¼ cup finely chopped fresh ginger

1 head cabbage, cored, leaves separated

1 Place the chicken in a small saucepan. Add cold water to cover (about 2 cups). Bring to a boil and then reduce the heat to maintain a simmer. Cook gently, breaking up the chicken with a wooden spoon as it cooks, until the chicken is opaque, 5 to 7 minutes. (Skim the foam that rises to the top while cooking. It's simply coagulated protein and doesn't mean there's anything wrong with the chicken.)

2 Remove the chicken from the heat and drain well, reserving the cooking liquid for another use. (You can use it as a light stock to cook with or even season it and sip it.) Transfer the well-drained chicken to a medium bowl and set aside to cool just slightly.

3 Add the mint, cilantro, peanuts, lime juice, fish sauce, chiles, shallots, green onions, carrot, and ginger. Stir to combine. To serve, spoon a few tablespoons or so of the larb into a cabbage leaf, fold the cabbage leaf somewhat like a taco, and eat.

Skillet-Baked Eggs in Tomato Gravy with Spinach

Serves 4

This recipe for tomato gravy is the kind of old-fashioned country cooking most commonly found in Appalachia. Typically, it would be served solo atop biscuits, but it seemed to be an open invitation for an addition of skillet-baked eggs, with the biscuits for sopping up this luscious combination.

2 slices bacon, cut into lardons (see page 32; optional)

2 tablespoons pure olive oil (optional)

1 sweet onion, chopped

1 garlic clove, very finely chopped

2 tablespoons all-purpose flour

3 fresh tomatoes (about 1½ pounds), peeled, seeded, and chopped (2 cups), or 1 (16-ounce) can whole tomatoes, chopped, with their juices

¾ cup 2% milk

2 cups loosely packed baby spinach (about 3 ounces)

1 tablespoon chopped fresh herbs, such as parsley, basil, or chives, plus more for garnish

1 teaspoon chopped fresh thyme leaves

¼ teaspoon Aleppo pepper, piment d'Espelette, or red pepper flakes, or to taste

Coarse kosher salt and freshly ground black pepper

4 large eggs

Cathead Biscuits (page 237) or toasted bread, for serving

1 Heat the oven to 350°F.

2 If using bacon, line a plate with paper towels. Heat a large ovenproof skillet over medium-high heat. Add the bacon to the skillet and cook, stirring occasionally, until crisp, 3 to 5 minutes. Use a slotted spoon to transfer the bacon to the prepared plate. You can use the bacon fat to cook the onion or, if you prefer, tip out the bacon fat and heat the olive oil in the skillet over medium heat. You can also just start with the oil and not use the bacon at all.

3 Add the onion to the fat (or oil) and cook until browned, 5 to 7 minutes. Add the garlic and cook until fragrant, 45 to 60 seconds. Add the flour and stir to combine. Add the tomatoes and milk and stir to combine. Bring to a boil and then reduce the heat to maintain a simmer. Cook until the tomatoes soften and the gravy thickens, 3 to 5 minutes. Add the cooked bacon (if using), the spinach, all of the herbs, and the Aleppo pepper; stir to combine. Taste and adjust the seasoning with salt and black pepper.

4 Using the back of a spoon, make four wells in the tomato-spinach mixture in the skillet. Break an egg into each indentation. Season the eggs with salt and black pepper. Transfer the skillet to the oven and bake until the whites are set and the yolks are to the desired doneness, 8 minutes for runny, 10 minutes for firm, and 12 minutes for fully set. Garnish with additional herbs. Serve immediately with the biscuits.

Weeknight Chicken and Andouille Jambalaya

Serves 4 to 6

Jambalaya traditionally contains sausage of some sort, often a smoked sausage such as andouille, along with some other meat or seafood, frequently pork, chicken, crawfish, or shrimp. Andouille is a coarse-grained smoked sausage made using smoked pork shoulder, garlic, pepper, onions, wine, and seasonings. The vegetable base is a combination of onion, celery, and green bell pepper known as the "holy trinity." I find that green bell peppers can be difficult to digest, so I use poblano peppers instead. They are far more flavorful and complex and less likely to cause digestive distress.

For generations, some the most flavorful rice Americans have eaten has been Jasmine rice imported to the United States from Asia. Twelve years ago, the Louisiana State University AgCenter started a project to increase rice production in Louisiana, and the state is now the third largest rice-producing state in the United States.

2 tablespoons pure olive oil

12 ounces andouille sausage, sliced into ¼-inch-thick rounds

6 bone-in, skinless chicken thighs (2 pounds)

1 tablespoon Homemade Creole Seasoning (page 219)

1 sweet onion, chopped

1 celery stalk, chopped

1 poblano pepper, seeded and chopped

1 garlic clove, very finely chopped

1½ cups long-grain rice, such as jasmine or basmati

½ cup tomato puree

2½ cups homemade chicken stock or reduced-sodium low-fat chicken broth

Coarse kosher salt and freshly ground black pepper

1 Heat the oven to 350°F.

2 Heat the oil in a large ovenproof skillet over medium-high heat until shimmering. Add the sausage and cook until the meat starts to brown and the fat renders, 3 minutes. Transfer the sausage to a plate. Add the chicken and sprinkle the Creole seasoning over the chicken. Cook until the chicken is just beginning to color, 3 minutes. Transfer the chicken to the plate with the sausage.

3 Reduce the heat to medium and then add the onion, celery, and poblano pepper to the residual oil in the skillet. Cook, stirring occasionally, until the vegetables start to color, 5 to 7 minutes. Add the garlic and cook until fragrant, 45 to 60 seconds. Add the rice and stir to coat. Stir in the tomato puree and stock and bring to a boil. Return the chicken and sausage to the skillet. Transfer to the oven and bake, uncovered, stirring once, until the rice is tender and the juices run clear when the chicken is pierced with the tip of a knife, 40 to 45 minutes. Transfer to a wire rack to cool slightly. Taste and adjust the seasoning with salt and pepper. Serve immediately.

Sorghum Butter Roast Chicken

Serves 4 to 6

Sorghum is Appalachia's version of maple syrup. It's the evaporated cane juice of a grain called sorghum that is pressed and then cooked in a shallow pan until it cooks down to an amber brown syrup that's a bit thicker than honey. Its flavor is vegetal, earthy, and sweet, with a hint of spice. It can be used in place of molasses, corn syrup, honey, or maple syrup on biscuits, pancakes, or sweet potatoes. The combination of sorghum, butter, and smoked paprika lacquers this bird into absolutely glowing, golden brown deliciousness.

Spatchcocking is the process of removing the backbone and opening the bird so that it is fairly flat—and therefore cooks quicker and more evenly. Brining the bird helps ensure a moist, tender dish. Make sure, however, not to buy a chicken that contains a "flavor solution" or "chicken broth," which are both essentially salted solution. Also, avoid kosher birds for this recipe, as they are soaked in water and salted to remove all traces of blood. Brining either of these types of bird will result in an overly salty bird.

1 (4- to 4½-pound) chicken, giblets and excess fat removed

½ cup coarse kosher salt

4 quarts hot water

8 cups ice cubes, or as needed

¼ cup sorghum syrup or honey

4 tablespoons (¼ cup) unsalted butter

1 teaspoon smoked paprika

Nonstick cooking spray

Freshly ground black pepper

1 To spatchcock the bird, place it on a clean work surface, breast-side down. Using poultry shears, cut lengthwise on both sides of the backbone from the neck to the tail. Remove the backbone and save it for stock or roast it along with the remainder of the bird for a cook's treat. Open the bird like a book and then place it open-side down on a clean work surface. Press firmly with both hands to flatten the bird.

2 Place the salt in a heatproof container large enough to hold the water and the bird. Add the hot water and stir to dissolve and then add the ice cubes and stir to cool. Add the chicken, cover, and refrigerate for at least 1 hour and up to 2 hours. (Do not brine any longer or the chicken will be too salty. If you can't cook it right at the 2-hour mark, remove the chicken from the marinade and refrigerate until ready to continue.) Remove the chicken from the brine, rinse well, and pat thoroughly dry with paper towels.

Recipe continues

3   Combine the sorghum syrup, butter, and paprika in a small saucepan. Heat over low heat just until the butter has melted and the sorghum syrup is fluid. Stir to combine. Set aside and keep warm.

4   Meanwhile, heat the oven to 350°F. Line a rimmed baking sheet with a double layer of aluminum foil. (Yes, double-lined. The sorghum will char as it drips and make a mess on the bottom of the pan. You will thank me.) Place a rack over the foil and spray with nonstick cooking spray.

5   Season both sides of the brined and dried chicken with pepper. For the best presentation and even cooking, tuck the wing tips under the bottom of the bird and arrange the drumsticks so that they are not askew. Brush the bottom of the chicken with the sorghum butter. Place on the rack, skin-side up. Roast for 45 minutes. Remove from the oven and baste all over with the sorghum butter, taking extra care to brush all the nooks and crannies. Continue roasting, basting occasionally, until an instant-read thermometer reads 155°F when inserted into the thickest part of the thigh. Let rest for about 5 minutes before carving and serving. Bring any remaining sorghum butter to a boil and then serve it drizzled over the top or on the side.

BRINING

Brining is a helpful technique when cooking white meats like chicken, turkey, pork, and even shrimp. (Red meat like beef and lamb do not respond well to brining.) Brine is simply a saltwater solution; although many types of brine also contain other ingredients such as sugar, herbs, and spices to add flavor, the science is all about the salt. How's it work? Think back to junior high science class. Remember osmosis? That's when water moves from an area of higher concentration (the brine) to an area of lower concentration (the meat). The salt in the brine causes the meat proteins to become denatured and unwind. The unwound protein coils form a mesh that traps the brine so the muscle fibers absorb liquid during the brining period. Essentially, the process adds moisture to the meat. I like to think of brining as a cup filled "over the rim." Then, when the meat cooks, the bonds break and the protein molecules unwind, and the heat shrinks the muscle fibers both in diameter and in length as water is squeezed out. Some of this liquid is lost during cooking, but because the meat is juicier at the start of cooking, it ends up juicier at the end.

Nashville Hot Grilled Chicken

Nashville is famous for many things—country music being at the top of the list. It's also famous for spicy-hot fried chicken, supposedly first made by a woman who was mad at her good-looking man for being out on the town all night. The story goes that Thornton Prince came home from carousing and wanted something to eat. His wife whipped up a batch of ultra-hot spicy chicken. But her plan backfired—he loved it. Prince's Hot Chicken was born and soon caught on to other chicken shacks. For many years, the picante poultry was solely found on the menu of African American establishments, but then some of those country singers found out about it and word got out. In a unique turn of events for the South at that time, because the restaurant was black-owned, white musicians would buy their chicken from the side door while blacks used the front entrance.

Typically, the breading mixture is hot with cayenne pepper, and then, to take the chicken over the top, the fried chicken is bathed in fiery-hot spiced oil. I've adapted the classic recipe for grilling instead of frying, so it's healthier and easier for weeknight cooking.

For the chicken and marinade

4 boneless, skinless chicken breasts (2 pounds), cut lengthwise into ½-inch strips

2 cups buttermilk

¼ cup hot sauce, or to taste

½ teaspoon cayenne pepper, or to taste

Coarse kosher salt and freshly ground black pepper

For the hot oil

¼ cup canola oil

1 tablespoon cayenne pepper, or to taste

1 tablespoon firmly packed dark brown sugar

1 teaspoon garlic powder

½ teaspoon smoked paprika

1   *To marinate the chicken,* combine the chicken, buttermilk, hot sauce, and cayenne in a resealable container. Refrigerate for at least 4 hours and up to 12 hours.

2   When ready to grill, drain the excess marinade off the chicken and discard the marinade. Season the chicken with salt and pepper. If using a charcoal grill, prepare a charcoal fire using about 6 pounds of charcoal and burn until the coals are completely covered with a thin coating of light gray ash, 20 to 30 minutes. Spread the coals evenly over the grill bottom, position the grill rack above the coals, and heat until medium-hot (when you can hold your hand 5 inches above the grill surface for no longer than 3 or 4 seconds). If using a gas grill, turn on all the burners to High, close the lid, and heat until very hot, about 500°F, 10 to 15 minutes. If using a grill pan, heat the pan over medium-high heat.

3   Grill the chicken until the juices run clear when pierced with the tip of a knife and the internal temperature registers 165°F when measured with an instant-read thermometer, 3 to 5 minutes per side.

Recipe continues

4   *Meanwhile, to make the hot oil,* heat the oil in a small saucepan over medium heat until hot, around 300°F, 5 minutes. Combine the cayenne, sugar, garlic powder, and paprika in a small bowl. Pour the hot oil over the spice blend and stir to combine.

5   Transfer the cooked chicken strips to a bowl and drizzle with some of the hot oil. Toss to coat. Serve immediately with the additional hot oil on the side.

Chicken and Butterbean Paella

Serves 6 to 8

Nestled alongside the Cumberland Plateau of the Appalachian Mountains is the town of South Pittsburg, Tennessee, home to Lodge Manufacturing Company, maker of cast-iron skillets since 1896. My most often used pan is my cast-iron skillet. I use it practically every day. It's beautiful, with a shiny satin finish, and black as the blackest coal. Once I use it, I wash it in warm soapy water, dry it well, and store it in the oven so it continues to dry in the residual heat of the oven. Some folks say you're not supposed to wash cast iron, but my grandmother Meme always did, so I do the same. I inherited my pan when my grandmother passed away, and it's well over seventy years old. It may be just a common skillet, but it is more precious to me than the finest bone china. It represents my love of food and family. It's more than a kitchen tool; it's my Southern talisman.

Lodge also has a line of seasoned carbon steel—including a 15-inch paella pan perfect for this recipe. I love that this century-plus-old Southern company has adapted, grown, and changed with the times.

3¾ cups homemade chicken stock or reduced-fat low-sodium chicken broth, plus more if needed

2 cups shelled fresh butterbeans (about 1½ pounds unshelled) or frozen butterbeans

Generous pinch of saffron

Coarse kosher salt and freshly ground black pepper

1 (4-pound) chicken, cut into 8 serving pieces

2 tablespoons pure olive oil

1 sweet onion, chopped

2 garlic cloves, mashed to a paste with salt (see page 22)

1½ cups long-grain rice

1 tomato, cored, seeded, and chopped

1 bay leaf, preferably fresh

1 tablespoon chopped fresh thyme

2 tablespoons parsley leaves

1 Heat the oven to 350°F.

2 Combine the stock, butterbeans, and saffron in a saucepan. Season with salt and pepper. Bring to a boil over medium-high heat, then reduce the heat to maintain a simmer. Cook until the beans are just barely tender, 15 minutes.

3 Season the chicken with salt and pepper. Heat the oil in a very large skillet or 15-inch paella pan over medium-high heat. Add the chicken without crowding. You may need to cook in batches. Cook until well browned on all sides, 5 to 7 minutes. Set aside.

4 Remove all but 1 tablespoon of the oil from the pan. Add the onion and cook until golden brown, 5 to 7 minutes. Add the garlic and cook until fragrant, 45 to 60 seconds. Add the rice and stir to combine.

Recipe continues

5   Add the tomato, bay leaf, and thyme. Pour in the stock with the butterbeans and stir to combine. Return the seared chicken to the skillet and nestle it into the rice. Make sure the stock covers the rice, and add more if needed. Transfer to the oven and cook until the rice is tender, the liquid has been absorbed, and the chicken is cooked through, 40 minutes. Remove and discard the bay leaf.

6   Return the pan to medium heat on the stovetop. Cook until the rice on the bottom is crispy, 5 minutes. Garnish with the parsley and serve immediately.

Latin Fried Chicken Chopped Salad

Serves 6

Sandra Gutierrez is a native Guatemalan, first-generation American, proud North Carolinian, fantastic cook, cookbook author, and a dear friend. She blends ingredients, traditions, and culinary techniques, creatively marrying Latin American cuisine with the food of the American South, as in this recipe for Latin Fried Chicken. The first time I tasted it was an absolute revelation. She cooks pieces on the bone, but I have adapted it to use boneless, skinless breasts for salad. Sandra has recounted stories about people assuming that because she is Latin American, she and her family are itinerant migrant workers. Not much could be farther from the truth! She attended Smith College, her husband is an international businessman, one of her daughters is a dentist, and the other daughter is a lawyer. Those sorts of assumptions—actually thinly veiled racism—are slowly changing as the region is becoming more diverse and more educated.

Self-rising flour is simply all-purpose flour that already contains baking powder and salt. If you are unable to find self-rising flour, you can make your own: For every 1 cup all-purpose flour, add 1½ teaspoons baking powder and ¼ teaspoon fine sea salt and whisk to combine.

For the chicken

¾ cup buttermilk

2 tablespoons chopped fresh cilantro

1 canned chipotle chile in adobo, finely chopped

¼ teaspoon garlic powder

Coarse kosher salt and freshly ground black pepper

4 boneless, skinless chicken breasts (2 pounds), cut lengthwise into ½-inch strips

1½ cups self-rising flour (see headnote)

1 teaspoon smoked paprika

½ teaspoon ground coriander

½ teaspoon cayenne pepper, or to taste

Canola oil, for frying

6 corn tortillas, cut into ¼-inch-wide strips

1. Line a rimmed baking sheet with paper towels. To make the chicken, combine the buttermilk, cilantro, chipotle, and garlic powder in a large glass bowl. Season with salt and black pepper. Add the chicken strips and stir to combine.

2. In a separate large bowl, combine the flour, paprika, coriander, and cayenne. Season with salt and black pepper.

3. Pour 1 to 2 inches of oil into a large Dutch oven and heat the oil to 350°F over medium-high heat. Add the tortilla strips and cook until crispy, 2 minutes. Use a slotted spoon to transfer the fried tortillas to the prepared baking sheet. (These may be done ahead. You may also simply use store-bought tortilla chips if you really want to make it easy for yourself.) Return the oil to 350°F.

For the salad

2 medium heads romaine lettuce, chopped

6 radishes, thinly sliced

1 red bell pepper, seeded and chopped

1 avocado, pitted, peeled, and chopped (see sidebar, page 103)

½ red onion, very thinly sliced

¼ jalapeño, or to taste, seeded and chopped

2 tablespoons chopped fresh cilantro

Salsa Buttermilk Ranch Dressing (recipe follows)

1 lime, cut into wedges, for serving

4 Working in batches, dredge some of the chicken strips in the seasoned flour. Fry the strips in the hot oil until the juices run clear when pierced with the tip of a knife and the temperature registers 165°F when tested with an instant-read thermometer, 5 to 7 minutes. Transfer to the baking sheet with the tortilla strips to cool slightly, then transfer to a cutting board and chop into 1-inch pieces.

5 *Meanwhile, to make the salad,* combine the romaine, radishes, bell pepper, avocado, onion, jalapeño, and cilantro in a large bowl. Toss to combine. Add the chicken and toss with a little of the Salsa Buttermilk Ranch. Top with the fried tortilla strips. Serve immediately with lime wedges and the remaining dressing on the side.

SALSA BUTTERMILK RANCH DRESSING Makes about 1 cup

¼ cup mayonnaise

¼ cup low-fat buttermilk

2 tablespoons 2% Greek or 0% Icelandic yogurt

1 green onion, chopped

1 tablespoon chopped fresh flat-leaf parsley

1 tablespoon apple cider vinegar

1 teaspoon Dijon mustard

1 garlic clove, very finely chopped

⅓ cup store-bought fresh salsa or pico de gallo

Coarse kosher salt and freshly ground black pepper

In a bowl, combine the mayonnaise, buttermilk, yogurt, green onion, parsley, vinegar, mustard, and garlic. Add the salsa, season with salt and pepper, and stir to combine.

Black Pepper Cornish Game Hens with Alabama White Sauce

Serves 4

Mayonnaise is practically a food group in the South. Alabama celebrates the Southern love of the condiment with a peppery concoction invented by Big Bob Gibson BBQ in Decatur called Alabama White Sauce, an anomaly in the predominantly tomato-based world of barbecue sauces. (Well, except for South Carolina, which is known for its potent mustard-based seasoning.) Drew Robinson of Jim 'N Nicks BBQ says he's always thought of it as a sort of barbecue hollandaise. He says, "The eggy, tangy flavor with the heavy black pepper kick works well with smoked meats." It's fantastic for drizzling and dipping, but really steals the show when used for basting smoked chicken. A magic alchemy occurs while cooking, and the seemingly pedestrian dressing is transformed, rendering the poultry mahogany and golden brown.

You can either grill the birds outdoors for an extra bit of smoky flavor, or start them in a grill pan on the stove and finish in the oven. Chicken is most often used for this dish, but I have adapted it to use with Cornish game hens. Quail are also exceptionally delicious.

1 cup mayonnaise

¼ cup apple cider vinegar

1 tablespoon Worcestershire

1 tablespoon garlic powder

1 tablespoon freshly ground black pepper, plus more as needed

1 teaspoon dry mustard powder

¼ teaspoon cayenne pepper

Nonstick cooking spray

2 Cornish game hens (about 2 pounds each)

1 tablespoon canola oil

Coarse kosher salt

1 Combine the mayonnaise, vinegar, Worcestershire sauce, garlic powder, black pepper, mustard, and cayenne in a medium bowl. Stir to combine. Reserve about ½ cup of the sauce for basting and set the rest aside for serving.

2 If using a charcoal grill, prepare a charcoal fire using about 6 pounds of charcoal and burn until the coals are completely covered with a thin coating of light gray ash, 20 to 30 minutes. Spread the coals evenly over the grill bottom, position the grill rack above the coals, and heat until medium-hot (when you can hold your hand 5 inches above the grill surface for no longer than 3 or 4 seconds). If using a gas grill, turn on all the burners to High, close the lid, and heat until very hot, about 500°F, 10 to 15 minutes. If using a grill pan, heat the pan over medium-high heat.

3 If cooking indoors, heat the oven to 350°F. Line a rimmed baking sheet with aluminum foil. Place a rack over the foil and spray with nonstick cooking spray.

4   Meanwhile, spatchcock the hens (see page 163). Brush both sides of the birds with the oil and season with salt and black pepper.

5   Place the birds skin-side down on the grill or grill pan and cook until seared on both sides, 3 to 5 minutes per side. If using the grill, move to a cooler part of the grill to cook over indirect heat; alternatively, transfer to the oven if cooking inside. Brush with the white sauce. Cook, basting generously with white sauce every 10 minutes or so, until the birds are golden brown, the juices run clear when pierced with a knife, and an instant-read thermometer registers 165°F when inserted into the thigh, 30 minutes total.

6   Place the birds on a clean cutting board. Using a large chef's knife, halve each bird down the middle of the breasts and backbone, so that each half contains both white and dark meat. Serve the halves with the reserved white sauce on the side.

Herb Roast Turkey with Apple and Onion Gravy

Serves
15 to 17

Some of my favorite memories are of Thanksgivings at my grandparents' house when I was a little girl. All the leaves would be inserted in the dining room table and a few card tables would be added at one end for the children. My grandmother, mother, and aunts would cook for days leading up to the celebratory meal, preparing rolls, cakes, pies, and ambrosia. Meme would remove the fine china from her cabinets and haul out the sterling silver from the chest. The pickles that had been put up in the summer found their way to crystal serving dishes and the scuppernong jelly was spooned into cut-glass crocks with lids. Each and every part of the meal was special. As kids we tried our best to stay out of the way, but for me, especially, all the excitement was happening in the kitchen.

Nicole Taylor, a Georgia native and author of *The Up South Cookbook*, spent her early twenties trying to distance herself from her Southern cooking roots, until a move "up" to Brooklyn gave her a fresh appreciation for the flavors of her childhood. She says, "Turkey was a Thanksgiving and Christmas tradition. For me, eating white meat meant you were special and grown up. I always grabbed the breast pieces." However, there's an innate problem with roasting a turkey—by the time the thighs are done, the breast is overcooked and dry. With this recipe, you'll never be intimidated by cooking a turkey again. I guarantee this will become your go-to recipe for perfect roast turkey.

1 cup kosher salt, plus more as needed

½ cup sugar

1 (12- to 15-pound) turkey, neck reserved for stock

8 cups homemade turkey stock, homemade chicken stock, or reduced-fat low-sodium chicken broth, plus more if needed

1 bunch fresh parsley

1 bunch fresh sage

1 bunch fresh thyme

5 small sweet onions, peels reserved, quartered

2 tablespoons unsalted butter, at room temperature, for the herb paste

2 tablespoons canola oil

2 garlic cloves, chopped

Freshly ground black pepper

2 apples, peeled, quartered, and cored

2 bay leaves, preferably fresh

5 tablespoons (about ⅓ cup)

unsalted butter or reserved fat from cooking the turkey, for the gravy

⅓ cup all-purpose flour

1 cup apple cider

½ cup apple cider vinegar

Recipe continues

When buying your turkey, estimate 1 pound per serving (this accounts for bone weight). For larger birds, a bit less is fine; they have a higher meat-to-bone ratio. But if your goal is to have ample leftovers—and who doesn't want a turkey sandwich with cranberry sauce the next day?—aim for 1½ pounds per person, whatever the turkey's size.

1   To brine the turkey, combine 2 gallons water, the salt, and the sugar in a large, nonreactive bucket or stockpot if storing in the refrigerator, or in an insulated cooler if not. (Two gallons water will be sufficient for most birds; larger birds may require three.) Submerge the turkey in the brine and refrigerate for up to 14 hours. If using a cooler, add ice or freezer packs to keep the bird very cold. Remove the bird from the liquid and rinse inside and out with cold water. Pat dry with paper towels and discard the brine.

2   Combine the turkey neck and stock in a medium saucepan. Set aside one sprig of each herb; strip the leaves from the remaining stems and chop (you should have about ¼ cup of each). Add the stripped herb stems and the onion skins to the stock. Bring the stock to a boil over high heat, then reduce the heat to maintain a bare simmer while the turkey cooks. (This little step will help you boost the flavor of the stock, especially if you are using store-bought stock.)

3   Meanwhile, combine the butter, oil, chopped herb leaves, and garlic in a food processor; pulse to combine. (You can also mix this herb paste in a small bowl as long as everything is finely chopped.) Season with salt and pepper.

4   Heat the oven to 450°F. Position an oven rack in the lowest part of the oven.

5   Season the turkey inside and out with pepper (no salt is necessary because of the brining). Place 1 quartered onion, 1 apple, and the reserved sprigs of parsley, sage, and thyme in the cavity. Add the fresh bay leaves.

6   Working from the cavity end, loosen the skin without tearing by running your fingers between the skin and flesh of the breast. Work the herb paste under the skin, then wipe any remaining herb paste on the outside of the bird. (This step is largely to clean your hands.)

7   Tie the drumsticks together with kitchen twine and fold the wings under the body to steady the bird and for best presentation. Transfer the turkey to a rack set in a large roasting pan. (I prefer a rack because it lifts the turkey and allows the bottom half of the bird to brown, too. However, you can roast your turkey without one.) Using a ladle and sieve, pour 3 cups of the prepared stock into the roasting pan. Scatter the remaining quartered onions and apple around the roasting pan.

8   Roast for 45 minutes. Decrease the oven temperature to 350°F. Baste the turkey with pan drippings, adding more strained stock as the pan becomes dry. (You'll likely need about 4 cups.) Roast, basting every 30 minutes, until an instant-read thermometer inserted into the thigh registers 165°F, 2½ to 3 hours.

9   Transfer the turkey to a rimmed cutting board. Tent it loosely with aluminum foil and let it rest for 30 minutes before carving to allow the juices to redistribute. Using a slotted spoon, transfer the onions to a medium bowl. Set aside. The apples have likely dissolved or become mush, so simply remove any larger pieces and discard.

10 Meanwhile, remove the rack from the roasting pan. Pour the juices from the roasting pan into a fat separator and set aside. The fat will rise to the top and the juices and dark drippings will stay at the bottom. (If you do not have a fat separator, pour the juices into a liquid measuring cup and remove the fat with a metal spoon; reserve the fat in a separate measuring cup or bowl.)

11 Pour the separated drippings into a large liquid measuring cup. Add enough stock to make 4 cups. Set aside.

12 Place the roasting pan across two burners on the stove over medium heat. Add the reserved turkey fat or ⅓ cup butter and the flour. Whisk to combine. Cook over low heat until foaming. Add the dripping-stock mixture, any turkey juices accumulated on the cutting board, the apple cider, and the vinegar; bring to a boil. Cook, stirring occasionally, until the gravy thickens enough to coat the back of a spoon, about 8 minutes. If the gravy is still too thin to hold a trail when you run your finger across the spoon, continue cooking. Taste and adjust the seasoning with salt and pepper.

13 *To serve,* carve the turkey and arrange on a serving platter. Scatter the onions around the bird. Transfer the gravy to a serving boat and pass it around with the turkey.

Stuffed Roast Quail with Mushrooms

Serves 4

James Beard Award–winning chef Anne Quatrano is one of the South's most respected chefs. Although she was raised in Connecticut, she attributes her passion for cooking to spending time with her grandmother in the kitchen and summers at her mother's family farm near Cartersville, Georgia. A longtime proponent of sustainability, Anne prides herself on using locally grown seasonal and organic produce, much of which is from her own garden at the same family farm that inspired her as a child, Summerland, where she now resides. She and her husband, chef Clifford Harrison, operate five of Atlanta's most celebrated restaurants. Her food and style of cooking is grounded in perfectly executed technique and the philosophy of using the best quality basic ingredients to produce something spectacular. This recipe is adapted from her beautiful cookbook, also named *Summerland*, based on a calendar year at her farm.

Quail meat is white and delicately flavored. Wild quail will taste stronger and a bit gamier than farm-raised quail.

1 tablespoon pure olive oil

4 ounces mixed mushrooms (such as white button, cremini, chanterelle, morel, and shiitake), chopped

1 shallot, very finely chopped

Coarse kosher salt and freshly ground black pepper

2 tablespoons bourbon or brandy

8 ounces ground chicken

1 tablespoon chopped fresh herbs, such as parsley, thyme, and chives

8 semiboneless quail (about 4 ounces each, or 2 pounds total)

2 tablespoons unsalted butter, melted

1 Heat the oil in a large skillet over medium-high heat. Add the mushrooms and shallot and season with salt and pepper. Cook, stirring occasionally, until all the liquid has cooked away and the mushrooms are tender, 5 minutes. Add the bourbon and cook until it has evaporated, 45 to 60 seconds. Transfer to a bowl and refrigerate to cool, 10 minutes. Once cooled, add the ground chicken and herbs. Season with salt and pepper. (To taste and adjust the seasoning, simply zap a teaspoon or so of the mixture in a bowl in the microwave to cook it through. Season with salt and pepper as needed.)

2 Heat the oven to 350°F.

3 Using a tablespoon, stuff the interior of each quail with the mushroom-chicken mixture. Using kitchen twine, tie the legs of each bird together, and then flip the wingtips under

the back of each bird to hold the wings in place. Brush the birds with the melted butter, and then season heartily with salt and pepper. Roast, basting occasionally with the melted butter, until the birds are pale golden brown and the interior of the stuffing registers 165°F when measured with an instant-read thermometer, 30 minutes.

4   Switch the oven to broil and place the birds under the broiler to darken the skin, if desired, for 45 to 60 seconds depending on the strength of your broiler. Serve immediately.

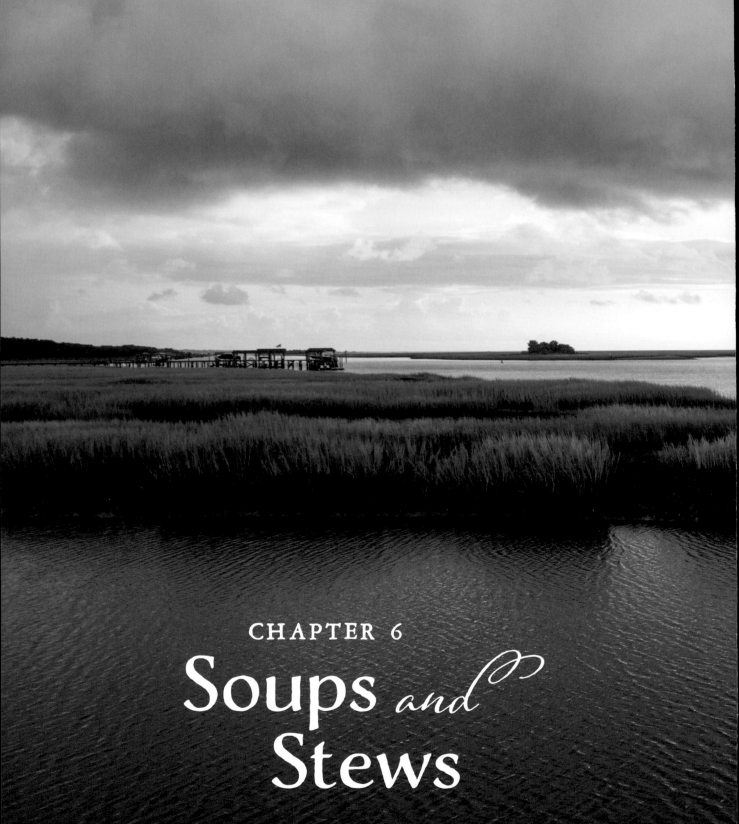

CHAPTER 6

Soups *and* Stews

MARSHES *and* "MERROIR"

There's nothing as primal and pulling as the ocean. I grew up fishing in the ocean and pretty much every body of water you can imagine. There was a pond at my grandparents' house surrounded by tall, swaying pines and flanked by wild dogwoods. I was practically born with a fishing rod in my hand. One of my first memories was falling into that dark, murky-brown water and the adults rushing to fish me out of the pond. Mama said the first time I caught a fish on my own, I jumped up and down so much that my diaper fell down around my ankles. Like I said, I was born to fish.

It was at that pond that my grandfather patiently taught me how to tie a line and bait a hook. I learned that the large-mouth bass hid under the overhanging branches at the pond's edge, while the bream liked to congregate around the flume of the dam. The pond was a source of wonderment as well as education. Many years ago, I read the book *Cod: A Biography of the Fish that Changed the World* by Mark Kurlansky. The book elucidates the concept of sustainable seafood and makes a pointed argument that we have overfished cod, a fish at the center of North American exploration and settlement. It had never occurred to me that we might overfish a species out of what I thought was the endless, bountiful ocean. I realized the ocean deserved the same respect my grandfather taught me to show our family pond.

My deference for the water is at the core of why I am meeting my friend chef Nico Romo at Garris Landing within the Cape Romain National Wildlife Refuge, a federally protected expanse of barrier islands, salt marshes, and intricate coastal waterways that harbors hundreds of at-risk and endangered species. We're going to spend the day with Dave Belanger, aka "Clammer Dave." Dave has been farming clams and oysters for more than fifteen years off a lease in the barrier island waters along Capers Island Wildlife Refuge. He harvests and sells about ten thousand shellfish each week, including uniquely grit-free, pressure-washed, and weight-graded clams and oysters, to restaurants in South Carolina, Georgia, Tennessee, California, and New York.

Nico has been a longtime customer of Clammer Dave and shares my passion for sustainable seafood. He and I are both on Monterey Bay Aquarium's Seafood Watch Blue Ribbon Task Force, a group of chefs, culinary educators, and food writers who care about the health of the oceans and advocate for sustainable seafood. Quality ingredients are important to Nico. He was born in Lyon, the culinary capital of France, and is the youngest-ever U.S. member of the French Culinary Academy (L'Académie Culinaire de France) and a French Master Chef (Maîtres Cuisiniers de

France). He is one of only sixty-five French Master Chefs in the United States and the only recipient who resides in South Carolina. He moved to the United States in 1999, working at grand hotels including the Peabody in Memphis and the Ritz Carlton flagship in Atlanta. His style of cuisine is a vibrant interpretation of classic French cuisine with delicate Asian touches.

The tide is out and we can easily see the oyster clusters near the dock. Skinny-legged plover flit between the patches of spartina grass, dipping their beaks into the pluff mud, searching for things to eat. For those of you that who don't know what pluff mud, or "plough mud," is, it's the slippery substance nearly the consistency of peanut butter found in the tidal flats and marsh grasses in the Low Country. It is a fertile, fecund, oozy combination of mud and water that defines the region. For locals, it smells like home; for others not as familiar with the particular aroma, it is more far likely to remind them of a potent combination of spoiled produce and rotten eggs. It is the "merroir" (the *terroir* of the sea) that gives Dave's bivalves their rich flavor.

The skies are dark and foreboding on the horizon. Dave scans a weather app on his phone. A little bad weather won't dissuade him from his work. He's a wiry fellow, moving sure-footedly and rapidly on the deck of his boat. As we leave the dock, Dave explains that the refuge is one of the most important ecosystems in the United States. (Later, I learn that it's actually a UNESCO "Man and the Biosphere" site, one of fewer than seven hundred sites in the entire world.) He then veers into a lengthy, passionate rant about the wealthy residents of the nearby Isle of Palms and how their pristine lawns and golf courses adversely impact the marsh. He says, "Everything that's sprayed on grass in the Low Country winds up in the ocean. The power company sprays weed killer around their poles and this eventually will wind up in the marsh where it kills single-cell blue algae—and it's pretty hard to get people excited about phytoplankton.

"Salt marshes are the nursery for the ocean," Dave continues. He takes a quick breath and describes what he calls "salt marsh terrorism," explaining how rolling waves from ski boats, WaveRunners, and parasail boats erode the shoreline. Dave explains that the waves break up the oyster clusters, which results in shoreline erosion, destroying the habitat for seabird nesting. As I listen I realize it is far more than a rant. It's abundantly clear that this is more than impacting his means to make a living—he, too, cares about the stewardship of the ocean.

We reach the clam beds and I ask him about his farming process. He explains that he seeds the beds with *Mercenaria mercenaria*, a clam indigenous to the region. They are planted like grass seed in the rich pluff mud and covered with mesh netting to keep the predators at bay. After three years of tending in nutrient-rich saline waters, the clams are ready. After the initial harvest, Dave places the clams in specialized racks floating in the highly oxygenated surface water. This purging

It is the "merroir" (the terroir of the sea) that gives Dave's bivalves their rich flavor.

method removes all grit from the shell and stomach and replaces it with pure algae, resulting in clean, sweet meat with abundant salty liquor. Finally, the clams are harvested for market, pressure washed, hand-graded by size, tightly packed in external compression bags to keep them from opening, and thermally tempered for shipping and enhanced shelf life.

Clammer Dave was born in New England and has a degree in animal science from Virginia Tech. He comments that he used to be a dirt farmer and the insight from that job helped him develop his oyster cultivation technique. He wades to the shore and grabs a cluster of wild oysters. In the Low Country, oysters are most often sold in clusters and roasted, not sold on the half shell. The small ones are simply discarded, but Dave says that's essentially throwing away next year's crop. With his method, the oysters are harvested and delivered to his processing plant, where they are separated by hand and sculpted into singles using a hammer and chisel, rather than sold in their original clusters. The bivalves then return to the water for six weeks for "finishing" as they plump up and become more richly flavored. A bushel of typical cluster oysters might contain 250 or so that are edible, but a bushel of Dave's sculpted oysters contains 500 to 600.

Dave's specialized techniques result in incredibly delicious—and sustainable—seafood. As we pull up to the dock, I ask Nico why sustainable seafood is so important to him. He says, "Sustainable seafood means protecting our waters so that they are wild and healthy for the long run. My grandfather was a fisherman in Algeria, where people went to the docks for the day's catch. The availability of fresh and local seafood has always been important—but even more so now that I have children. I want them to be able to grow up eating the same fish that we enjoy today, and for many more years to come."

The GOSPEL *of* HAM

The three of us stand in the small screened-in patio at the entrance of the smokehouse. Nancy carefully removes the thick, black magnetic strips from around the heavy metal door. Every possible precaution is taken to protect the curing hams—including a large crucifix attached to the entryway. As she tugs at the heavy magnets, she recounted the "troubles" she experienced just after her daddy died: That there had once been a "pest house" (a quarantine home for contagious tuberculosis patients) around the corner and a Cherokee graveyard just down the hill, and on several occasions she had felt a haunting presence at the entryway. Nancy, however, is a strong Christian Kentucky woman, and folks (dead or alive) shouldn't mess with her—or her hams. As she continues to peel away the safeguards, she recalls that she stood one morning and firmly and loudly told "them" to leave her alone. And they did.

We enter and quickly shut the door behind us. The fans and dehumidifier hum. The ethereal aroma of smoke surrounds me. The soles of my shoes slip against the slick fat on the hard floor. It takes a moment for my eyes to adjust to the dim light. Then the darkness slowly warms to golden. I can identify the blue-gray concrete block walls and see the tightly built wooden rafters that extend from the ground to the high ceiling. The grease-darkened wooden boards are pierced with nails, and from the orderly spikes hang multitudes of honey-brown legs of pork. The sight is breathtaking and positively surreal, like nothing I have ever seen. It's like I'm basking in the glory of a ham church.

My guide and host is Nancy Newsom of Newsom Country Hams, also known as Nancy the Ham Lady. She, and now her son, John Carl Mahaffey, use a centuries-old family recipe to produce Col. Bill Newsom's Aged Kentucky Country Ham. Their meat-curing method was originally used by her ancestors, who settled in Surry County, Virginia, in 1635. Newsom's Country Hams are consistently ranked as some of the finest handcrafted hams in the United States.

How did ham become a secret of the Southern table—and why is a ham bone such a good thing for soup? Turns out, there's more to ham than picking one up at the grocery. In the days before refrigeration, salting and smoking hams were a means to preserve meat. True to country cooking, every last bit of the ham is used, including the bone, which often winds up in the soup pot. The word *ham* itself refers to the back leg of a pig. Hams can be fresh, cured, or cured and smoked. Fresh ham is essentially a pork roast on the bone. It's simply the upper hind leg of a pig, not

processed, cured, or smoked. In the meat market, fresh hams look like (and are) raw pork. Cooked fresh ham tastes like a really moist pork loin.

Cured hams are sometimes labeled "fully cooked," "ready-to-eat," or "heat-and-serve." Also known as "city ham," these hams are wet-cured, meaning that they are submerged in or injected with brine, then smoked and sold fully cooked to be glazed and warmed at home. They may be eaten as is, but are more often heated to an internal temperature of 140°F for fuller flavor. These are the spiral-sliced varieties that grace holiday tables. Wet-cured ham is a deep rosy-pink with a moist, slightly chewy texture. A whole cured ham is the entire back leg of a hog and weighs about 20 pounds. You'll often see these hams in the meat department around the holidays. Half hams are also available and come as butt end and shank end. The butt end comes from the upper thigh and has a rounded end, whereas the shank end comes from the lower portion of the leg and has a pointed or tapered end. Look for bone-in cured hams over boneless cured hams for more flavor (and a bone for the soup pot).

Nancy the Ham Lady makes country hams, a specialty of the American South. Tennessee, Virginia, North Carolina, and Kentucky have a tradition of curing and smoking hams; only a handful of producers take as much time and care with those country hams as Newsom's Country Hams.

Ordering or purchasing a country ham can be a bit confusing. There are uncooked and cooked versions. Uncooked country hams are salted, smoked, and hung to cure. Nowadays, more and more folks are enjoying thinly sliced handcrafted uncooked country ham much in the same way they savor Italian prosciutto or Spanish Serrano. Cooked country hams, on the other hand, have been salted, smoked, and hung to cure; they're then scrubbed, soaked, and boiled to rehydrate the meat. Cooked country ham is what is traditionally served on a ham biscuit.

We start our ham pilgrimage on a hot summer afternoon at Newsom's Country Store, established January 1, 1917, by H. C. Newsom, Nancy's grandfather, in Princeton, Kentucky. It's an old-fashioned country store with wide plank wooden floors and an ancient white enamel refrigerated cooler. Nancy sells a smattering of local produce, honey, jams and jellies, hard candy, and, of course, cured meats, smoked sausage, and hams. There are various tin buckets of seeds for planting, each tagged with a paper label telling the name and the intended results.

Nancy leans against the well-worn counter of her country store and presents me with various salty, sweet samples to taste, all laid out on opaque waxed paper. My first taste is of the traditional country ham. I place a wafer-thin sliver on my tongue. The salt is bracing and the tannins cause my mouth to water. A wave of intense, savory umami gives way and sweetness floods my palate at the finish. The entire experience is positively blissful. It's amazing that a little piece of ham is so infinitely complex—and tastes so good. I then sample her version of prosciutto, which is drier than the traditional country ham, a feat achieved by its higher, hotter placement in the rafters of the smokehouse and longer curing time. I also nibble a specialty she calls "preacher ham," a less salty, smoked cooked ham that got its name from its past of being served for Sunday dinner.

She explains how the various hams are created and how all hams aren't the same. She says, "Mass-produced hams use nitrates for curing and are sold at the minimum eighteen percent moisture loss." By contrast, once her hams have cured for twelve months, they exhibit a 26 to 36 percent moisture loss. What's so important about moisture loss? It's all about flavor. Nancy carefully controls the cure so the ham absorbs only enough salt to preserve it. By the end, her trimmed ham will have lost more than a quarter of its weight through moisture loss, helping to concentrate the flavor.

However, it's not just the action of the salt that cures the ham. It's also a matter of time and temperature. Big companies, she explains, raise the curing room temperature to speed up the process and cure hams for as little as the government-regulated minimum of twenty-five days. Newsom Country Hams aren't sold a day before they've cured for at least seven months. She laments that her hams aren't ready for the State Fair at the end of August. Large companies, she says, crank out four hundred hams a day; she's hoping with the addition of her newest smokehouse to reach three thousand hams a year.

She leads me out the back door to the packing room and explains that the hams are hand-rubbed in the winter with a combination of salt and brown sugar to flavor the meat and extract moisture. When the weather starts to warm in the spring, the hams are hand-washed and transported to be hung in the smokehouse. At that time, Nancy lights a slow, smoldering hickory fire in an old iron kettle, which gives them their honey amber color and distinctly smoky flavor. Over time, a fine layer of greenish-gray mold develops on the exterior, which adds to the distinctive flavor, and as the meat ages, it develops white specks, a result of salt pulling moisture from the meat. She tells me that she records every ham by hand in a notebook: when it was salted, when it was hung, and when it was sold. Newsom's hams are a hand-crafted product, limited in number and accompanied by a hand-numbered certificate. These hams are the result of serious dedication and commitment.

When the meat is gone, the ham keeps giving. Whether fresh, cured, or country, ham bones are one of the best ingredients for soup and stews, especially slow-cooked ones that simmer long enough for the flavor to be extracted from the bone. When you're lucky enough to work with a country ham like Nancy Newsom's, you need to make sure to enjoy every last tasty bite.

A smoldering hickory fire gives them their honey-amber color and distinctly smoky flavor.

Country-Style Oyster Stew with Potatoes

Serves 6

Wintzell's Oyster House was founded in 1938 by J. Oliver Wintzell as a small, six-stool oyster bar in Mobile, Alabama. It is known far and wide for "Oysters—fried, stewed, or nude." Their oyster stew is a simple combination of milk and oysters. This version isn't nearly as minimalist, yet it is still simple enough that the fresh oysters are the stars of the show.

Oysters take on the flavor of the seas where they are grown. This means that oysters grown in different regions have their own unique taste. Gulf of Mexico oysters are harvested in several locations in the Southeastern United States, including Texas, Louisiana, Mississippi, Alabama, and eastern Florida. Gulf oysters generally have a sweeter flavor and softer texture than their northern counterparts. According to the Gulf States Fisheries Commission, even with wild populations on the decline, 70 percent of all wild-caught Eastern oysters are from the Gulf of Mexico. And oyster farming is just beginning in the Gulf, but it shows huge promise. In the Gulf of Mexico, wild Eastern oysters are harvested with tongs and small dredges. Both are used on bottom habitat that is covered by oysters, living and dead, and therefore there is no by-catch. So the best news is that both wild and farmed oysters are deemed sustainable by Seafood Watch.

2 tablespoons unsalted butter

1 sweet onion, finely chopped

Coarse kosher salt and freshly ground black pepper

2 garlic cloves, mashed to a paste with salt (see page 22)

¼ cup all-purpose flour

1 quart whole or 2% milk

2 (8-ounce) containers oysters, drained, juices reserved

8 fingerling potatoes (8 ounces), sliced into ¼-inch-thick coins

1 bay leaf, preferably fresh

1 tablespoon chopped fresh chives

1 teaspoon chopped fresh dill

1 Melt the butter in a large pot over medium-low heat. Add the onion and season with salt and pepper. Cook, stirring often, until soft and translucent, 3 to 5 minutes. Add the garlic and cook until fragrant, 45 to 60 seconds. Sprinkle over the flour and stir to combine. Whisk in the milk and reserved oyster juice. Add the potatoes and bring to a gentle boil over high heat. As soon as bubbles start to appear at the edge of the pan, reduce the heat to maintain a very gentle simmer. Add the bay leaf, cover, and cook until the potatoes are tender, 10 minutes. Add the oysters and simmer, uncovered, until they are heated through and their edges begin to curl, 3 minutes. Remove the bay leaf and discard. Add the chives and dill. Taste and adjust the seasoning with salt and pepper. Ladle into warmed bowls and serve immediately.

Shrimp and Roasted Corn Chowder

Serves 6

There's nothing quite as sweet as super-fresh shrimp purchased at the dock or a roadside stand. Along the coast all across the South you will find pickup trucks pulled off to the side of the road, tailgates open, the beds filled with coolers packed with ice and shrimp for sale. Head-on shrimp must be incredibly fresh, as they start to deteriorate the minute they are taken from the water. Most often, these shrimp are so fresh that their long threadlike antennae and sharp needlelike projections called rostrums are still intact. Only a few miles off the coast, it's nearly impossible to purchase fresh shrimp.

While it's hard to beat shrimp that are only hours out of the ocean, it doesn't mean frozen shrimp are bad. Increasingly, shrimp are actually frozen on the boat. (Keep in mind that the "fresh" shrimp at your market very well may be frozen and then defrosted.) However, all frozen shrimp is not the same. Make sure the bag is labeled "IQF," which stands for "individually quick frozen." The packaging should also note whether the shrimp is farmed or wild, and where it came from. Consult the Seafood Watch website or app to determine if it's sustainable. Be sure to buy shrimp in the shell, which protects the actual meat of the shrimp; in addition, peeled shrimp has often been treated with chemical preservatives that you'll want to avoid.

This shrimp chowder celebrates summer's bounty. Taking the time to make a quick corn and shrimp stock elevates this dish from simple to spectacular.

4 ears corn, shucked

1 pound unshelled large (21/25-count) shrimp, peeled and deveined, shells reserved

3 sweet onions, chopped

1 carrot, coarsely chopped

4 cups water

1 tablespoon pure olive oil

2 poblano peppers, seeded and chopped

2 celery stalks, chopped

2 garlic cloves, chopped

12 red potatoes (about 1 pound), quartered

1   Heat the oven to broil. Broil the corn, rotating it every 5 minutes, until charred, 15 minutes. Set aside to cool. To cut the corn from the cob, set each ear of corn on its side and, using a chef's knife, slice away the kernels on four "sides," squaring off the round ear. The kernels will fall away, but not scatter. Then stand the ear on one end and cut away the "corners" of the cob. Set the kernels aside in a bowl. Finally, using the back of the knife, scrape the milky remainder from the cob and add to the kernels in the bowl. Break the cleaned cobs in half and set aside.

2   Place the shrimp shells in a medium pot and add one-third of the chopped onions, the carrot, and the halved corncobs. Add the water. Bring to a boil over medium-high heat, and then decrease the heat to maintain a simmer. Cook until the

Ingredients and recipe continue

Leaves from 3 sprigs thyme

2 bay leaves, preferably fresh

2 tablespoons all-purpose flour

1 cup 2% milk

Coarse kosher salt and freshly ground black pepper

¼ cup chopped fresh flat-leaf parsley

broth is slightly colored and smells lightly sweet, 5 minutes. Strain into a bowl, discarding the solids, and set aside; you should have 4 cups stock.

3 Heat the oil in a large pot over medium heat until shimmering. Add the remaining chopped onion, the poblanos, and the celery. Cook until the onion is soft and translucent, 3 to 5 minutes. Add the garlic and cook until fragrant, 45 to 60 seconds. Add the potatoes, corn, thyme, and bay leaves and stir to combine. Stir in the flour until incorporated, 2 minutes. Stir in 3 cups of the shrimp stock, reserving 1 cup to use if the chowder seems too thick. Add the milk. Cover and bring to a boil over medium-high heat. Uncover, reduce the heat to medium-low, and gently simmer until the vegetables are tender, 15 minutes. Remove from the heat. Discard the thyme sprigs and bay leaves.

4 Taste and adjust for seasoning with salt and pepper. Stir in the raw shrimp; cook until the shrimp are opaque, 2 minutes. Add the parsley; taste and adjust for seasoning with salt and pepper. Divide among warmed bowls and serve immediately.

If you are reading this cookbook, you're likely to be familiar with the concept of "farm to table." We have learned that food is best when produced on a small scale in accordance with the rhythms of the planet. Seafood deserves the same kind of respect and awareness. We've lost touch with seafood seasonality because the fish counter is always full. Shrimp used to be a luxury—now it's all-you-can-eat due to cheap farm-raised shrimp from Asia, and farm-raised shrimp is a problem. Mangroves are cut down to create the farms, which results in environmental destruction. The shrimp are fed a meal made from ground wild fish, and the meal is laced with antibiotics to prevent disease. According to the Centers for Disease Control, antibiotics must be used judiciously in humans and animals because both uses contribute to the emergence, persistence, and spread of resistant bacteria. What can you do? It's easy. Buy wild American shrimp. With your purchase, you support the U.S. seafood industry, advocate for sustainability, and get fresh, seasonal shrimp with every delicious bite.

Catfish Mulldown

Catfish can grow to an enormous size; there are photos of my grandfather as a young man with a catfish hanging from a tree on the banks of the Savannah River. The fish was nearly as long as my grandfather's strapping six-foot height. His brother was a fishing guide, and although he passed away before I was born, I got the impression that Uncle Marshall was rough around the edges, and probably ate his share of catfish mulldown, an old-fashioned recipe that would be found at a fish camp. It's a very thick, layered catfish stew made of bacon, onions, potatoes, and often ketchup, slowly cooked until the fish is falling apart. Typically, the catfish was cut into steaks because the large fish were too big and tough to fry.

This adaptation is more gratin than stew, soulfully filling, decadently rich, stunningly delicious, and more likely to be found at the table of a fine restaurant than a roughneck cabin in the woods.

1 tablespoon unsalted butter, at room temperature, for the baking dish

1¼ pounds Yukon Gold potatoes, thinly sliced

Coarse kosher salt and freshly ground black pepper

1 sweet onion, very thinly sliced

1 pound catfish fillets, thickly sliced on an angle

¾ cup heavy cream

¼ teaspoon paprika

1 Heat the oven to 350°F. Butter a large ovenproof casserole. Arrange half the potato slices in the prepared dish, overlapping them to cover the bottom of the dish. Season with salt and pepper. Scatter half the onion over the potatoes and then arrange the fish slices over the onion in a single layer, overlapping the slices as necessary. Top with the remaining onion and then with the remaining potatoes. Season with salt and pepper. Pour the cream evenly over the layers. Cover with a tight-fitting lid or aluminum foil and bake for 40 minutes.

2 Remove from the oven and spoon some of the cooking liquid over the top of the gratin to moisten the potatoes and help them brown. Sprinkle with a few shakes of the paprika. Remove the lid and bake until the top layer of potatoes is tender when pierced with a sharp knife, 20 minutes. Let stand for 10 to 15 minutes before serving.

Chicken Posole Soup

Serves 4 to 6

Although we often associate California and Texas with large Hispanic populations, the Southeast has a fast-growing Hispanic presence, with Alabama leading the way. According to the Pew Research Center, Alabama's Hispanic population grew 158 percent between 2000 and 2011—more than any other state. Latin markets have opened all across the South, selling everything from soccer jerseys to phone cards to hard-to-find spices and other ingredients. It's a bonus if there's a little restaurant attached, featuring dishes such as flavorful cow cheek tacos; tender, freshly made *sopas* topped with refried beans and cabbage; and hearty, homey soups like this one.

Posole, also known as hominy, is corn that has been soaked in a lye solution so that the pericarp, or outside of the corn kernel, dissolves. Dry posole is available in Latin markets and online, but the more user-friendly canned version is widely available even in more traditional grocery stores. This hearty soup is rib-sticking comfort food—and gets even better a day or so after making it.

4 cups homemade chicken stock or reduced-fat low-sodium chicken broth

4 boneless, skinless chicken thighs (about 2 pounds), cut into 1-inch cubes

½ cup pepitas (shelled pumpkin seeds)

1 pound tomatillos, husks removed

1 sweet onion, thickly sliced

4 large garlic cloves, smashed

2 jalapeños, or to taste, seeded and sliced

1 teaspoon dried oregano

1 (15.5-ounce) can hominy, drained and rinsed

¼ cup chopped fresh cilantro

Coarse kosher salt and freshly ground black pepper

3 radishes, thinly sliced

Green onions, chopped

1 Place the stock and chicken in a medium pot. Bring just to a simmer over medium-high heat. When bubbles just start forming around the edge of the pot, cover and reduce the heat to medium-low. Cook, occasionally skimming any foam from the surface with a spoon, until the chicken registers 160°F on an instant-read thermometer, 10 to 12 minutes. (If your pot is too broad and the stock level is too low to submerge the chicken, you may need to turn the chicken halfway through cooking so it cooks completely on both sides and all the way through.) Once the chicken is cooked, turn off the heat and set aside.

2 Meanwhile, toast the pumpkin seeds in a dry skillet over medium heat until lightly browned and plumped, 3 to 5 minutes (see Note). Transfer the toasted seeds to a blender.

3 Wipe the skillet clean and place over high heat until very hot—if you flick a droplet of water on the surface it should dance quickly and then evaporate. Add the whole tomatillos and cook them on all sides, without moving them too much, until lightly charred, 8 to 10 minutes.

Ingredients and recipe continue

2 avocados, pitted, peeled, and chopped (see sidebar, page 103), for serving

Lime wedges, for serving

Tortilla chips, for serving

4 Scoot the tomatillos to one side of the skillet and add the onion. Cook until the onion slices are browned, 3 to 5 minutes. Transfer the tomatillos and onion to the blender with the pumpkin seeds. Drop in the smashed garlic, jalapeños, and oregano. Add 1 cup of the stock that was used to cook the chicken. Puree until smooth, about 4 minutes.

5 Wipe the skillet clean once again and heat over medium heat. Add the pureed tomatillo mixture. Cook, stirring often, until the mixture is thick, reduced, and darker green, 10 to 12 minutes. (You'll be able to draw a spoon through the bottom of the pan and hold a trail.)

6 Add the reduced tomatillo mixture and hominy to the saucepan with the chicken and remaining stock; stir to combine. Bring the soup to a boil over medium-high heat. Reduce the heat to a simmer and cook until everything is heated through, 5 minutes. Stir in the cilantro. Taste and adjust for seasoning with salt and pepper. Ladle into warmed bowls and top with radishes, green onions, and avocado. Serve lime wedges and tortilla chips on the side.

Some markets carry toasted, salted pumpkin seeds in the dried fruit and nut section, in which case, there's no need to toast them again. Simply place them in the jar of the blender.

West African Chicken Stew with Collard Greens and Peanuts

Serves 6 to 8

The peanut likely originated in South America and spread throughout the New World via Spanish explorers. It now grows in tropical and subtropical regions throughout the world, including the American South. The first known printed recipe for peanut stew comes from an 1847 cookbook by Sarah Rutledge, a housewife from South Carolina, who published a recipe for "Ground Nut Soup."

However, it's important to understand that enslaved Africans introduced peanut stew to the South. There's perhaps no greater expert on the food and foodways of the African diaspora than Dr. Jessica B. Harris. She is the author of twelve critically acclaimed cookbooks documenting the food and culture of Africa in the Americas. According to Jessica, peanut stews are found across West Africa, originally made with indigenous groundnuts before the peanut arrived from the New World in the sixteenth century.

The list of potential ingredients in this hearty stew often extends to okra, tomatoes, hot peppers, and ginger, but it's the indispensable peanut that gives this dish its essential earthy character.

4 cups homemade chicken stock or reduced-fat low-sodium chicken broth

¼ cup tomato paste

1 tablespoon canola oil

1½ pounds boneless, skinless chicken thighs, cut into 1-inch pieces

Coarse kosher salt and freshly ground black pepper

1 sweet onion, chopped

2 carrots, diced

1 red bell pepper, seeded and chopped

3 garlic cloves, finely chopped

1 tablespoon finely chopped fresh ginger

1 Combine the stock and tomato paste in a large measuring cup or bowl. Whisk or stir until no lumps of tomato paste remain. Set aside.

2 Heat the oil in a large pot over medium-high heat until shimmering. Season the chicken with salt and pepper. Add the chicken to the pot and sear it, in two batches if necessary to avoid crowding, until brown on all sides, 8 minutes. Transfer the chicken to a plate. Set aside.

3 Add the onion, carrots, and bell pepper to the pot and cook, stirring, until the onion is soft and translucent, 3 to 5 minutes. Add the garlic and ginger; cook until fragrant, 45 to 60 seconds. Add the stock mixture, peanut butter, Scotch bonnet, bay leaf, coriander, cumin, and cinnamon; stir until smooth. Add the chicken, collard greens, and sweet potatoes.

Ingredients and recipe continue

1 cup crunchy peanut butter

1 Scotch bonnet or habanero pepper, seeded and finely chopped

1 bay leaf, preferably fresh

½ teaspoon ground coriander

¼ teaspoon ground cumin

¼ teaspoon ground cinnamon

4 cups loosely packed chopped collard greens

2 sweet potatoes, peeled and cut into ½-inch cubes

4 Reduce the heat to medium-low and cook until the vegetables are tender, 25 minutes. Taste and adjust for seasoning with salt and pepper. Ladle into warm bowls and serve immediately.

There are many different techniques to chop a pepper. I find the most simple to be what I refer to as the "box cut." For a bell pepper, place the pepper stem-side up on the cutting board. Using a chef's knife, cut off all four sides of the pepper, leaving the seeds and core at the center, attached to the stem. Then, turn the pepper core on its side and cut off the bottom. Discard the stem and seedy core. Working with a quarter pepper or one side at a time, use the tip of your knife to remove any interior white pith and tap it against the cutting board to remove any stray seeds. Slice into strips or cut into dice, as needed. This same technique may be used with more pointed peppers that won't stand up on the board such as jalapeño and serrano as well. Simply lay them on the board and slice off one quarter of the pepper, then turn and remove the second quarter or side. Repeat until no sides remain. Discard the stem and seeds.

Ginger Chicken Bog

Serves 6 to 8

Every October just inland from Myrtle Beach in Loris, South Carolina, giant cast-iron cauldrons are pulled out of storage for the "Bog-Off." Nope, there's no swamp involved. A bog is a chicken and rice dish, and according to my friend cookbook author Nancie McDermott, a bog belongs in the family of dishes traditional in South Carolina known as pilau and *perloo*—meaty rice-centered main dishes with ancient Persian and South Asian roots. Why is it called a bog? Perhaps because it's moist and boggy, or maybe because chicken gets all bogged down in the rice-and-broth goodness. As Nancie says, "It's so good, nobody really knows or cares."

Her passion is researching and celebrating traditional food in its cultural context, and her beloved subjects are two seemingly different places with much in common: the cuisines of Asia and of the American South. Nancie gained her Southern kitchen wisdom as a North Carolina native and her knowledge of Asian cuisine as a Peace Corps volunteer in Thailand. In honor of her multiple talents, I'm adapting her recipe for chicken bog from her book *Southern Soups and Stews*, and adding a congee-like Asian twist.

5 green onions

1 (4-pound chicken), cut into 8 serving pieces, including back and neck

1 carrot, coarsely chopped

1 celery stalk, coarsely chopped

6 (¼-inch) slices fresh ginger, plus 1 tablespoon very finely chopped fresh ginger

½ cup sherry

8 ounces smoked sausage, such as kielbasa or andouille, halved lengthwise and cut crosswise into ½-inch pieces

1½ cups long-grain rice

Coarse kosher salt and freshly ground white pepper

1 tablespoon fish sauce (optional)

¼ cup fresh cilantro leaves, for garnish

1 Cut three of the green onions in half lengthwise and smash them with the flat side of a knife. Slice the remaining two on an angle and set aside for garnish. Place the chicken in a stockpot with the three halved and smashed green onions, the carrot, celery, sliced ginger, and sherry. Add enough water to cover the chicken by 2 inches (about 16 cups). Bring the water to a rolling boil over medium-high heat. Skim off and discard any foam that rises to the surface. After 10 minutes, when the foam has subsided, lower the heat to maintain a gentle but visible simmer. Cook until the chicken is tender and the juices run clear when pierced with the tip of a knife, 45 minutes to 1 hour.

2 Transfer the chicken to a rimmed baking sheet and let rest until it is cool enough to handle. When the meat has cooled, pull it in large chunks from the bones and set it aside, discarding the skin and bones.

3 Meanwhile, strain the broth though a fine-mesh sieve, reserving the liquid and discarding the solids. Measure 8 cups of chicken broth, reserving the rest for another use.

Clean the pot and return the broth to the pot; add the chicken meat, sausage, and rice. Season with 1 teaspoon salt and white pepper to taste. Place the pot over medium-high heat and bring it to a lively boil.

4   Reduce the heat to maintain a simmer and cook, stirring occasionally, until the rice is tender but not split, 30 to 35 minutes. Add the fish sauce (if using); taste and adjust for seasoning with salt and white pepper. Stir in the chopped ginger. The rice will thicken as it stands. Thin with reserved broth as necessary. Serve ladled into warm bowls and garnished with cilantro and the reserved chopped green onions.

Kentucky Soup Beans with Chow Chow

Serves 6

My friend Joyce Pinson, known for her outrageous red hat, pointy-toed shoes, and cast-iron skillet, is a farmer, community leader, and farm-to-fork advocate, and a trusted voice of agriculture and food-ways in central Appalachia. She told me that to this day in her corner of Kentucky, there is always a kettle of soup beans on the stove, or in the refrigerator ready to rewarm; and they are always served with cornbread. "In company settings, cornbread is eaten by the hunk, but if it's just family, the bread is crumbled into the beans," she says. "As Mexican dishes have become more popular, some folks serve soup beans one day and use the remainder in the pot for refried beans or for tacos."

To salt or not to salt? According to the Bean Growers Association, dry beans cook faster when salt is added because salt helps break down the cell walls, so the notion of salt slowing down the cooking process is a myth. However, go easy on the salt, especially if cooking with salt pork, which is simply salted pork belly; it looks like side or slab bacon, but it's not smoked. If you cannot find salt pork, bacon is a fine substitute.

1 pound dried pinto beans

1 tablespoon canola oil

2 sweet onions, finely chopped

2 garlic cloves, very finely chopped

12 ounces salt pork or bacon

Coarse kosher salt and freshly ground black pepper

Chow Chow (recipe follows), for serving

1 Place the beans in a large bowl. Remove and discard any stones. Add cold water to cover by several inches. Soak for 8 hours or up to overnight. (Or, for a quick soak, wash and sort the beans. Place in a large stockpot and add water to cover, about 3 quarts. Bring to a rolling boil over high heat. Remove from the heat and let soak for 1 hour.) Drain the soaked beans, discarding the water.

2 Heat the oil in a large pot over medium heat until shimmering. Add half the onion and cook until soft and translucent, 3 to 5 minutes. Add the garlic and cook until fragrant, 45 to 60 seconds. Add the beans and water to cover by 1 inch. Add the salt pork and bring to a boil over high heat. Season with 1 teaspoon salt. Reduce the heat to maintain a simmer and cook, stirring occasionally, until the beans are very tender and beginning to burst, 1½ to 2 hours. If necessary, add ½ to 1 cup water while simmering to keep the beans just submerged in cooking liquid.

Recipe continues

3 When the beans are tender, transfer the salt pork to a cutting board. Using a knife or two forks, pull the meat into bits. Return the meat to the pot. Using a potato masher, mash to break up some of the beans. Taste and adjust for seasoning with salt and pepper. Serve with the remaining raw onion and the chow chow.

CHOW CHOW Makes 4 cups

Chow chow is a spicy pickled relish that uses the produce at the end of the harvest, and it is the traditional condiment for Soup Beans (page 212). The vegetables can vary from recipe to recipe and can include green tomatoes, sweet peppers, onions, carrots, cucumber, and even apples or pears. For this recipe, you'll need 8 cups raw vegetables to make 4 cups pickles.

1 red bell pepper, seeded and chopped

1 poblano pepper, seeded and chopped

1 sweet onion, chopped

½ cabbage, cored and chopped

2 tablespoons coarse kosher salt

2 cups white vinegar

1 cup sugar

1 teaspoon mustard seeds

½ teaspoon dry mustard powder

¼ teaspoon ground turmeric

¼ teaspoon celery seed

Freshly ground black pepper

1 *Place the peppers, onion, and cabbage in a resealable container. Add the salt and stir to combine. Cover and refrigerate for at least 4 hours and up to 12 hours. Drain well in a colander and rinse under cold running water to remove any excess brine. Shake well to remove any excess moisture.*

2 *Combine the vinegar, sugar, mustard seeds, dry mustard, turmeric, and celery seed in a large stainless steel or enamel-coated cast-iron pot and bring to a boil over medium high heat. (You need to use a nonreactive pot because you'll be cooking vinegar.) Whisk to dissolve the sugar. Add the drained vegetables and stir to combine. Return to a boil, then reduce the heat to maintain a simmer. Cook until the vegetables are just tender and become translucent, 30 minutes. Season with pepper. Pack the vegetables and liquid into clean, sterilized jars and let cool slightly. Seal with a tight-fitting lid and refrigerate for up to 6 weeks.*

Cream of Anything Soup

Serves 4 to 6

Cream of Anything Soup is one of the easiest of soups to make. It can be practical and money saving, too. Do you have some vegetables lingering in the fridge that are too limp for sautéing or too bruised for salad? They are perfect for Cream of Anything Soup. Think cream soups are too rich and fatty? You actually don't need any cream, other than perhaps an optional few drops at the end, to make velvet-smooth, silky soups. This technique works for butternut squash, sweet potatoes, carrots, and all sorts of root vegetables. Do you think soups are just for winter? How about chilled cream of asparagus in the spring or cream of corn or zucchini in the summer? The only difference in technique is that when you're using vegetables like mushrooms and summer squash that exude liquid, you need to cook the vegetables a bit to reduce the moisture and concentrate the flavor before adding the stock.

2 tablespoons unsalted butter

1 sweet onion, finely chopped

2 pounds mixed fresh mushrooms (such as white button, cremini, shiitake, morel, and chanterelle), or other vegetable, sliced

Bouquet garni: 5 sprigs thyme, 4 sprigs flat-leaf parsley, 2 bay leaves (preferably fresh), and 10 whole black peppercorns, tied together in cheesecloth

4 cups homemade chicken stock or reduced-fat low-sodium chicken or vegetable broth, plus more if needed

¼ cup heavy cream (optional)

Coarse kosher salt and freshly ground black pepper

1   Melt the butter in a large pot over medium heat, then add the onion. Cook until the onion is translucent, 3 to 5 minutes. Add the vegetable—in this case, mushrooms—and the bouquet garni. Cook the mushrooms until they're just tender and have given off some of their moisture, about 5 minutes. Add enough stock just to cover the vegetable pieces. If you think about standing in the deep end of the pool, add stock just up to the "shoulders" of the vegetable. And remember, you can always add more, but it's not as easy to take out.

2   Bring to a boil, then decrease the heat to maintain a simmer. Simmer until the mushrooms are very soft, 30 minutes. The cooking time depends on the vegetable; mushrooms will take less time than butternut squash, for example.

3   Remove and discard the bouquet garni. Use an immersion blender (or a regular blender) to puree the soup. Leave the vegetables coarse for a more rustic soup, or puree until smooth for a more elegant soup. You can serve the soup plain or with a bit of heavy cream on the side. (It's better to use heavy cream than milk, as milk will dilute the soup. And be cautious if you're looking for lighter substitutes for the cream; yogurt may curdle.) Taste and adjust for seasoning with salt and pepper. Ladle into warmed bowls and serve immediately.

Grillades Stew with Creole Rice

Serves 6

My friend and colleague chef Kelly English is the executive chef and owner of Restaurant Iris and The Second Line in Memphis. His style of cooking is deeply rooted in his Louisiana upbringing and heavily influenced by his world travels. As a New Orleans native, I asked him how he felt about the traditional beef and gravy dish known as *grillades*. He responded, "I have strong *grillade* feelings. My father used to make it almost every Sunday for us when I was a kid. It is served for brunch and is the official midnight meal at Mardi Gras balls. It doesn't fit in the one definition of any meal, but is appropriate at all of them."

These *grillades* have absolutely nothing to do with the grill. Pronounced *"gree-ahds,"* they are traditionally a cutlet of veal, pork, or beef simmered in Creole gravy. I've adapted the basic flavors of *grillades* into a rich, savory stew that can be made in the oven or on the stovetop, although I prefer the oven. It's less likely to scorch on the bottom and produces a silky-smooth gravy.

For the grillades

3½ pounds chuck roast, cut into 2-inch pieces

1 cup red wine

1 cup all-purpose flour

1 tablespoon Homemade Creole Seasoning (recipe follows), or to taste

⅓ cup canola oil, plus more if needed

1 sweet onion, chopped

2 celery stalks, chopped

1 red bell pepper, seeded and chopped

1 poblano pepper, seeded and chopped

3 garlic cloves, finely chopped

2 tablespoons tomato paste

2 cups homemade chicken stock or reduced-fat low-sodium chicken broth

3 sprigs thyme

1 ***To make the grillades,*** place the meat in a resealable container and pour the wine over the meat. Refrigerate for 4 hours or up to overnight.

2 When ready to prepare the grillades, transfer the beef from the wine to a plate, reserving the wine. Heat the oven to 350°F if cooking in the oven.

3 Pat the beef dry with paper towels. Place the flour in a shallow plate. Stir in the Creole seasoning. Heat the oil over medium-high heat in a large heavy Dutch oven until shimmering. Dredge the beef in the flour on all sides, shaking off the excess. Add the beef to the oil and sear on all sides until dark brown, 3 minutes per side. Transfer to the plate. (Using the same plate is fine with regard to food safety since you're going to cook the meat again.)

4 Reserve ½ cup of the seasoned flour and discard the rest. Add the onion, celery, and peppers to the residual oil in the

Ingredients and recipe continue

2 tablespoons unsalted butter

1 shallot, chopped

2 cups long-grain rice, such as
Carolina Gold, jasmine,
or basmati

1 teaspoon Homemade Creole
Seasoning (recipe follows)

3 cups homemade chicken stock,
reduced-fat low-sodium chicken
broth, or water

1 bay leaf, preferably fresh

1 teaspoon coarse kosher salt

Freshly ground black pepper

Dutch oven and stir to coat and combine. Cook, stirring often, until the vegetables wilt and color, 5 to 7 minutes. Add the garlic and cook until fragrant, 45 to 60 seconds. Add the reserved seasoned flour and cook until the flour turns brown, 3 minutes. (The mixture will be thick and pasty.) Combine the reserved wine marinade and tomato paste. Whisk to combine so that there are no lumps of tomato paste and then add the marinade-paste mixture and the stock to the pot. Stir to combine.

5 Return the seared beef and any accumulated juices to the pot and turn the meat in the gravy to coat. Toss the thyme sprigs on top and cover the pot with its lid. If cooking on the stovetop, reduce the heat to medium-low. Or, at this point, transfer the pot to the oven. Cook, spooning sauce over the meat occasionally, until the meat is very tender and falling apart like a stew, 1½ to 2 hours.

6 Meanwhile, about 30 minutes before the beef is ready, prepare the Creole Rice. Heat the oven to 350°F if you haven't already. Melt the butter in a large ovenproof saucepan with a lid over medium heat until foaming. Add the shallot and cook until translucent, 2 to 3 minutes.

7 Add the rice and stir to combine. Cook, stirring continuously, until the rice is coated with butter and lightly toasted. Add the Creole seasoning, stock, and bay leaf; stir to combine. Bring the mixture to a boil. Cover with the lid and transfer to the heated oven. (You can also cook the rice on the stovetop, but I find that baking produces better results for individual, separate grains of rice.)

8   Bake or cook on the stovetop until the liquid has been absorbed and the rice is tender, 17 minutes. Remove from the oven and let stand, covered, for 5 minutes before serving. Fluff with a fork just before serving.

9   **To serve the grillades,** taste and adjust for seasoning with the salt and pepper. Spoon a heaping serving of the Creole rice into a shallow bowl. Top with a spoonful of the tender meat and the rich gravy.

HOMEMADE CREOLE SEASONING

Makes about ½ cup

This is a handy blend of herbs and spices that can easily be doubled or tripled. It's great for turkey and chicken cutlets or to give some kick to pot roast, as I've done here. This will keep in an airtight resealable container for about 6 months.

- 2 tablespoons freshly ground white pepper
- 2 tablespoons cayenne pepper, or to taste
- 1 tablespoon coarse kosher salt
- 1 tablespoon dried thyme
- 2 teaspoons freshly ground black pepper
- 2 teaspoons paprika
- 1 teaspoon dried sage
- ½ teaspoon onion powder
- ½ teaspoon garlic powder

Combine all the ingredients in a small airtight container or mason jar. Shake to combine. Store in a cool, dry place for up to 3 months.

Gumbo Z'herbes

Serves 6 to 8

This hearty vegetable gumbo is traditionally eaten on Holy Thursday to fortify worshipers for Good Friday, a day of fasting and abstinence from meat. I've seen recipes that contain everything from chicken wings to spicy chaurice sausage (a Cajun cousin of chorizo) to smoked brisket. Custom also dictates that the gumbo is supposed to have an odd number of greens—five or seven or nine and as many as fifteen—for luck. Many recipes include foraged herbs such as peppergrass, as well as the green tops from radishes, carrots, and beets. Leah Chase, the Grande Dame of NOLA, is world famous for her Gumbo Z'herbes. At her restaurant, Dooky Chase, there are three lunch seatings on Holy Thursday, serving nearly five hundred guests.

Most recipes are quite the production, featuring multiple pots and pureeing vast quantities of simmered greens. I've streamlined the recipe by using baby greens and prechopped greens to avoid pureeing them at the end. Aim for the odd number in any combination of "z'herbes" you'd like. This amount of liquid is suitable for 3 pounds of greens.

6 tablespoons pure olive oil, canola oil, or rendered bacon fat

1 pound chaurice, fresh chorizo, or hot pork Italian sausage, removed from casing

16 ounces andouille sausage, sliced

⅓ cup all-purpose flour

1 sweet onion, chopped

1 poblano pepper, chopped

1 celery stalk, chopped

6 garlic cloves

2 quarts homemade chicken stock, reduced-fat low-sodium chicken broth, or water

1 smoked ham hock (about 8 ounces)

1 (16-ounce) bag chopped collard greens, or 1 (1½-pound) bunch collard greens, stems removed and leaves coarsely chopped

1. Heat 1 tablespoon of the oil in a large heavy pot over medium heat. Add both kinds of sausage; cook until the sausage is cooked through and the fat has rendered, about 5 minutes. Use a slotted spoon to transfer the meat to a plate.

2. Add the remaining 5 tablespoons oil to the pot. Add the flour and cook, stirring continuously with a wooden spoon, until deep golden brown, about 15 minutes. Add the onion, poblano, and celery and cook, stirring often, until onion is translucent, 3 to 5 minutes. Add the garlic and cook until fragrant, 45 to 60 seconds. Add the stock and stir to combine.

3. Plop the ham hock in and bring to a boil over high heat. Add the collard greens, kale, spinach, cabbage, green onions, and thyme. (You may need to let the greens cook a bit between additions so they will all fit in the pot. Don't be tempted to add additional liquid too soon: It's easy to add but hard to remove, and you want the gumbo to be dense and like stew,

1 (12-ounce) bag chopped kale or baby kale

1 (16-ounce) box baby spinach leaves

½ cabbage (about 8 ounces), cored and thinly sliced

6 green onions, chopped

2 teaspoons chopped fresh thyme

Coarse kosher salt and freshly ground black pepper

Hot sauce, for serving

Cooked white rice, for serving

not soup.) Reduce the heat to maintain a simmer. Cook until the greens are tender, about 45 minutes. Taste and adjust for seasoning with salt and pepper. Add hot sauce to taste. Serve ladled over cooked white rice with hot sauce on the side.

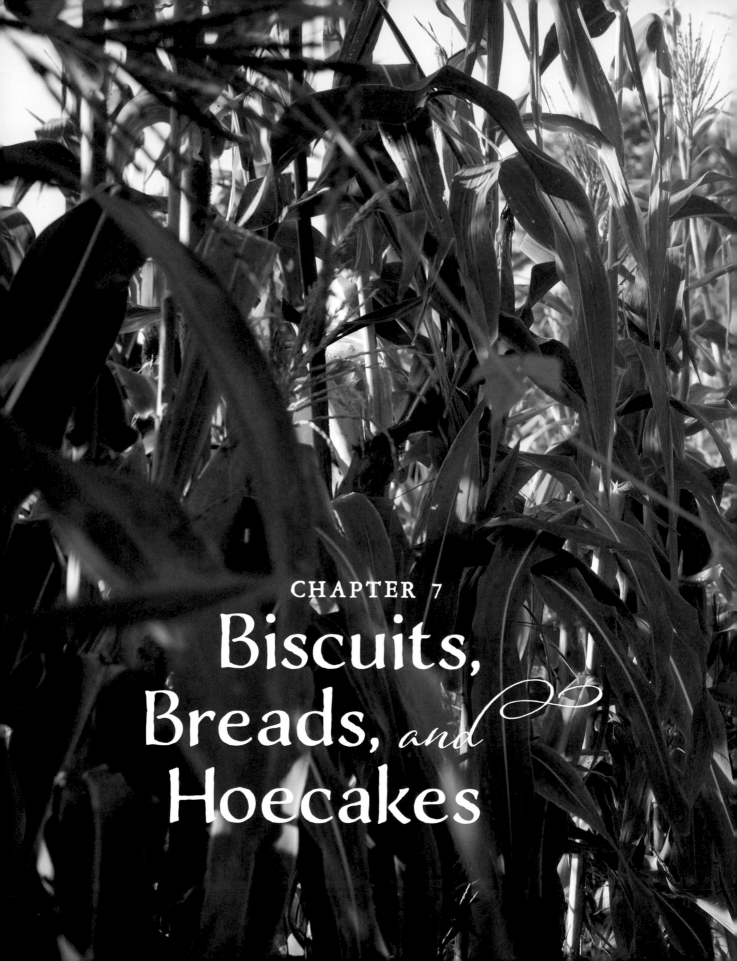

CHAPTER 7

Biscuits, Breads, and Hoecakes

ANSON MILLS *and* HEIRLOOM GRAINS

"Listening to Glenn Roberts talk is like trying to drink water out of a fire hose," proclaims Hal Hanvey, farm manager for the Clemson Coastal Research and Education Center. Having spent the previous day with Glenn, I have a very real understanding of what Hal means. Glenn Roberts is the founder of Anson Mills, an artisan milling company that specializes in organic heirloom and landrace grains. (*Landrace* refers to a crop cultivar or animal breed that has been developed through traditional farming practices for many years in a particular area without influence from modern agricultural science.) Glenn is seemingly equal parts historian, plant geneticist, food activist, conservationist, and farmer—and each sentence that rapidly flows out of his mouth reflects that particular combination of skills.

Hal and I are standing in a wizened patch of straw-colored Jimmy Red corn, drying in a process known as field ripening. Jimmy Red corn, also known as James Island corn, named for a large island adjacent to the Charleston peninsula, is an heirloom, open-pollinated, blood red dent corn that makes incredibly nutty and flavorful grits with a subtle red hue. The corn grows between six and ten feet tall and produces on average two ears of corn per stalk. Field ripening is when the corn is allowed to dry completely on the stalk in the field, which gives ground corn more flavor. Commercial milling typically demands that the corn be harvested unripe and dried with forced and sometimes heated air. Hal explains that this historical corn is "nice and oily, good for making cornbread and whiskey." I say, "Well, you can't get much more Southern than that." Laughing, he explains that some of the ancient corn was saved from extinction by small family farms—as well as bootleggers and moonshiners.

The previous day I'd visited with Glenn Roberts in Columbia, South Carolina, at the actual mill of Anson Mills; there I'd seen Jimmy Red corn and a plethora of other heirloom grains with names like Guinea Flint corn, Henry Moore Yellow hominy, Hickory King, Carolina Gourd Seed, and Red May wheat. Glenn is tall with bright blue eyes, and he's boyishly handsome, even with the shock of white hair falling across his forehead. As a chef and food professional, I had met Glenn at culinary events over the years. He's a bit of a rock star for foodies and chefs. I had long enjoyed his products and was aware of the great conservation work he does, but I'd never seen him on his home turf. He greeted us and we entered the milling rooms. Over the cacophony of the

Everything in the mill is done carefully, in small batches, and by hand.

loud machinery, he explained that Anson Mills cold-mills all the grains to order, immediately chills and vacuum packs them, and then ships them the same day for maximum flavor retention. It's a proprietary process that grinds the flour while the seed is still alive and active, not dormant. The resulting flours and meals are more flavorful and contain more nutrients. Together, we entered a second room where a group of men were hand-sieving the cornmeal in stainless steel tamis, drumlike fine-mesh sieves. Glenn explained that all the men also farm for Anson Mills, and they work both in their fields as well as the mill. In another area, a man worked a bank of ovens, toasting French Huguenot peelcorn oats. The oats are so moist, fresh, and packed with natural oils that they must first be toasted in order to be hulled. Except for the electricity, Glenn explained that the toasting process is a traditional colonial method. Everything in the mill is done carefully, in small batches, and by hand.

It's not just the processes that are so different at Anson Mills. It starts with the grains themselves. There's a natural tremendous varietal diversity in the plant world. The easiest way to conceptualize diversity is to think about the apple selection in the produce department. Even smaller markets will have at least three or four different kinds of apples, and large markets may have a dozen or so. That diversity exists in nearly every plant—literally apples to oranges—wheat and corn included. Colonial and antebellum seedsmen and farmers bred for flavor, not for transport, visual appeal, shelf life, or even disease resistance. With industrial agriculture, however, crops that were susceptible to insects or disease, or that didn't ship well, simply ceased to be farmed. With that, we sadly also lost flavor and taste. For example, there are thousands of different kinds of wheat, but 95 percent of the wheat grown in the United States is red winter wheat. In contrast, Anson Mills offers thirty-four different types of landrace wheat varieties.

Radiating energy, Glenn was eager to show me some of the many varieties of grains used at Anson Mills. We were off on a tear through the warehouse filled with more than one hundred white chest freezers. As we raced from freezer to freezer filled with bags of heirloom grain and corn, his words flying fast and furious, my mind became quickly saturated. He's a veritable encyclopedia. He grabbed a handful of emmer and placed it on the surface. Wide-eyed, he emphatically pointed to the kernels and explained that this grain, shockingly, is twenty thousand years old. At another freezer he explained that the terrorist group ISIS achieves much of its success in acquiring territory because members provide people with good bread made with heirloom wheat—for free. At yet another, he explained that before the medieval guilds took control, women, not men, were brewsters—the primary makers of ale and beer. Motioning to a freezer full of corn, he explained that to Native Americans, corn was seen as alive, as a person. Holding his hand up open, palm facing forward, he rattled off the five ways to prepare and consume corn: parched, germinated, soured, alcohol fermented, and nixtamalized (soaked and cooked in an alkaline solution, usually limewater, and hulled). As he presented and touched bag after bag of grain during our visit, he poured forth historical facts about the various grains and their properties. It was, indeed, like trying to drink water from a fire hose.

After a thorough tour of the mill, we headed out to a field to see Sea Island Guinea Flint corn. It's farmed by one of the men who had been sifting the corn at the mill. Buckwheat grows at the edge of the field, a patch of heirloom Bradford watermelons sit plump and ripe, and rumlike aromas waft from the grain sorghum being pounded by the hot summer sun. This corn is still green in the husk and on the stalk. The grain lessons continued as Glenn explained that this corn originated in the Americas and was exported to Africa, then reintroduced to the United States, where it became a source of provisions for enslaved Africans. Native Americans, primarily in the coastal areas, he explained, grew Sea Island Guinea Flint. It was regarded "as the finest, as food for man, of all the known varieties," according to the U.S. Census of 1880, and yet was saved from extinction only a handful of years ago.

Why is the resurrection of one particular type of corn so important? It's not solely for flavor or to create fun ingredients for chefs to play with. Glenn believes diversity is important for other reasons. There are two main considerations: crop and varietal. Loss of crop diversity means more people are dependent on fewer crops, leaving them vulnerable to harvest failure. Loss of varietal diversity has similar implications: If people are increasingly dependent on only one variety, what happens if it succumbs to pestilence or disease, climate change, or limited or changing habitats? Poof, gone. Breeding multiple varieties of crops enables the creation of strains able to withstand these challenges. Depending on a continually diminishing number of varieties of a diminishing number of crops threatens global food security.

Under the leadership of Glenn Roberts, Anson Mills grows and mills one of the most diverse collections of heirloom grains in America. The company's mission is to return what has been lost and repatriate the flavors of antiquity to promote the well-being of all. I can drink in that kind of knowledge all day long.

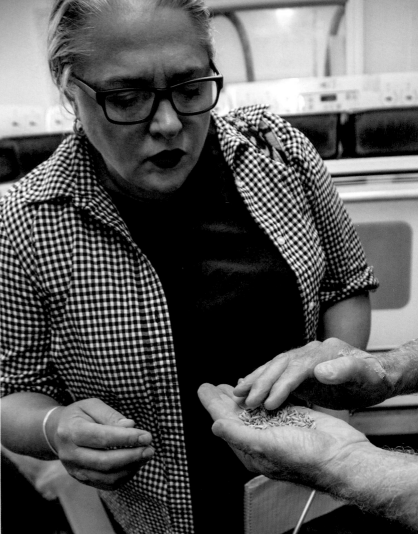

Ben-s

SEA ISLAND
BENNE SEEDS

Unenriched

[STORE IN FREEZER]

WHAT'S ON YOUR BISCUIT? PRESERVING *with* APRIL McGREGER

"It's a sensual process and yet very hard work; the only way I can stand it is to be in beauty. I need beauty—I married an artist," says April McGreger.

Sunshine streams through the bank of windows and skylights above, bathing the large open room in soft winter light. Honey-colored wooden floors glow with a well-worn patina. Colorful embroidered tapestries hang as curtains, a bright and cheerful Mexican oilcloth covers a long farm table, sunshine-yellow walls are punctuated with shocking blue trim, and a turquoise expanse of wall features large framed prints and paintings. Crayon scribbles on sheets of crinkled paper cover the fridge, interrupted by magnetic letters of the alphabet shaped for tiny fingers in primary colors. A glass-front cabinet holds an assortment of handcrafted pottery—bowls, plates, and platters. Shelves of books line the walls—all the walls, every wall—and a variety of musical instruments rests in stands about the living room awaiting their next chord. The broad kitchen island hosts a myriad of heirloom winter squash alongside pale yellow poached lemon halves resting in a glass bowl. On the stove a slope-sided French copper confiture pan houses vivid orange chips, strips of lemon, and thinly sliced ginger that gently bubbles, emitting a spicy, seductive sweetness.

Preserving in the South is both a time-honored tradition and a necessity. From the glistening spoonful of jelly on a warm buttery biscuit to the sharp pungency of colorful chow chow on soup beans (see page 214), preserves permeate our cuisine and culture. My grandparents and mother prepared quarts upon quarts of fruits and vegetables when I was a child. My grandparents' cellar was filled with orderly jars of reddish-gold scuppernong jelly, pale amber orbs of preserved pears, verdant green relish, spears of pickles, ruby-red plum jam, and bushel upon bushel of green beans packed into mason jars. "Putting up" was a way of life. I have a vague memory of asking for scuppernong jelly instead of the popular grape variety at a childhood friend's dinner table. I cannot imagine what my friend's mother wanted to say to me.

Growing up, I wasn't allowed to be underfoot in the actual process of making preserves. My chores were relegated to the sidelines of peeling and chopping, as

"I started Farmer's Daughter Preserves
because I wanted to preserve Southern culture."
—APRIL MCGREGER

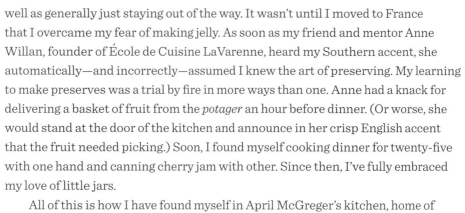

well as generally just staying out of the way. It wasn't until I moved to France that I overcame my fear of making jelly. As soon as my friend and mentor Anne Willan, founder of École de Cuisine LaVarenne, heard my Southern accent, she automatically—and incorrectly—assumed I knew the art of preserving. My learning to make preserves was a trial by fire in more ways than one. Anne had a knack for delivering a basket of fruit from the *potager* an hour before dinner. (Or worse, she would stand at the door of the kitchen and announce in her crisp English accent that the fruit needed picking.) Soon, I found myself cooking dinner for twenty-five with one hand and canning cherry jam with other. Since then, I've fully embraced my love of little jars.

All of this is how I have found myself in April McGreger's kitchen, home of Farmer's Daughter Brand Preserves. I first met April at an event for the University of North Carolina Press Savor the South series at the majestic O'Henry Hotel in Greensboro, North Carolina. I was immediately struck by her broad smile, sparkling brown eyes, and joyful laughter—and knew instantly she was one of those Southern country girls who likes to have fun. One look told me her mama had a hard time getting her in a dress when she was a little girl and that she was a wild child who liked to hang out in the woods over more "ladylike" pursuits.

April really is a farmer's daughter. Her father grows sweet potatoes in her home state of Mississippi. She grew up cooking and first learned the art of preserving in the kitchen with her mother, but her path to being a food professional was rocky— quite literally. She has an undergraduate degree in geology from Millsaps College in Jackson, Mississippi, and moved to Chapel Hill to pursue an advanced degree in the same field. That's not entirely true. She moved to North Carolina for graduate school, but her love of music what brought her specifically to the area known as the Piedmont Triangle. And singing music is how she met her husband, Phil. They were both attending a "Food Not Bombs" meeting and he was playing old-time music on his banjo. She walked up to the group and started singing along, and that romantic story, as they say, is history.

While April was writing her master's thesis, she started working as a prep cook at chef Andrea Reusing's nationally acclaimed Lantern Restaurant. Eventually, April ascended to the position of pastry chef, where part of her responsibilities involved being in tune with the seasons and sourcing local foods, particularly those that were associated with Southern identity; she also was tasked with attempting to use Southern ingredients in non-Southern ways. On her own time, she studied preserving traditions around the world and experimented in her home kitchen. When she returned from a graduate research trip to Stromboli, Italy, she realized her focus had been more on food and not geology. She also realized that her degree was grooming her for a position in the oil industry. The result of these personal revelations led to her founding Farmer's Daughter in 2007.

I settle in on a stool to watch her prepare the pumpkin chip preserves. Pumpkin chip preserves are not chips in the sense of fried and crispy potato chips; they are winter squash pieces—this time, butternut squash—that have been sliced and cooked with sugar. As she peels the butternut squash, she tells me, "I started Farmer's Daughter Preserves because I wanted to preserve Southern culture. The pressure to make hits and only feature things with the widest appeal is how we got to the fake-biscuits-and-barbecue stage of Southern food." As she works, we bounce between her technique, her personal story, and her overarching assessment of Southern food. She is constantly reaching for a spoon, tasting every ingredient at every step along the way. In the midst of the rapid flow of words and work, she prepares a cup of hot tea. Distracted, she lets it steep a bit too long and I watch, quietly astonished, as she reaches for a tasting spoon before serving it. It's very clear that April believes nuances are important, whether it's a big-picture observation or a detailed study.

The subtle flavors in her line of products speak to her attention to detail and life as a pastry chef; Blackberry Rose Geranium Jelly, Ginger Jalapeño Jelly, Bourbon Fig Jam, and Orange Marmalade with Rye Whiskey are but a few of her tantalizing combinations. Beyond the preserves, Farmer's Daughter produces a line of locally sold barrel-fermented krauts, including a yellow cabbage–collard kraut and salsa verde. Additional limited batches of products, including Arkansas Black Apple Butter and Hinkelhatz Hot Pepper Jelly, are featured on the Ark of Taste, Slow Food's living catalog of culturally significant foods in danger of extinction.

Steam fogs the windows as April stirs the simmering pan of squash. As she pours over the lemon juice, she explains, "Adding the acid early helps maintain the texture and shape of the pumpkin." This commitment to small-batch preserving is what prevents her from working with an outside company to produce her line of preserved goods. "I couldn't pay a co-packer to do what we do." Her dedication extends to her purpose of supporting local farmers and local agriculture, which extends to the ginger, sourced from a local Hmong farm, that she's using in the pumpkin chips.

We cook and talk until the bright orange slices have become translucent, nearly jewel-like. She hand-packs the mixture into jars and pours over the hot sugar syrup. April's husband, Phil, walks behind her as their son, Moe, bounds into the door from school. Moe has had a rough day: Naptime has just been eliminated from the daily schedule. April walks over and pats his tousled ash-blond head. "Honey, do you want a biscuit?" His troubled face breaks into a smile. Mine does, too.

farmer's daughter

PUMPKIN &
GINGER PRESERVES

Cathead Biscuits

Makes about 9

My friend and colleague Dr. Marcie Cohen Ferris is a professor in the Department of American Studies at the University of North Carolina. Her research and teaching interests include Southern history and culture—particularly the foodways and material culture of the American South and the history of the Jewish South. In her excellent book *The Edible South* she writes, "In contemporary worlds of popular and consumer culture, Southern food has become untethered from the complex historical narrative responsible for this cuisine. Think of buckets of Southern fried chicken and cathead biscuits like culinary spacecraft set adrift from the mother ship of southern history, culture, and experience." I wholeheartedly agree. Many people outside the South think all Southern food is unhealthy and/or fried.

The term *cathead biscuit* is an authentic one, indicating that it's a biscuit as large as a cat's head, and a phrase my grandfather once used. This extra-large biscuit would not have been the norm on the everyday table, but it has become the standard size for fast-food biscuits. Ferris continues, "Fried chicken, biscuits, and sweet tea—the icons of Southern food—have become so 'super-sized,' enriched, sweetened, and filled with butter that they are almost unrecognizable to native Southerners." *This* cathead biscuit is the real deal.

There are a few secrets to a tender biscuit: First, flours vary in their protein levels. Reach for a low-protein flour for light-as-air biscuits. After that, you want cold butter—when the cold butter is transferred to the hot oven it melts and produces steam, which helps produce flaky biscuits. Lastly, avoid overworking the dough, which activates the gluten and will produce a tough, heavy biscuit. The perfect biscuit should be golden brown and slightly crisp on the outside, with a light, airy interior.

4 cups White Lily or other Southern all-purpose flour, or cake flour (not self-rising), plus more for rolling out

2 tablespoons baking powder

2 teaspoons fine sea salt

8 tablespoons (½ cup) cold unsalted butter, cut into cubes and chilled

2 cups buttermilk

1 Heat the oven to 500°F. Line a baking sheet with a silicone baking mat. (You can also bake the biscuits on an ungreased baking sheet.)

2 In a bowl, combine the flour, baking powder, and salt. Using a pastry blender or two knives, cut the butter into the flour mixture until it resembles coarse meal. Pour in the buttermilk and mix until just barely combined. It will be a shaggy mass. (Alternatively, you can mix the dough in a food processor: Pulse to combine the flour, baking powder, and salt.

Recipe continues

Using a pastry blender, cut the chilled cubed butter into the flour mixture. The butter coats the flour and will prevent the absorption of moisture, therefore lessening the activation of the gluten.

Stop cutting when the butter bits are about the size of small peas. The butter will melt during baking, creating pockets of steam that give biscuits their flakiness.

Add the buttermilk and stir to combine, but do not stir until it is a smooth dough. You don't want to overwork the dough and activate the gluten.

Turn the shaggy mass out onto a floured work surface. Flour is your friend!

Using a bench scraper, turn the dough a few times until it starts to come together.

Shape the dough into a rectangle. Try not to touch the dough with your warm hands so the butter stays cold.

Using a floured rolling pin, start at the middle of the dough and roll backward without coming off the edge. Then start in the middle of the dough and roll forward without coming off the edge. This will help keep the dough even.

Using your bench scraper, rotate the dough so it does not stick to the work surface. Add more flour, if needed.

Using a floured circular cutter, punch out the biscuits. Do not twist as you punch, as that would seal the edges and possibly inhibit the biscuit's rise.

Place the biscuits on the baking sheet. If the biscuits touch, the sides will be soft and tender. If they do not touch, the sides will be crispier.

Do not ball the scraps of dough in a knot. Instead, layer the scraps and pat them together. Reroll following the same procedure and punch out the remaining biscuits.

The biscuits are ready for the oven! A very hot oven is essential to create the biscuits' ideal texture inside and out.

3   Add the butter and pulse until it resembles coarse meal. Pour in the buttermilk through the feed tube and pulse until just barely combined. It will be a shaggy mass.)

4   Turn the shaggy mass out onto a lightly floured surface. Knead lightly, using the heel of your hand to compress and push the dough away from you, then fold it back over itself. Give the dough a small turn and repeat four or five times. (It's not yeast bread; you want to just barely activate the gluten, not overwork it.)

5   Using a lightly floured rolling pin, roll the dough out 1 inch thick. Cut out rounds of dough with a 3½-inch round cutter dipped in flour; press the cutter straight down without twisting so the biscuits will rise evenly when baked.

6   Place the biscuits on the prepared baking sheet. If the biscuits are baked close together, the sides will be tender. If the biscuits are baked farther apart, the sides will be crisp. (I always say biscuits are like people: If you are close to your neighbor, you will be tender, and if you aren't close to your neighbor, you will be crisp!)

7   Once you've punched out the first round from the dough, you can reroll the scraps. However, do not simply roll them into a ball; this will create a knot of gluten strands. Instead, place the pieces one on top of the other in layers. Then roll out and repeat punching out the biscuits.

8   Bake until golden brown, 10 to 12 minutes. Transfer to a rack to cool just slightly. Serve warm.

Wheat flour contains two proteins, glutenin and gliadin. Gluten is a strong and elastic sheet produced by these proteins by the combination of moisture and motion. When you combine flour with liquid, the proteins produce gluten. Gluten gives structure and chewiness to yeast breads, but you don't want to develop gluten in tender biscuits.

Summer Hoecakes

Hoecake, griddle cake, corncakes, corn pone, johnnycake, cornbread, corn dodger . . . the list of names goes on and on. There's a misconception that the term *hoecakes* comes from slaves cooking corncakes on a hoe in the field, alluding to their lack of cooking equipment. In truth, *hoe* was a colloquial term for "griddle" dating back to at least the 1600s in parts of England, where baking cakes on boards or griddles was commonplace. Cornbread was for many years the basic bread of the poor, rural South for many reasons. Compared to wheat, corn is four times more productive per acre, requires only one-tenth the seed, and takes one-third the time from planting until it can be used as food. Also, corn is a crop that can be harvested over a period of time instead of all at once. Lastly, corn can be eaten fresh during the summer and ground into grits or meal to eat throughout the year.

At their most simple, hoecakes can be a mixture of ground corn, fat, and water. I love doubling up on the corn flavor by including fresh corn kernels, and believe me, canned corn just isn't the same. I've also added some chile peppers for a bit of heat.

2 cups finely ground whole-grain white or yellow cornmeal

2 teaspoons baking powder

1 teaspoon fine sea salt

1 large egg, lightly beaten

1½ cups water, more if needed

2 green onions, chopped

Kernels from 1 ear fresh sweet corn (about ½ cup; see page 201)

½ jalapeño, or to taste, seeded and chopped

½ bird's-eye or other Thai red chile, or to taste, seeded and chopped

Canola oil, for frying

1 In a large bowl, whisk together the cornmeal, baking powder, and salt. In a second bowl or large liquid measuring cup, combine the egg and 1½ cups water. Stir until smooth. Stir the wet ingredients into the dry ingredients; add the green onions, corn, and chiles. The batter should be pourable, not stiff; you may need to add a little more water depending on the texture of the cornmeal. (If it's fine, you might need to add more water.)

2 Heat a thin sheen of oil in a cast-iron skillet or large griddle over medium heat. Ladle 2 tablespoons of the batter onto the heated skillet. Repeat with additional batter, filling the pan without crowding.

3 Cook the cakes until the bottoms are a rich brown and bubbles form on the tops and along the edges, 2 to 3 minutes. Turn and brown the other side, an additional 2 to 3 minutes. Serve each batch immediately while you continue to fry up the remaining cakes, adding oil to the skillet as needed between batches.

Brown Butter and Thyme Whole-Grain Cornbread

Makes 1 (12-inch) skillet bread

A great debate about sugar and Southern cornbread rages. Although people often think of it in terms of North and South, it turns out that the debate divides pretty much on racial lines. Typically, African American cornbread contains sugar; white Southern cornbread most often does not. *Charlotte Observer* food editor Kathleen Purvis wrote an award-winning article on black versus white cornbread. In it she asks, "So many Southern food traditions are shared by both races. Most Southerners, black and white, revere fried chicken, pursue pork barbecue and exalt their grandmothers' garden vegetables. So why is there such a fundamental difference between two styles of one basic bread?"

Until early in the twentieth century, Southern cornmeal was made from sweeter-tasting white corn stone-ground in a water-powered mill. But higher-yielding yellow corn varieties, which are not as sweet, are more suited for industrial agriculture. As African Americans left the South during the Great Migration, the sweeter white cornmeal they were used to wasn't readily available; the industrially milled yellow cornmeal was cheaper and easier to access. But because it was not as sweet as the white cornmeal they were used to, African Americans started adding sugar to compensate. You can use either white or yellow cornmeal for this recipe.

3 tablespoons unsalted butter

1½ cups cornmeal, plus about 2 tablespoons for the skillet

1 tablespoon fresh thyme leaves

¾ teaspoon fine sea salt

¾ teaspoon baking soda

1 large egg

1 cup buttermilk

Freshly ground black pepper

1 Heat the oven to 450°F. Once the oven is hot, place the butter in a large cast-iron skillet or ovenproof baking dish and heat in the oven until brown, 10 to 15 minutes. (Preheating the skillet ensures that when the batter is poured into the skillet, it swells and instantly crisps; it also browns the butter.)

2 Meanwhile, in a bowl, combine the cornmeal, thyme, salt, and baking soda. Set aside. In a large measuring cup, combine the egg and buttermilk. Add the wet ingredients to the dry ingredients and stir to combine.

3 Remove the skillet from the oven and pour the hot melted butter into the batter. Working quickly, sprinkle the hot skillet with the remaining 2 tablespoons coarse cornmeal.

4 Stir the batter to combine and then pour it into the hot skillet. Top with a few grinds of pepper. Bake until golden brown, about 15 minutes. Cut into wedges to serve.

Lace Cornbread Crepes

My dear friend and colleague Rebecca Lang is a ninth-generation Southerner. She's as Southern as a glass of iced tea—and nearly as sweet! She also had a close connection with her grandmother, whom she called "Tom." According to Rebecca, Tom cooked daily until she was one hundred, never had a problem with arthritis, and often wore Nike running shoes in the last few years of her life. I know that Rebecca's love of food and cooking started in her grandmother's kitchen, as did mine. The grandmother-granddaughter relationship is a powerful one, I know.

This recipe was inspired by Tom's recipe for lace cornbread, although I have to admit I found the batter easier to maneuver by adding a tablespoon of flour to Tom's original recipe. It's an old-fashioned crisp, lacy, brown wafer best enjoyed a few seconds after it leaves the skillet.

½ cup fine-ground white or yellow cornmeal

1 tablespoon all-purpose flour

½ teaspoon fine sea salt

Pinch of cayenne pepper (optional)

¾ cup boiling water

Canola oil, for frying

1 Combine the cornmeal, flour, salt, and cayenne (if using) in a medium bowl. Add the boiling water and stir to combine. Let sit for 5 minutes.

2 Heat a teaspoon or so of oil in a nonstick skillet or cast-iron skillet over medium heat until shimmering. (More oil produces more lace and crispier edges, just know that it also sputters and spatters more.) Working one crepe at a time, at least for this first one, add 1 tablespoon of batter to the skillet. The batter will immediately look lacy and bubbly.

3 Cook until the edges are brown, 1 to 1½ minutes. Turn and cook until the second side is browned, 1 to 1½ minutes more. Transfer to a wire rack or a plate lined with paper towels. Repeat the procedure with the remaining batter, adding more oil to the pan between batches and moderating the heat as needed. Serve immediately.

Dulce de Leche
Pecan Sweet Rolls

Makes 12 rolls

Dulce de leche is caramelized sweet milk. My friend and colleague Von Diaz, a writer, radio producer, and self-taught cook who explores Puerto Rican food and culture in her work, calls dulce de leche a "rich, decadent, and sweet concentrated burst of caramel in your mouth." Loosely translated, it means "sweet jam of milk" and I can pretty much guarantee it would improve the flavor of shoe leather. This recipe makes about 1½ cups, a little more than is needed for the rolls, but I promise you will put the leftovers to good use. It will keep in a resealable container in the refrigerator for up to 2 weeks.

My grandmother used to make quick bread rolls instead of yeast-based rolls, which speeds up the time it takes to get the rolls on the table—this dough is very user-friendly and can be thrown together quickly on a Saturday morning. The dulce de leche, however, does take more time and patience; I suggest making it the night before. If you want the rolls without the dulce de leche, you can simply use caramel sauce or the glaze from Apple Stack Cake (page 294).

For the dulce de leche

4 cups 2% or whole milk

1¼ cups granulated sugar

¼ teaspoon baking soda

1 teaspoon pure vanilla extract

Pinch of fine sea salt

For the dough

3 cups all-purpose flour, plus more for rolling and shaping the dough

3 tablespoons granulated sugar

1½ teaspoons baking powder

½ teaspoon baking soda

½ teaspoon fine sea salt

1½ cups buttermilk

6 tablespoons unsalted butter, melted

1 teaspoon pure vanilla extract

¼ cup firmly packed dark brown sugar

½ cup coarsely chopped pecans

1 **To make the dulce de leche,** combine the milk, granulated sugar, and baking soda in a heavy-bottomed medium saucepan. Bring to a boil, then reduce the heat to medium-low and simmer, uncovered, stirring occasionally, until caramelized and thickened, 1½ to 1¾ hours. (After about 1 hour, stir more often as the milk caramelizes to avoid burning.) Stir in the vanilla and a small pinch of salt. Transfer to a bowl to cool. (This can be made ahead and refrigerated overnight to ensure a smooth start to the next day.)

2 Heat the oven to 400°F. Line a rimmed baking sheet with a silicone baking mat.

3 **To make the dough,** stir together the flour, granulated sugar, baking powder, baking soda, and salt. Combine the buttermilk, 5 tablespoons of the butter, and the vanilla in a bowl or measuring cup. Add the buttermilk mixture to the dry ingredients and stir to combine.

Recipe continues

4   Transfer the dough to a well-floured surface and roll it into a 12-inch square just under ½ inch thick. Brush the dough with the remaining 1 tablespoon butter. Sprinkle evenly with the brown sugar and ¼ cup of the pecans. Roll the dough into a log, starting with a longer edge. Pinch the seam closed as well as you can; it'll be a bit messy, with filling spilling out. That's okay. It might also stretch out a bit when you roll it, so push it back together at both ends to return it as close to 12 inches as possible.

5   Using dental floss or a serrated knife, cut the log into 1-inch slices (see sidebar). Transfer the slices to the prepared baking sheet. Bake the buns until they're golden brown, 25 to 30 minutes, covering them with foil near the end of baking if the exposed pecans start to darken too much.

6   Drizzle over the cooled dulce de leche and top with the remaining ¼ cup pecans. Serve immediately. These are best served the same day that you make them.

One challenge with any sweet roll or cinnamon roll recipe is cutting the log of rolled-up dough into individual buns without squeezing out the filling in the process! Unflavored, unwaxed dental floss solves this problem. Section off a 10-inch length of floss and slide it under the roll where it needs to be cut. Grab both ends of the floss in each hand, crossing over the top of the roll, moving your hands in opposite directions. Pull it taut to cut through the roll and form a slice.

Apple Cheddar Pancakes

Makes 5 cups batter to make 16 pancakes

Commercial apple production in the Southeast is concentrated in the mountain regions of Georgia, North Carolina, South Carolina, and Tennessee. North Carolina, the country's seventh-largest apple producing state, produces 8 million bushels of apples a year! In autumn, many of the mountain towns host apple festivals, and all along the winding roads folks can stop and buy apples, as well as apple butter, apple jelly, apple bread, apple cake, fried apple hand pies, apple pie, dried apples, apple cider, and more, to take home.

My friend and colleague Ronni Lundy is perhaps the best-known champion of Appalachian foodways. She is the author of *Victuals: An Appalachian Journey, with Recipes.* In the chapter titled "Apple-achia," Ronni writes that at one time between 1,000 and 1,600 different varieties of apples flourished in the mountain South, and it's likely that at least 600 still remain.

For the apples

2 or 3 apples, such as Honeycrisp (about 1½ pounds), peeled and cored

1 tablespoon unsalted butter

2 tablespoons sugar

¼ teaspoon ground cinnamon

Pinch of kosher salt

For the pancakes

2 cups all-purpose flour

2 tablespoons sugar

2 teaspoons baking powder

1 teaspoon baking soda

1 teaspoon fine sea salt

2 cups buttermilk

2 large eggs, lightly beaten

5 tablespoons unsalted butter, melted

1 cup grated sharp cheddar cheese (4 ounces)

1 tablespoon canola oil

Cane syrup, sorghum syrup, or maple syrup, for serving

1 **To prepare the apples,** cut them into slices just under ½ inch thick, and then halve them again horizontally so you have a chunk smaller than a slice and larger than a dice. Melt the butter in a skillet over medium-high heat. Let the butter sizzle until it just starts to brown, then add the apple chunks. Sprinkle with the sugar, cinnamon, and salt. Reduce the heat and cook, stirring occasionally, until the apples are just tender to the point of a knife and starting to brown on the edges, 8 to 10 minutes. (If the apples are super fresh, this might not take as long.)

2 Heat the oven to 200°F.

3 **To make the pancakes,** sift together the flour, sugar, baking powder, baking soda, and salt into a large bowl. In another bowl or a liquid measuring cup, whisk together the buttermilk, eggs, and 4 tablespoons of the melted butter. Add the buttermilk mixture to the dry ingredients and whisk just until combined. Add the cheese and the apples. Stir until combined.

Recipe continues

4 In a small bowl or measuring cup, stir together the remaining 1 tablespoon butter and the oil. Heat a large nonstick skillet over medium-low heat and lightly brush with the melted butter–oil mixture. Ladle about ⅓ cup of the batter into the pan for each pancake. Cook until the bubbles on the top burst and the bottoms are golden brown, about 2 minutes. Flip the pancakes and cook until golden, about 2 minutes. Transfer to a baking sheet and place in the oven to keep warm. Repeat with the remaining batter, adding more of the butter-oil mixture to the pan as necessary. Transfer to warmed serving plates. Drizzle with the syrup of your choice and serve immediately.

Crispy Rice Waffles

Waffles are most often thought of as something served at breakfast or brunch. Historical cookbooks, however, indicate that waffles weren't always breakfast fare and were simply another kind of bread, just as likely to be served with chicken and gravy as powdered sugar and sweet syrup. Many Southern colonial waffle recipes started with rice cooked until soft, falling apart, and almost batterlike before being bound with egg and additional wheat or rice flour, but here I take a simpler approach and use only rice flour. The flavor of yeast waffles is so rich and distinctive—and making the batter the night before seems a lot more user-friendly than having to do it first thing in the morning. Naturally gluten-free, these delicate waffles are incredibly light on the outside and tender on the inside.

2¼ cups brown rice flour

½ teaspoon fine sea salt

1 (¼-ounce) packet active dry yeast (2¼ teaspoons)

½ cup warm water

½ teaspoon sugar

6 tablespoons unsalted butter

1 cup buttermilk, plus more if needed

2 large eggs, lightly beaten

¼ teaspoon baking soda

Cane syrup, sorghum syrup, or maple syrup, for serving

1 In a large bowl, whisk together the rice flour and salt; set aside.

2 Combine the yeast, warm water, and sugar in a liquid measuring cup. Set aside to proof. The mixture will become creamy and foamy after about 5 minutes.

3 Meanwhile, melt 4 tablespoons of the butter in a small saucepan over medium-low heat, allowing it to brown just a little bit, about 4 minutes. Remove from the heat and stir in the buttermilk. Set aside to cool slightly.

4 Whisk the yeast mixture and the buttermilk mixture into the flour mixture. Cover the bowl with a clean kitchen towel and leave on the counter to rise for at least 2 hours or overnight.

5 When ready to cook, whisk in the eggs and baking soda. If the batter feels a bit thick, add up to 2 tablespoons more buttermilk.

6 Melt the remaining 2 tablespoons of butter. Coat a waffle iron with the melted butter and preheat. Spoon in enough batter to cover three-quarters of the surface (about ½ cup for an 8-inch round waffle iron). Cook until the waffles are crisp and golden brown and no steam escapes from the edges, about 5 minutes. Repeat with the remaining batter. Serve immediately, drizzled with the syrup of your choice.

Black Pepper Cream Cheese Biscuits

Makes 36 (1½-inch) biscuits

Callie White was once a much-sought-after caterer in Charleston, and one of her most popular menu items were cream cheese biscuits stuffed with minced country ham and slathered with Dijon mustard–spiked butter. For years, customers clamored for her to sell her biscuits on the side, but she was always too busy. The biscuits became so popular that her daughter, Carrie Morey, finally convinced her mom they needed to go into the biscuit business. Now, ten years later, they've baked more than 4 million biscuits, each and every one by hand!

Carrie and her team of bakers use White Lily self-rising flour—and since White Lily doesn't sell in bulk, the bakers are forced to use 5-pound bags! Why is Carrie so attached to White Lily? Southern all-purpose flour is milled from soft winter wheat that has less gluten-forming protein than national brands of all-purpose—approximately 9 grams per cup of flour for White Lily versus 11 or 12 grams per cup for other brands. Gluten gives structure to yeast breads, but is not what you want for tender biscuits. If you live outside the South, White Lily is available online or in some specialty shops. Or, for results similar to those of Southern flour, substitute equal parts all-purpose flour and cake flour.

These black pepper biscuits were inspired by the flavor and texture of Callie's Charleston Biscuits. I split them and stuff them with thinly sliced country ham, too, and here I've topped them with Pear Mostarda.

4 cups all-purpose flour, plus more for rolling out the biscuits

2 tablespoons baking powder

1½ teaspoons fine sea salt

8 tablespoons (½ cup) unsalted butter, at room temperature

1 (8-ounce) package cream cheese, at room temperature

¾ to 1 cup buttermilk, plus more for brushing the biscuits

2 teaspoons freshly ground black pepper, plus more for the top

Sliced ham, for serving (optional)

Pear Mostarda (recipe follows)

1 Heat the oven to 500°F. Line a baking sheet with a silicone baking mat.

2 In a food processor, pulse together the flour, baking powder, and salt. Add the butter and cream cheese and pulse to combine. Add ¾ cup of the buttermilk and the pepper; process until the dough starts to come away from the sides of the bowl, adding the remainder of the buttermilk, if necessary. The dough should pull from the sides of the bowl. (In testing, I found that 1 cup was necessary with King Arthur all-purpose flour and ¾ cup was more appropriate for White Lily flour.)

3 Turn the dough out onto a floured work surface. Knead lightly, using the heel of your hand to compress and push the

Recipe continues

dough away from you, and then fold it back over itself. Give the dough a small turn and repeat four or five times. (It's not yeast bread; you want to just barely activate the gluten, not overwork it.)

4   Using a lightly floured rolling pin, roll the dough out to a 9-inch square about ³⁄₄ inch thick. Using a chef's knife or a long utility knife, cut the biscuits into 1¹⁄₂-inch squares. (Don't drag the knife through the dough, but instead press the knife directly through the dough. This will help prevent pinched edges.)

5   Use an offset spatula or pancake turner to move the biscuits to the prepared baking sheet, keeping them close together. Brush with buttermilk and sprinkle with additional pepper.

6   Transfer the baking sheet to the oven and immediately reduce the oven temperature to 450°F. Bake, rotating the pan once, until nicely browned and the temperature registers 205°F, about 17 minutes. Transfer to a wire rack to cool slightly. Serve warm with sliced ham and Pear Mostarda.

PEAR MOSTARDA   Makes 2 cups

½ cup white vinegar

1 cup sugar

1 tablespoon mustard seeds

6 firm Bosc pears, cored, peeled, and diced (about 6 cups)

2 tablespoons Dijon mustard

Coarse kosher salt and freshly ground white pepper

Combine the vinegar, sugar, mustard seeds, and ½ cup water in a medium saucepan. Add the pears and bring to a boil over medium-high heat, stirring occasionally. Reduce the heat to maintain a simmer. Cook until the pears are tender but still hold their shape and most of the liquid has cooked away, 30 to 35 minutes. Remove from the heat and stir in the Dijon mustard. Season with salt and pepper. Let cool completely before serving. The mostarda is best made a few days before serving so that the flavors can meld and intensify. It keeps well in the refrigerator for up to 3 months.

Moravian Sugar Cake

Moravians, a religious group originally from what is now the Czech Republic and Slovakia, are acknowledged as the first Protestants, predating Martin Luther and the Protestant Reformation by one hundred years. After a failed attempt to settle in Savannah, Georgia, they settled in Bethlehem, Pennsylvania, in 1740, where they played a large and important role in the colonies. Then in the 1750s, a group of families moved from Pennsylvania to North Carolina. A large group of Moravians still live in the area, and Old Salem is a beautifully restored living history town that meticulously re-creates the town of Salem, North Carolina, as it was from 1766 to 1840.

Like many religions, the Moravian faith has associated food customs, including crisp, paper-thin ginger cookies, chicken pie, and this sweet yeast bread. Part of the Moravian worship service is a "love feast" that consists of singing hymns and sharing coffee and sweet buns. My dear godmother, whom I call Aunt Jenny, is Moravian. She and her husband lived in Winston Salem, North Carolina, for many years, and it was there where they converted to the faith. When I was a child, it seemed wildly exotic to my seemingly pedestrian Methodist upbringing—they got to eat cake at church and all we had were communion wafers and Welch's grape juice.

For the dough

1 russet potato (about ½ pound), peeled and cut into ½-inch pieces

1 (¼-ounce) packet active dry yeast (2¼ teaspoons)

½ cup warm water

½ cup granulated sugar

8 tablespoons (½ cup) unsalted butter, melted and cooled

1 large egg

1½ teaspoons fine sea salt

2½ to 3 cups unbleached all-purpose flour, plus more for dusting

For the topping

8 tablespoons (½ cup) cold unsalted butter, cut into bits

½ cup firmly packed light brown sugar

2 teaspoons ground cinnamon

1   *To make the dough,* combine the potato and enough cold water to cover in a small saucepan. Bring to a boil over high heat and reduce the heat to maintain a simmer. Cook, stirring occasionally, until very tender, 10 to 15 minutes. Remove 2 tablespoons of the cooking liquid and set aside. Drain the potato and return to the pot. Add the reserved cooking water and, using an old-fashioned potato masher or a sturdy whisk, mash the potatoes until very smooth. Set aside.

2   In the bowl of a stand mixer fitted with the dough hook, combine the yeast and warm water; let sit for 5 minutes, or until the mixture is foamy. Add the mashed potato, granulated sugar, butter, egg, and salt. Add 2½ cups of the flour and mix the dough on low speed until it is well combined, 3 to 5 minutes. Turn the dough out onto a floured surface and knead it by hand for 8 to 10 minutes, adding as much of the remaining ½ cup flour as is necessary to form a smooth and elastic dough. Transfer the dough to a buttered large bowl,

Recipe continues

turning the dough to coat it with the butter. Cover the bowl with plastic wrap and let the dough rise in a warm place for 1½ to 2 hours, or until it is double in size. Punch down the dough.

3 Press the dough evenly into a buttered 9 by 13-inch baking pan. Cover the pan with a kitchen towel and let the dough rise in a warm place for 30 to 45 minutes; the dough will be puffed and risen. Meanwhile, heat the oven to 400°F.

4 Using your thumb, make indentations all over the top of the dough and then scatter the butter over the dough and into the indentations.

5 *To make the topping,* in a small bowl, stir together the brown sugar and the cinnamon and sprinkle the mixture evenly over the dough. Bake the cake in the middle of the oven until an instant-read thermometer inserted into the cake registers 190°F and the cake is dark brown, 25 to 30 minutes. Check it around 20 minutes; if it starts to become too dark, cover it with aluminum foil.

6 Transfer to a wire rack to cool slightly, about 5 minutes, then, using a serrated knife, cut into squares and serve.

Spiced Sweet Potato and Pecan Breakfast Bread

Makes 1 (8½ by 4½-inch) loaf

Sweet potatoes and pecans are harvested in the fall, so they make a natural pairing. To increase the nutritional density in this recipe, I've subbed out oil for applesauce and suggest using whole wheat pastry flour, found in the baking section of most supermarkets. This moist, tender breakfast bread will keep for up to a week when tightly wrapped in plastic or in an airtight container. Serve it toasted and spread with honey, cream cheese, or nut butter for a healthy start to your day.

1 sweet potato

1½ cups whole wheat pastry flour

2 teaspoons baking powder

1 teaspoon baking soda

1 teaspoon fine sea salt

½ teaspoon ground cinnamon

½ teaspoon freshly grated nutmeg

¼ teaspoon ground cardamom

¼ teaspoon freshly ground black pepper

Nonstick cooking spray

½ cup firmly packed brown sugar

½ cup unsweetened applesauce

2 large eggs, lightly beaten

½ cup chopped pecans

2 tablespoons flaxseeds

1　Heat the oven to 350°F. Place the sweet potato in an ovenproof pan or skillet. Roast the sweet potato until tender, 45 to 60 minutes. Transfer to a bowl and cover with a lid or a plate. As the sweet potato cools, the steam will help loosen the skin. Once it's cool enough, trim the tough ends and peel, discarding the skin.

2　Meanwhile, combine the flour, baking powder, baking soda, salt, cinnamon, nutmeg, cardamom, and pepper in a bowl.

3　Reduce the oven temperature to 325°F. Spray an 8½ by 4½-inch loaf pan with nonstick cooking spray. Line the loaf pan with parchment paper, letting the excess hang over the sides. Spray the parchment with nonstick cooking spray.

4　Place the sweet potato in a medium bowl. Using an old-fashioned potato masher, mash the potato until smooth. Add the brown sugar, applesauce, and eggs. Stir to combine. Add the flour mixture, half the pecans, and the flaxseeds; stir to combine. Pour into the prepared pan and top with the remaining ¼ cup pecans. Bake until rich brown and the temperature registers 200°F when an instant-read thermometer is inserted into the center, 65 to 70 minutes. (You may need to cover the loaf with aluminum foil if it becomes too dark toward the end of baking.) Transfer to a wire rack to cool slightly. Lift the bread out of the pan using the parchment "wings." Let cool until at least warm, then, using a serrated knife, slice into ½-inch-thick slices and serve.

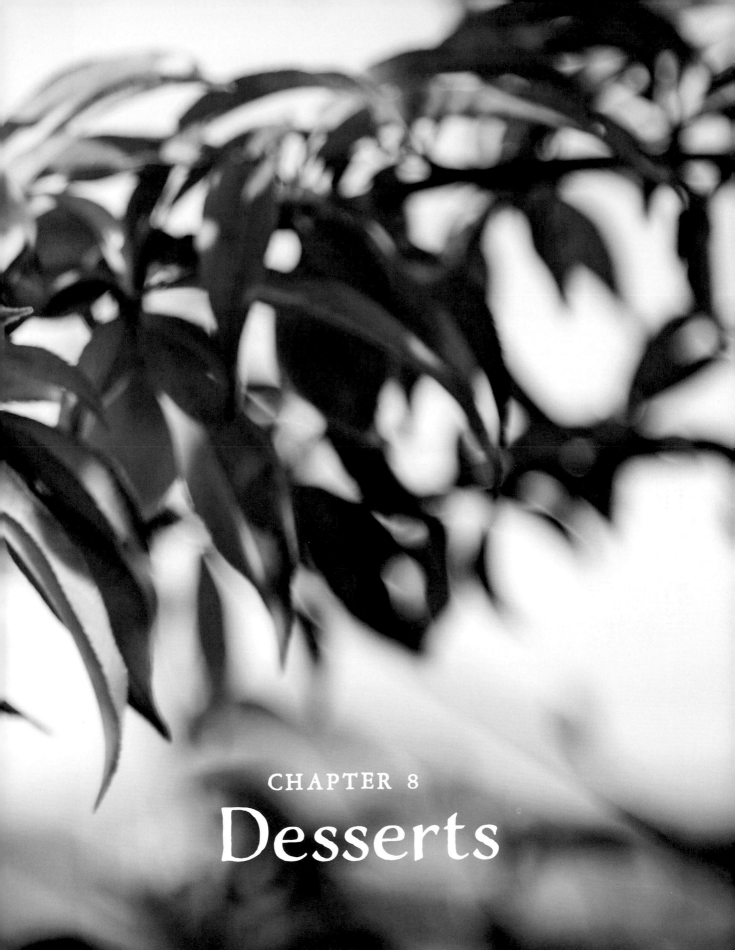

CHAPTER 8

Desserts

AN HEIRLOOM APPLE *a* DAY

I
t hasn't rained in eight weeks. I can feel the hard earth beneath my boots as we walk the steep hill of the apple orchard. Small tufts of wild cress poke through the dormant silver-gray grass and fallen leaves. Long, dark, lead-colored branches reach into the dreary sky, and there's a slight breeze coming up through the valley. I'm in Carroll County, Virginia, tucked in the southwest corner of the state in the Blue Ridge Mountains with farmer Diane Flynt, owner of Foggy Ridge Cider. Looking about the dry orchard, she says hopefully, "It's supposed to rain tomorrow." She reaches out to inspect a branch. Harvest ended several weeks ago, and I ask if she's able to take a break. Laughing, she lists off winter pruning, followed by training the branches in the spring when the sap is running and the wood is pliable, and seeding the orchard floor to provide food for the pollinators. She continues that summer brings fighting pests and culminates in fall harvest. Apple farming, like most farming, is a year-round job.

Apples became a major commercial crop in parts of the South in the late 1800s, and Virginia still ranks sixth in terms of apple production in the United States. Since before the founding of the country, Southerners have grown apples as a year-round food source, developing varieties adapted to the various climates and soils of the region, as well as tailoring cultivars for winter storage, apple butter and preserves, drying, and hard cider. Dried apples are a touchstone of Appalachian cooking, and cider has a long history in the South. Since the days of Washington and Jefferson, the state of Virginia has been a key player in alcohol production. In seventeenth-century colonial America, hard cider and whiskey were consumed more often than water. In the cities, water was often contaminated, and alcohol-based drinks were less likely to spread disease and had a longer shelf life than nonalcoholic beverages.

You've heard of Johnny Appleseed? He's not just a mythical character in a children's story, but a real person whose name was John Chapman. In the late 1700s, he traveled the frontier planting apple orchards, and then would return several years later to sell the orchard and the surrounding land. The small, tart apples his orchards produced were used primarily to make hard cider and apple brandy. Johnny never made it below the Ohio River, but many others like him did.

Diane came of age in the 1970s, when many of her college buddies were seeking a "back to the land" experience. A former finance executive, Diane admits to loving her

Heirloom apples are often bitter or tart, and that's part of what makes a good cider: bold tannins, bracing acidity, and complex flavor.

life in banking, insisting she's not a corporate escapee. Yet she had always wanted a farm—a real farm, not a hobby farm. Being a businesswoman, she set about acquiring a farm in an orderly fashion. At the time, she didn't know she wanted to grow apples—or that she would become one of the foremost authorities on heirloom apples.

As we walk through the orchard, Diane explains to me the birds and the bees of apple trees. (I'll use more commonly known cultivars as examples—although Diane did derisively refer to the ubiquitous Granny Smith as an "apple potato.") First, understand that cross-pollination is the transfer of pollen from the stamen (male) of a flower of one plant to a stigma (female) of a flower of another plant of the same species. Apples require cross-pollination between *two different* varieties of apple trees. For example, a Granny Smith must be pollinated by any other apple that's *not* a Granny Smith, such as a Honeycrisp. Second, you can grow an apple from seed, but the seed from a Granny Smith apple will not produce a pure Granny Smith apple tree. This is because the seed is the product of two different trees. A tree grown from seed and its future fruit may display characteristics from past generations of both parent trees. (To understand this concept, think about a human baby, who often shows characteristics from the sides of both parents. That's how little Jack looks like Grandpa Will.) Therefore, fruit trees cannot be reproduced true to the original cultivar from seed; they can only be reproduced by grafting.

As we're walking, Diane points at the trunk of a tree near the ground. I can see a noticeable difference in the wood. She explains that grafting involves taking plant tissue called a scion from the desired parent tree (for example, a Granny Smith apple tree) and placing it on a compatible rootstock. The Granny Smith scion is allowed to grow into the new tree. Because only one parent is involved in the process, the grafted tree will be a true-to-name Granny Smith and bear Granny Smith fruit.

We arrive at part of the orchard where trees are noticeably smaller. She explains that apple trees in their natural state can grow to be very large. Over the centuries, horticultural techniques were developed so that apple scions were grafted onto dwarf or semidwarf rootstock to create smaller trees, resulting in high-density orchards. In fact, Diane says that one of the best pieces of advice ever given to her was "grow a stick with fruit on it, don't grow wood."

My big question is, where did the grafting branch originate? Diane explains that it's a process of selection, which farmers have been doing for centuries. Countless apple seeds were planted over the centuries since the time that Europeans landed in North America. Some of those trees would grow to produce small and tasteless apples or apples that would not keep well or produce good cider. Those apples would likely be fed to the hogs. However, some of those seeds would produce outstanding-quality fruit. To preserve those exceptional trees, rootstock would be shared and eventually branches would be grafted, nurseries were developed, and the apple cultivar would spread.

Through that process, Southerners developed more than 1,800 apple varieties that grew across the entire South, of which it is estimated today that well over 80 percent are extinct. What caused the demise? Prohibition had a lot to do with the eradication of some of those early nurseries, since apples for producing alcohol were abandoned in favor of apples for eating. The apple industry focused its efforts on promoting a handful of varieties, such as the ones found in the grocery store today, and the rest were forgotten. We lost an entire apple culture.

There's now an effort underway to bring back that culture. There's an undeniable romance to heirloom apples. How could there not be with names like Winter White Pearmain and Blacktwig? Yet many of the apples don't taste good eaten fresh, as they were bred for other uses. Heirloom apples are often bitter or tart, and that's part of what makes a good cider: bold tannins, bracing acidity, and complex flavor. Some of Diane's apples are heritage Southern apples such as Grimes Goldman, an apple that's long been considered excellent for making apple butter and cider, or Ralls Janet, an apple grown by Thomas Jefferson and traditional for winter keeping. Other Foggy Ridge apples include Northern and European apples that grow well in the mountainous region, like Roxbury Russet, a seventeenth-century apple that is the oldest named variety of apple grown in North America; Dabinett, a classic English cider apple; and Rhode Island Greening, an apple that originated near Newport around 1650 and that Diane reports is excellent for cooking.

We head back up to the rambling country home that Diane shares with her husband, Chuck. In front of a toasty fire crackling in the fireplace and fortified with a bit of cheese, we taste a sampling of her ciders. Many mass-produced ciders are sweet and considered an alternative to beer. Not the ones produced at Foggy Ridge. These ciders are high-acid, fruit-forward, and dry—more like a crisp white wine. Much of the history and culture of the agrarian South has been lost for reasons both good and bad. Our cider tasting is both refreshing and heartwarming. To see a Southern tradition reclaimed and homage paid to the past in these very modern times feels incredibly good.

The next morning, the fog marches into the valley in wave after wave of ghost-like sheets, bringing the much-needed rain Diane had hoped for.

THE SWEET LIFE *at* MUDDY POND

An aroma similar to the intermingling of green beans and peanuts cooking fills the air. It's mildly sweet, but also vegetal, earthy, and, more than anything, intoxicating. Before me is a large shallow metal cooker laced with channels, all feeding into a smaller pan about the size of a kitchen table. Steam billows off the top of the simmering sorghum juice. I am at the Muddy Pond Sorghum Mill to visit the Guenther family, artisan makers of sorghum syrup. Mark, the eldest brother, says hello and offers his hand. They've been at work since four thirty a.m., preheating the juice and firing up the steam engine with logs of split wood. Mark's brother Pete stands at the lower pan, moving continuously in an elaborate rhythm, skimming the juice, adjusting the tilt of the larger pan, moving juice into the smaller pan, stirring the thick viscous amber-colored syrup, and releasing the finished syrup to be pumped into the cooling trays.

Muddy Pond lies deep in the hills of Tennessee, midway between Nashville and Knoxville on the western edge of the Cumberland Plateau. The rough topography of the surrounding mountains resulted in small, isolated settlements like Muddy Pond and Hanging Limb, just down the way. The church signs I had sighted on the small winding country roads en route to this sequestered hamlet made me smile: "When life is not a bed of roses, remember who wore the thorns" and "Need a lifeguard? Remember who walks on water." There are a lot of church signs and steeples in this part of the South. In Monterey, Tennessee, where Muddy Pond is located, there are thirty-five churches for roughly 2,800 people. There seems to be a direct correlation in the South with folks—both black and white—who always seem to be on hard times and who live in the fullness in faith. I was once told by a Baptist preacher, "If you don't have much on this Earth, you want to believe there's something waiting for you in the next."

Indeed, the majority of the churches are Baptist, but there is a small community of Mennonites in the area. Similar to the Amish, the Mennonites are a group of Christian Anabaptist denominations committed to nonviolence, nonresistance, and pacifism. The reasons the Mennonites migrated to Tennessee include the search for affordable land, concern over school consolidation, and compulsory school attendance laws that were instituted after World War II in the Middle Atlantic and Midwestern states. Many Mennonites at the time did not believe in schooling after the

Muddy Pond is a family business, and when it's time to cook and bottle the sorghum, the entire family participates.

middle school years; hands were needed on the farm, not studying at a desk.

The Guenther family was part of this immigration, moving to the area from Pennsylvania in 1965. At the time, Muddy Pond was an old-fashioned horse-and-buggy community and Mark and Pete were raised in the traditional way. Part of their way of life included the community efforts of producing sorghum syrup. Their parents, John and Emma Guenther, started the Muddy Pond family operation in the early 1980s. It's now a family business, and when it's time to cook and bottle the sorghum, the entire family participates. An hour or so after we arrive, Mark's and Pete's wives, Sherry and Doreen, arrive with breakfast: foil-covered plates of fried farm-fresh eggs with thick-cut bacon and toast. As Mark douses the plate in steaming-hot syrup fresh from the cooker, Sherry laughs and says, "Mark eats sorghum on everything, even pizza!"

Doreen sets out sorghum cookbooks, luminous jars of honey, brightly colored jelly, sorghum barbecue sauce, and golden brown baked goods. Rows of pumpkins are lined up outside on the rock wall. Cousin Jenelle arrives in a bright red dress to bottle the cooling sorghum and sell the bottles to passersby. The scene is picture-perfect. One of the ways community farms like this one generate income is by selling homemade goods. With a few exceptions, the Mennonite experience in North America has been, and continues to be, predominantly rural. However, tourism has long been part of the Mennonite story, and the bucolic setting is perfect for weekend drives in the country—and the search for a simpler way of life. The elder Guenthers own a variety store and other family members own Bauman's Harness & Leather Shops and Muddy Pond General Store, with quilts, crafts, natural foods, and a deli.

While Mark enjoys his sorghum-doused breakfast, he explains the origins of sweet sorghum. "Sorghum is not indigenous to North America and was brought to the United States from Africa." He explains that some people call it "sorghum molasses." However, sweet sorghum syrup is made from 100 percent pure, natural juice extracted from sorghum cane; in contrast, molasses is a by-product of making sugar from sugarcane. Sorghum syrup retains all its natural sugars and other nutrients. It is 100 percent all-natural and contains no chemical additives of any kind. Mark tells me sorghum became a popular sweetener because, unlike sugarcane, it could be grown and harvested without supporting the slave trade—a point of distinction for members of his faith. In the 1860s, sorghum cultivation was concentrated in the Midwest, but by the 1890s it had become predominately a southern crop. According to the National Sweet Sorghum Producers and Processors, the syrup was an important sweetener for many small communities well into the 1900s, and then declined over the next century in the face of competition from glucose syrups. With corn thoroughly dominating American agriculture, it's unlikely sorghum will ever resume its former elevated status, but chefs, food writers, and people who care about local handcrafted foods are bringing it back.

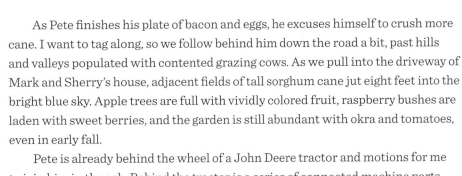

As Pete finishes his plate of bacon and eggs, he excuses himself to crush more cane. I want to tag along, so we follow behind him down the road a bit, past hills and valleys populated with contented grazing cows. As we pull into the driveway of Mark and Sherry's house, adjacent fields of tall sorghum cane jut eight feet into the bright blue sky. Apple trees are full with vividly colored fruit, raspberry bushes are laden with sweet berries, and the garden is still abundant with okra and tomatoes, even in early fall.

Pete is already behind the wheel of a John Deere tractor and motions for me to join him in the cab. Behind the tractor is a series of connected machine parts, making the tractor appear as if it is part of a caravan. A farmhand oversees a modified scythe that cuts the cane and feeds it into mechanical rollers for crushing; the farmhand periodically rakes the spent cane from the bottom. Pete explains that as the cane is crushed, the juice drains into a tray. A hydraulic pump forces the juice through a tube into the third element of the elaborate system, a 1,000-gallon receiving tank on wheels.

While I ride in the tractor with Pete, it's clear he's proud of the modernization. He explains that when he and his brother were younger, they had to cut the cane by hand and it was manually fed into a horse-powered mill; that mill is now only a demonstration for tourists, festivals throughout the mountains, and during the fall at Dollywood. Motioning behind him, he smiles and says, "With this setup, I can fill that tank in one and a half hours." He explains that it's a four-month process to plant and grow sweet sorghum.

Once the cane is crushed, the juice will be transported back to the mill, preheated, and held in a tank. During the harvest through September and October, the Guenthers cook the juice into syrup every two days. Cooking the juice is a controlled evaporation that occurs in a 22-foot-long shallow pan controlled by a hydraulic lift. (The pan is shallow so it's less likely to boil over.) The juice is then channeled into a smaller pan where it transforms into syrup. The process is measured by sight and taste, but also by the measurement of Brix, or the percent of sugar in an aqueous solution. Once the Brix consistency is correct, the syrup is pumped through a series of pipes into cooling trays and then into a large metal tank.

I turn my attention to Sherry, who is noting the production in a spiral-bound notebook—the amount of juice they start with and the number of resulting gallons of syrup. "In general," she tells me, "it takes roughly ten gallons of juice to make one gallon of syrup, but the juice does vary in sugar content. Our last batch ratio of juice to syrup was 7 to 6." I ask Mark how many gallons of syrup they produce and he answers, "About three thousand. It's not enough to get rich, but it's enough to make a good living." After spending the day in this beautiful setting, learning about this traditional syrup and meeting these generous, kind people, I'd say the Guenthers are living the sweet life, indeed.

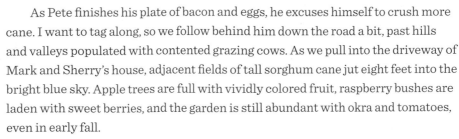

As Pete finishes his plate of bacon and eggs, he excuses himself to crush more cane. I want to tag along, so we follow behind him down the road a bit, past hills and valleys populated with contented grazing cows. As we pull into the driveway of Mark and Sherry's house, adjacent fields of tall sorghum cane jut eight feet into the bright blue sky. Apple trees are full with vividly colored fruit, raspberry bushes are laden with sweet berries, and the garden is still abundant with okra and tomatoes, even in early fall.

Pete is already behind the wheel of a John Deere tractor and motions for me to join him in the cab. Behind the tractor is a series of connected machine parts, making the tractor appear as if it is part of a caravan. A farmhand oversees a modified scythe that cuts the cane and feeds it into mechanical rollers for crushing; the farmhand periodically rakes the spent cane from the bottom. Pete explains that as the cane is crushed, the juice drains into a tray. A hydraulic pump forces the juice through a tube into the third element of the elaborate system, a 1,000-gallon receiving tank on wheels.

While I ride in the tractor with Pete, it's clear he's proud of the modernization. He explains that when he and his brother were younger, they had to cut the cane by hand and it was manually fed into a horse-powered mill; that mill is now only a demonstration for tourists, festivals throughout the mountains, and during the fall at Dollywood. Motioning behind him, he smiles and says, "With this setup, I can fill that tank in one and a half hours." He explains that it's a four-month process to plant and grow sweet sorghum.

Once the cane is crushed, the juice will be transported back to the mill, preheated, and held in a tank. During the harvest through September and October, the Guenthers cook the juice into syrup every two days. Cooking the juice is a controlled evaporation that occurs in a 22-foot-long shallow pan controlled by a hydraulic lift. (The pan is shallow so it's less likely to boil over.) The juice is then channeled into a smaller pan where it transforms into syrup. The process is measured by sight and taste, but also by the measurement of Brix, or the percent of sugar in an aqueous solution. Once the Brix consistency is correct, the syrup is pumped through a series of pipes into cooling trays and then into a large metal tank.

I turn my attention to Sherry, who is noting the production in a spiral-bound notebook—the amount of juice they start with and the number of resulting gallons of syrup. "In general," she tells me, "it takes roughly ten gallons of juice to make one gallon of syrup, but the juice does vary in sugar content. Our last batch ratio of juice to syrup was 7 to 6." I ask Mark how many gallons of syrup they produce and he answers, "About three thousand. It's not enough to get rich, but it's enough to make a good living." After spending the day in this beautiful setting, learning about this traditional syrup and meeting these generous, kind people, I'd say the Guenthers are living the sweet life, indeed.

Benne Seed Crisps

Immediately after college, I moved to Charleston, South Carolina, where I soon met my friend and colleague John Martin Taylor. I was in my early twenties and was absolutely intrigued by John. He was quite the bon vivant and seemed to have a magical life filled with food, fellowship, and famous people. He owned Hoppin' John's, a culinary bookstore that was a mecca to me. I had not yet gone to culinary school or thought about a career in food, so his bookstore seemed to contain the keys to the universe. He had also been a friend of The B-52s, he introduced me to veal sweetbreads, and I attended a very smoky party at his home with guest Allen Ginsberg. The whole scene felt like a Southern version of a European salon. I didn't know how, what, why, or when, but I knew there was something about the whole situation that I wanted in my life.

He very well should be credited with creating the spark that began the transformation of Low Country cooking more than twenty-five years ago with his award-winning book *Hoppin' John's Lowcountry Cooking*, to this day one of the most significant explorations of regional cuisine written. When the book was published in 1992, most white-tablecloth restaurants in Charleston and through-out the South were French or Italian, and no one gave much thought to regional cuisine; the restaurants that have driven Charleston's thriving dining community—McCrady's, Hominy Grill, FIG, and Husk—were years away. Of course, he included a recipe for benne seed wafers, the signature cookie of Charleston. These rich, sweet brown cookies will last for weeks in an airtight container.

½ cup white sesame seeds

⅓ cup all-purpose flour

¼ teaspoon baking soda

½ teaspoon fine sea salt

3 tablespoons unsalted butter, at room temperature

¾ cup firmly packed dark brown sugar

1 large egg, lightly beaten

¼ teaspoon pure vanilla extract

1 Heat the oven to 325°F. Adjust the oven rack to the middle position. Line two rimmed baking sheets with silicone baking mats or parchment paper. Scatter the seeds on one of the baking sheets and bake until lightly toasted, 8 to 10 minutes. Transfer the pan to a rack to cool.

2 In a medium bowl, whisk together the flour, baking soda, and salt; set aside. In the bowl of a stand mixer fitted with the paddle attachment, or in a large bowl using a handheld mixer, beat together the butter and brown sugar to the consistency of wet sand, about 2 minutes. Reduce the speed to medium and beat in the egg and vanilla until combined. Using a wooden spoon or rubber spatula, add the flour mixture, and then fold in the cooled toasted sesame seeds.

Recipe continues

3   Drop level teaspoon-size portions of the dough onto the prepared baking sheets, spacing the cookies about 2 inches apart. (Allowing space is important, as the cookies will spread.)

4   Bake for 7 to 8 minutes total, until the tops of the cookies bubble and the edges turn deep brown, rotating the baking sheets once during baking. Transfer the baking sheets to a wire rack to cool slightly, and then use an offset spatula to transfer the cookies to the rack to cool completely. (If you leave the cookies on the baking sheet to cool completely, they will be harder and more crisp; if you remove them immediately, they will be slightly softer.) Repeat with the remaining dough. Store the cookies in an airtight container for up to 1 week.

Lemon Icebox Tart with Saltine Cracker Crust

Makes 1
(9-inch) tart

I first tasted this pie at Crook's Corner, the legendary Chapel Hill restaurant that's had my friend and colleague chef Bill Smith at the helm for more than two decades. The first forkful was a revelation, the sort of otherworldly gustatory experience that involuntarily causes heads to tilt back and eyes to roll—the OMG kind of reaction. It's a perfectly crafted balance of sour, salty, bitter, and sweet. The best thing about it isn't the bright lemon flavor, but its salty, savory cracker-crumb crust, which distinguishes it from sweet piecrusts made with crushed cookies or graham crackers. Best of all? It's dead simple to make. Bill doesn't take credit for inventing the pie, but he has single-handedly revived a vintage recipe.

Bill is that kind of man, that kind of chef. He's very modest, yet in 2011 the James Beard Foundation named Crook's Corner an "America's Classic," and Bill has been listed twice in the final five for the award for Best Chef Southeast by the same foundation. He's unassuming, riding his bike with the beat-up metal basket around Chapel Hill, but the truth is that Bill Smith is one of the most influential chefs in the Southeast. Chef Bill Neal, truly a groundbreaking chef in regard to Southern cuisine, was the chef-owner for the first ten years of Crook's Corner. With his passing, Bill Smith took the toque—or well-worn baseball cap—and has been there ever since. I didn't know Bill Neal, and while I understand his legacy, I have the opinion that if Bill Smith weren't so good at what he does at Crook's Corner, that legacy might not still shine so bright. Bill Smith has not only proudly carried on Bill Neal's legacy, but also created one of his very own.

1½ sleeves saltine crackers
(about 6 ounces/68 crackers)

8 tablespoons (½ cup) unsalted
butter, melted

3 tablespoons sugar

4 large egg yolks, lightly beaten

1 (14-ounce) can sweetened
condensed milk

Zest and juice of 3 lemons
(about ½ cup juice)

1 cup heavy cream

⅛ teaspoon fleur de sel
or fine sea salt

1   Heat the oven to 350°F.

2   Place the crackers in a zip-top plastic bag. Using a rolling pin or the bottom of a skillet, crush the crackers until fine, but not powder. Transfer to a bowl. (Alternatively, you can simply put them in the bowl and crush them with your fingers.) Add the butter and sugar and stir to combine. You should have about 3 cups of the saltine mixture.

3   Transfer the saltine mixture to a 9-inch fluted tart pan with a removable bottom. Use the bottom of a measuring cup or the back of a large metal spoon to press the crumbs into the pan and ensure the crumbs are evenly packed. Chill for at

Recipe continues

least 15 minutes and then place on a rimmed baking sheet. Bake for 15 minutes, or until the crust is golden brown. Transfer to a wire rack.

4   Using a whisk, gently beat the egg yolks into the condensed milk without incorporating air bubbles. Add the lemon zest and juice to the egg-milk mixture. Gently whisk until completely combined, being careful not to create air bubbles as you mix. Pour into the warm shell and return to the oven to bake until the filling has set, about 10 minutes.

5   Transfer the tart to a wire rack to cool until cool enough to touch. Transfer to the refrigerator and refrigerate until completely cooled, about 1 hour. (To cool the tart even faster, place it on a rack rather than a solid shelf in the refrigerator, so air can circulate underneath the pan.) Go ahead and wipe out the bowl you used for making the crust and place it and a clean whisk in the refrigerator for whipping the cream later.

6   When ready to finish and after the tart is completely cooled, place the chilled cream in the chilled bowl and whisk vigorously until the cream holds soft peaks. (Alternatively, you can use a handheld mixer. Either way, it's important the bowl and the cream are well chilled.)

7   Remove the tart from the pan. (An easy way to do this is to place a bowl smaller than the outer ring underneath the center of the tart so the outer ring will simply fall away.) Using the flat side of a chef's knife or a large offset spatula, remove the tart from the removable bottom and slide it onto a serving plate. Make sure to collect any crumbs that accumulate to scatter as a garnish on top of the tart.

8   Spoon the whipped cream onto the top of the lemon filling. Sprinkle over the fleur de sel and any crust crumbs. Using a chef's knife, cleaning with a damp towel between each slice, cut the tart into wedges. Serve immediately. Astonishingly, the tart keeps fairly well if refrigerated in an airtight container for up to 2 days.

Chocolate Chess Pie

Makes 1
(9-inch) pie

When I was a little girl, my family would travel from our home in Louisiana to Georgia for holidays and summer break to visit our family back east. My parents would load us up in the big, green Oldsmobile and my father would drive through the night as my sister and I slept in the expansive back seat. It was an extravagant production moving a family across four states, and very exciting business for my sister and me. The car was packed to the gills and even had a bulging cargo box on the roof. My sister and I fought sleep—and each other—for as long as we could. As the sun rose we would stop for breakfast at a truck stop on the Georgia-Alabama border. The bright fluorescent lights in the diner caused me to squint after the long, dark night. Tall, weathered men in baseball caps sipped coffee and smoked cigarettes at the counter. It was another universe. The illuminated multisided rotating glass tower of pie truly enchanted me. It seemed otherworldly, a shining beacon of pie lined with lace doilies and filled with white saucers of picture-perfect wedges. Sadly, since our trip always timed with a breakfast visit, the enticing pies were decidedly off-limits.

One of the best parts about being a grown up is that you can have a slice of this traditional Southern favorite whenever you want it.

8 tablespoons (½ cup) unsalted butter

¼ cup bittersweet chocolate chips (1½ ounces)

4 large eggs, at room temperature

1½ cups sugar

¼ cup cocoa powder

2 tablespoons yellow cornmeal

¼ teaspoon fine sea salt

½ cup buttermilk, at room temperature

1 teaspoon pure vanilla extract

1 French Pie Pastry crust (recipe follows), blind baked for 20 minutes and still warm

1   Heat the oven to 325°F.

2   Melt the butter and the chocolate in the microwave and set aside to cool. In a bowl, whisk the eggs until smooth. Add the sugar, cocoa powder, cornmeal, and salt. Whisk well to combine. Add the butter-chocolate mixture, buttermilk, and vanilla. Whisk well to combine. Pour into the warm piecrust.

3   Bake until set and not wiggling, 45 minutes. During the last 15 minutes of baking, cover the pie with aluminum foil if the pie starts to become too dark. The pie may puff and crackle during baking, which is fine. It will settle as it cools. Transfer to a wire rack to cool completely, at least 2 hours, then slice and serve.

French Pie Pastry

2 cups all-purpose flour

1 teaspoon fine sea salt

8 tablespoons (½ cup) unsalted butter, cut into cubes and chilled

2 large egg yolks

5 to 6 tablespoons ice water

1 Combine the flour and salt in the bowl of a food processor fitted with the metal blade. Add the butter. Process until the mixture resembles coarse meal, 8 to 10 seconds. Add the egg yolks and pulse to combine.

2 With the processor on pulse, add the ice water, 1 tablespoon at a time. Pulse until the mixture holds together as a soft but not crumbly or sticky dough. Shape the dough into a disk, wrap in plastic wrap, and refrigerate until firm and evenly moist, about 30 minutes.

3 Lightly flour a clean work surface and a rolling pin. Place the dough disk in the center of the floured surface. Roll out the dough, starting in the center and rolling up to, but not over, the top edge. Return to the center and roll down to, but not over, the bottom edge. Give the dough a quarter turn and continue rolling, repeating the quarter turns until you have a disk about ⅛ inch thick.

4 Drape the dough over the rolling pin and transfer to a 10-inch tart pan with a removable bottom or a 9-inch pie plate, unrolling over the pan. With one hand, lift the pastry and with the other, gently tuck it into the pan, being careful not to stretch or pull the dough. Let the pastry settle into the bottom of the pan. Take a small piece of dough and shape it into a ball. Use the ball of dough as a tool to press around the bottom edges of the tart pan, snugly shaping the pastry to the pan without tearing it. If using a tart pan, remove any excess pastry by rolling the pin across the top of the pan. If using a pie plate, crimp or flute the edge. Prick the bottom of the pastry all over with the tines of a fork to help prevent shrinkage during baking. Chill until firm, about 30 minutes.

5   Heat the oven to 425°F. Crumple a piece of parchment paper and then lay it out flat over the bottom of the pastry. Fill the paper with pie weights, dried beans, or uncooked rice. This will keep the unfilled piecrust from puffing up in the oven as it bakes.

6   For a partially baked (blind-baked) shell that will be filled and baked further (such as for the Chocolate Chess Pie on page 280), bake for 20 minutes. Remove the paper and weights. (You can reuse the rice or beans for blind-baking a number of times, but not for cooking.) The shell can now be filled and baked further, according to the recipe directions. For a fully baked shell that will hold an uncooked filling, bake the empty shell until a deep golden brown, an additional 10 minutes, or 30 minutes total.

Mexican Chocolate Pudding with Bourbon Cream

Makes 6 (½-cup) servings

Sometimes Mama would make chocolate pudding after school, and my sister and I would watch her measure and prepare the ingredients, combine everything, and then cook until the dark mixture would suddenly thicken. She'd pour the molten chocolate pudding into those glass cups with thick ruffled edges and let us swipe our little fingers against the side of the pan to get every last bit.

The stereotype of Appalachia—a region that stretches from the southern tip of New York to northern Mississippi—is a mountainous area sparsely populated by poor whites. But there has always been a lot more to that region—including a well-established Mexican community. Spanish is the second most commonly spoken language in the region. One wonderful and unique Mexican treat is Mexican chocolate, enhanced with spices such as cinnamon and cayenne, which my friend and colleague, chef Anthony Lamas of Seviche in Louisville, Kentucky, calls "truly a one-of-a-kind chocolate." Although I'll always love the chocolate pudding of my childhood, in homage to the Latin influences in the region, I've kicked up the flavor of these decidedly adult pudding cups with a bit of spice and heat to go along with the Kentucky bourbon cream.

For the pudding

6 tablespoons firmly packed light brown sugar

3 tablespoons cornstarch

1½ tablespoons cocoa powder, plus more for dusting

1 teaspoon instant espresso powder

¼ teaspoon ground cinnamon

Pinch of cayenne pepper

Pinch of fine sea salt

1¼ cups heavy cream

1¼ cups milk

1 teaspoon pure vanilla extract

6 ounces best-quality bittersweet chocolate, finely chopped, or 1 cup bittersweet chocolate chips

1 tablespoon unsalted butter, cut into small pieces

1 *To make the pudding,* whisk together the brown sugar, cornstarch, cocoa, espresso powder, cinnamon, cayenne, and salt in a saucepan. In a large measuring cup, combine the cream, milk, and vanilla. Add the wet mixture to the dry ingredients in the saucepan and whisk until smooth.

2 Place the saucepan over medium heat. Cook, whisking continuously, until the mixture comes to a boil and thickens, about 5 minutes. Add the chocolate and cook, whisking continuously, until the chocolate has melted, 1 to 2 minutes.

3 Remove the saucepan from the heat. Whisk in the butter until melted. Divide the mixture equally among six serving dishes such as dessert coupes or ramekins. To prevent a skin from forming, place plastic wrap directly against the surface of each pudding. Refrigerate until set, about 1 hour.

Ingredients and recipe continue

For the bourbon cream

½ cup heavy cream

1 tablespoon bourbon

4 ***Meanwhile, to make the bourbon cream,*** combine the cream and bourbon in a large bowl. Refrigerate, along with a whisk, for at least 15 minutes. Once chilled, beat the cream with the chilled whisk until it holds soft peaks, 3 to 5 minutes.

5 When the pudding is chilled completely, top each glass with a spoonful of bourbon cream and dust with cocoa powder. Serve immediately.

Sweet Potato Bread Pudding with Peanut Streusel

Serves 8 to 10

This delicious dessert is my homage to George Washington Carver (see page 40). Soul food scholar Adrian Miller is the author of *Soul Food: The Surprising Story of an American Cuisine, One Plate at a Time.* He says, "George Washington Carver is one of the most underappreciated OGs ('Original Gardeners') in Southern food. I'm thrilled that he gets a lot of love for his innovative scientific research on peanuts and sweet potatoes, but he should be known for so much more. The agricultural bulletins he authored while at Tuskegee University showed countless people myriad ways to grow crops and utilize wild foods. George Washington Carver's legacy of growing and teaching should long be celebrated."

8 tablespoons (½ cup) butter, plus more for the baking dish

3 large sweet potatoes

3 cups milk

1 cup heavy cream

1¾ cups firmly packed light brown sugar

8 large eggs

½ teaspoon fine sea salt

1 teaspoon ground cinnamon

1 teaspoon ground ginger

½ teaspoon freshly grated nutmeg

2 baguettes (about 1 pound), cut into 1-inch cubes

½ cup golden raisins

½ cup peanuts

¼ cup granulated sugar

Whipped cream or ice cream, for serving

1 Heat the oven to 350°F. Butter a large casserole or baking dish.

2 Place the sweet potatoes on a baking sheet and roast until fork-tender, about 45 minutes; set aside to cool. While the sweet potatoes are cooling, melt 4 tablespoons of the butter in a small saucepan.

3 When the potatoes are cool enough to handle, peel and place the flesh in a large bowl. Using an old-fashioned potato masher, mash to a coarse consistency. Add the milk, cream, brown sugar, the 4 tablespoons melted butter, the eggs, salt, cinnamon, ginger, and nutmeg; mix well. Add the baguette and raisins; stir to combine and make sure all the bread is coated with the custard mixture. Set aside to soak for at least 15 minutes while you make the streusel.

4 Combine the remaining 4 tablespoons butter, the peanuts, and the granulated sugar in a food processor. Pulse until the mixture resembles cookie dough.

5 Pour the bread mixture into the prepared baking dish, making sure the custard is evenly dispersed. Dot the peanut streusel over the top. Bake until risen and set, about 45 minutes. Serve warm with whipped cream or ice cream.

Almond Jelly with Blueberry-Ginger Compote

Makes 1
(8-inch) pan

The Mississippi Delta has been described as the "most Southern place on earth." It also boasts a sizable Chinese population, descended from merchants who immigrated to the Delta during Reconstruction. These immigrants occupied a place between white and black in a deeply segregated society. But because the immigrants were mostly men, with a shortage of women, they intermarried with African Americans. Chinese children were not allowed to attend white schools. According to Dr. Charles Reagan Wilson, the director of the Center for the Study of Southern Culture, by the 1930s many of the Delta Chinese had become Baptists, with the church serving as a center for wedding banquets, community service projects, fund-raising activities, funerals, and other occasions that brought the extended Chinese community together.

Almond jelly is a popular Chinese dessert, especially during the hotter summer months—and there are plenty of those on the Mississippi Delta. Typically, the Americanized version would be served with canned fruit cocktail, but here I use homemade Blueberry-Ginger Compote. It would be equally delicious with fresh or grilled peaches or plums. The jelly is ready when it barely wiggles.

For the almond jelly

1½ cups water, divided

2 (¼-ounce) pouches unflavored gelatin

½ cup sugar

Pinch of fine sea salt

1 cup cold milk, or store-bought or homemade almond milk

1 teaspoon pure almond extract

For the compote

½ cup water

½ cup sugar

3 thin slices fresh ginger, cut into julienne

2 cups blueberries (10 ounces)

Finely grated zest of 1 lemon

1½ tablespoons freshly squeezed lemon juice

Pinch of fine sea salt

Mint sprigs, for garnish

1 *To make the almond jelly,* bring 1 cup of the water to a boil in a small saucepan. Sprinkle the gelatin over the remaining ½ cup water in a medium bowl; stir until dissolved. Pour the boiling water over the gelatin and stir to combine. Add the sugar and salt; stir until dissolved. Stir in the milk and almond extract. Pour into an 8-inch square glass baking dish. Refrigerate until set, at least 1 hour.

2 *Meanwhile, to make the compote,* combine the water, sugar, and ginger in a 1-quart heavy saucepan; bring to a boil and cook, uncovered, for 5 minutes. Stir in the blueberries and simmer, stirring occasionally, until the blueberries begin to burst, 3 to 5 minutes. Remove from the heat and stir in the lemon zest, lemon juice, and salt. Transfer to a bowl and refrigerate or freeze until cold before serving.

3 Slice the jelly into 2-inch squares and place in serving bowls or cups. Spoon the compote, with its juices, over the almond jelly. Garnish with mint and serve immediately.

Buttermilk Pound Cake with Roasted Strawberries

Makes 1 (10-inch) cake

There are many classic Southern cakes—hummingbird, lane, red velvet, angel food, and many more—but in my mind, a pound cake is the ultimate Southern cake. Nothing beats its rich, buttery flavor. It has been my mother's go-to cake my entire life. Many years ago, my partner, Lisa, and I went to my mother's for Christmas. Mama had prepared her pound cake, knowing that it was Lisa's favorite dessert, and she left it in a Tupperware cake carrier on her kitchen table. Lisa knew the pound cake was there, but didn't want to be rude by just helping herself. My mother, in turn, was incredulous as to why Lisa was ignoring the cake that she had specifically made for her! Believe me, they've now gotten on the same page, and if there's cake, Lisa has no shyness about helping herself to a slice!

This recipe is buttery rich and tangy due to the buttermilk and lemon zest. Try a slice toasted in a skillet with a bit of butter—you won't believe how good it is! This pound cake will easily keep for up to a week if stored in an airtight container.

For the pound cake

24 tablespoons (1½ cups) unsalted butter, at room temperature, plus more for the pan

3 cups all-purpose flour

2 teaspoons baking powder

½ teaspoon baking soda

½ teaspoon fine sea salt

1 cup buttermilk, at room temperature

5 large eggs, at room temperature

1 vanilla bean, split and seeds scraped, or 1 tablespoon pure vanilla extract

Zest of 1 lemon

3 cups sugar

1 **To make the pound cake,** heat the oven to 300°F. Generously grease a 16-cup (measure to the rim) Bundt pan with butter.

2 Sift together the flour, baking powder, baking soda, and salt into a bowl. Set aside. In a large liquid measuring cup, whisk together the buttermilk, eggs, vanilla bean seeds, and lemon zest. Set aside.

3 In the bowl of a stand mixer fitted with the paddle attachment, cream together the butter and sugar on medium speed until light and fluffy. Add the flour mixture to the butter mixture in three batches, alternating with two batches of the buttermilk mixture and ending with the flour mixture, occasionally scraping down the sides of the mixing bowl. Fill the prepared pan with the batter (it should be no more than two-thirds full).

For the roasted strawberries

1 pound strawberries, hulled, halved, and quartered if large

2 tablespoons sugar, or to taste

½ vanilla bean, split and scraped

Pinch of fine sea salt

4 Bake on a rack in the middle of the oven for 15 minutes. Increase the oven temperature to 325°F and bake for 45 minutes more, or until the cake is golden brown and pulls away from the sides of the pan. Transfer to a wire rack to cool for 10 minutes. Invert the cake onto the rack to cool completely. Increase the oven temperature to 425°F.

5 While the cake is cooling, to make the roasted strawberries, toss the halved strawberries with the sugar, vanilla, and salt in a bowl. Place in a single layer in a large glass baking dish or on a rimmed baking sheet lined with a silicone baking mat. Transfer to the oven and roast until the juices are bubbling and the strawberries are soft to the touch, 12 to 15 minutes.

6 *To serve,* using a serrated knife, slice the cake into wedges and top with the roasted strawberries.

Apple Stack Cake

Makes 1 (8-inch) cake

Apple Stack Cake is legendary in the mountains of the American South. Traditionally it is a dense, almost cookielike cake. Some stories suggest that women would each bring a single layer for marriage celebrations and they would be assembled onsite for the wedding cake, held together with a spread of stewed dried apples, applesauce, or apple butter. Then it was necessary to wait a few days so the crumb would soften and take on the flavors of the applesauce. Lordy mercy, who has the patience or time for that?

This version has the flavor profile of the traditional cake and is indeed stacked, but is ready to enjoy once it's made. No patience required.

For the filling

8 ounces dried unsulfured apple rings (2 cups)

½ cup firmly packed brown sugar

½ teaspoon ground cinnamon

½ teaspoon ground ginger

½ teaspoon freshly grated nutmeg

For the cake

Nonstick cooking spray

2 cups all-purpose flour

1½ teaspoons baking powder

2 tablespoons ground ginger

1 teaspoon ground cinnamon

¼ teaspoon freshly grated nutmeg

½ teaspoon fine sea salt

1 cup apple cider

1 cup dark molasses

½ teaspoon baking soda

1 cup packed dark brown sugar

1 cup granulated sugar

½ cup unsweetened applesauce

¼ cup canola oil

3 large eggs

1 **To make the filling,** combine the apple rings, brown sugar, cinnamon, ginger, nutmeg, and 3 cups water in a medium saucepan. (A deep and narrow saucepan is better than a shallow one to ensure the water covers most of the apples.) Bring to a boil and reduce the heat to maintain a simmer. Cover and cook, stirring occasionally, until the apples are completely tender, about 1 hour.

2 **Meanwhile, to make the cake,** heat the oven to 350°F. Coat three 9-inch round cake pans with cooking spray and line the bottom of each with a round of parchment paper cut to fit.

3 Sift together the flour, baking powder, ginger, cinnamon, nutmeg, and salt into a bowl. Set aside.

4 Bring the apple cider and molasses to a boil in a large saucepan and remove from the heat; carefully whisk in the baking soda—it will foam up. Let cool to room temperature.

5 In a large bowl, whisk together both sugars, the applesauce, and canola oil. Whisk in the eggs, then whisk in the cooled molasses mixture. Add the dry ingredients. Stir until just combined.

Ingredients and recipe continue

2 cups confectioners' sugar, sifted

1 teaspoon pure vanilla extract

2 to 4 tablespoons whole milk

6 Divide the batter among the prepared cake pans. Bake for 18 to 22 minutes, until a toothpick inserted into the center of the cake comes out clean. Let cool in the pans on a wire rack for 5 minutes, and then turn the cakes out onto the rack, carefully remove the parchment paper (it will be sticky), and turn the cakes right-side up. Let cool completely.

7 Place the first cake layer on a cake stand. Spread with half the apple mixture (about 1½ cups); top with the second layer and spread with the remaining apple mixture. Top with the third cake layer.

8 *To make the glaze,* combine the confectioners' sugar, vanilla, and milk in a small bowl. Using a spoon, drizzle the glaze over the top of the cake.

9 To serve, slice with a serrated knife into individual slices and serve immediately. The cake will keep in an airtight container for up to 1 week.

Peach Upside-Down Cake

Serves 10

Southern peaches are something special. The trouble is, you pretty much have to live in the South to understand what the fuss is about, because peaches bought elsewhere are most often picked green and hard before shipping. When ag-entrepreneur Stephen Rose moved to Nashville in the summer of 2010, he made a disheartening discovery: No one was selling fresh, flavorful peaches like the kind he'd grown up with in Peach County, Georgia. He had an idea. He and his wife bought a 1964 Jeep truck and started selling big, beautiful, juicy Georgia peaches out of their cab in Nashville. Within five weeks, the city had consumed over ten tons of their brown-bagged peaches. Now the Peach Truck Tour travels through Tennessee, Kentucky, Ohio, Indiana, and Pennsylvania!

Pineapple upside-down cake is a Southern classic and is most often made with canned pineapple. This version uses fresh peaches and is a vast improvement, in my opinion. You can use all-purpose flour instead of the cake flour, but the results will be a bit heavier and slightly dense.

4 medium peaches (about 1½ pounds), unpeeled and cut into ⅓-inch-thick wedges

Juice of 1 lemon

1 cup cake flour, not self-rising

¾ teaspoon baking powder

¼ teaspoon baking soda

1 cup granulated sugar

10 tablespoons (½ cup plus 2 tablespoons) unsalted butter, at room temperature

1 vanilla bean, split and seeds scraped

2 large eggs

½ cup sour cream

Bourbon Cream (see page 286)

1 Heat oven to 350°F. Line a rimmed baking sheet with a silicone baking mat or parchment paper. (This step helps with cleanup.)

2 Toss the peaches with the lemon juice in a large bowl. In a separate bowl, whisk together the flour, baking powder, and baking soda.

3 Cook ¼ cup of the granulated sugar over medium heat in a 10-inch cast-iron skillet, stirring occasionally with a wooden spoon, for 10 minutes, or until the sugar melts and turns a deep amber color. Remove from the heat. Immediately add 2 tablespoons of the butter and stir vigorously. Arrange the peach wedges in concentric circles over the sugar mixture, overlapping them as needed.

4 In the bowl of a stand mixer fitted with the paddle attachment, beat the remaining ¾ cup granulated sugar, ½ cup butter, and vanilla bean seeds on medium speed until smooth. Add the eggs, one at a time, beating until blended after each addition. Add the sour cream and beat until blended. With the mixer running on low speed, gradually

Recipe continues

add the flour mixture, beating just until blended and stopping to scrape bowl as needed. Spoon the batter over the peaches in the skillet and spread to cover. Place the skillet on the prepared baking sheet.

5 Bake until golden brown and a wooden toothpick inserted into the center of the cake comes out clean, 40 to 45 minutes. Let cool in the skillet on a wire rack for 10 minutes. Run a knife around edge to loosen.

6 Carefully pour out any excess liquid from the skillet into a measuring cup and set aside. (It's okay if you don't have any excess liquid—it all depends on how juicy your fruit is.) Carefully invert the cake onto a serving plate and drizzle with any reserved liquid. Let cool slightly, about 10 minutes. Cut into wedges using a serrated knife. Top with bourbon cream and serve immediately.

Blackberry
Bourbon Dumplings

Serves 4 to 6

Throughout the South, wild blackberry patches can be found at the edge of fields, on the sides of roads, in ditches, through vacant lots, and in the undergrowth of woods. In late spring, the impenetrable thickets are covered in delicate white, lacelike flowers that belie the arching fiercely barbed canes—and possible venomous snakes that might be found hiding in the bramble! I can still hear my grandmother telling me not to get too close to the edge of the woods lest I "get on a snake." (By the way, it was not unreasonable advice, as every single species of deadly poisonous snake that lives in North America can be found throughout the South.) Free for the picking and gloriously sweet when warmed by the summer sun, blackberries are the taste of summer where I grew up in Georgia.

My friend and colleague chef Jeremy Ashby of Lexington, Kentucky, shares a similar story of food and cooking. His began just as mine did, by the side of his grandmother named Sally B. (I'd bet money she fussed about snakes, too.) He shared with me this old-fashioned recipe that has a decidedly Kentucky twist.

For the blackberry syrup

2 pints fresh blackberries

1½ cups sugar

¼ cup freshly squeezed lemon juice

3 tablespoons unsalted butter

Pinch of fine sea salt

For the dumplings

1½ cups all-purpose flour, plus more for rolling

2 tablespoons sugar

1 tablespoon baking powder

1 teaspoon fine sea salt

2 tablespoons unsalted butter

5 tablespoons Kentucky bourbon

1 cup milk

Vanilla ice cream, for serving

1   *To make the blackberry syrup,* set aside 4 to 6 blackberries for garnish and combine the remaining blackberries, sugar, lemon juice, butter, and salt in a large saucepan. Bring to a boil over medium-high heat and then reduce the heat to maintain a simmer. Cook, stirring occasionally, until the berries have broken down and form a syrup, about 10 minutes.

2   *Meanwhile, to make the dumplings,* in a food processor, pulse together the flour, sugar, baking powder, and salt. Add butter and 1 tablespoon of the bourbon and pulse to combine. While the machine is running, pour the milk though the feed tube until the dough pulls away from the sides of the bowl.

3   Tip the dough out onto a lightly floured work surface. Using a lightly floured rolling pin, roll the dough out to ¼ inch thick. Using a pastry wheel or a knife, cut into long strips about 1½ inches wide, then cut crosswise at 1½-inch

intervals to create squares. (You're making dumplings, so the squares don't have to be perfect, but they should be about the same size so they cook at the same rate.)

4   Transfer the dumplings to the simmering blackberry syrup. Cover and cook until puffed and cooked through, 10 to 12 minutes. To serve, spoon a few dumplings into a bowl and top with cooked berries and syrup. Top with a scoop of ice cream. Splash each bowl with a tablespoon or so of the bourbon. Garnish with the reserved blackberries and serve immediately.

ACKNOWLEDGMENTS

While my name is on the cover and these are my words and recipes, there is no doubt in my mind that these stories would not be expressed nearly as well without the beautiful artistry and flat-out hard work of my dear friend and the photographer of this book, Angie Mosier. For nearly a year we explored the South in sweltering heat, bitter cold, soaking rain, and yes, gloriously beautiful, picturesque days. We traversed the region on trails ranging from winding, rutted, single-path red dirt roads to traffic-clogged multi-lane interstates, and journeyed through the flat intercoastal waterways of the salty tideland marshes to the lofty, smoky ridges and peaks of the oldest mountains in the United States. We met Southerners of every race, color, religion, creed, sexual orientation, age, and ancestry. Our trips were a study in demographics and a veritable education in equal opportunity law. We met friends old and new, moved along quickly from bigotry, and were greeted with open arms by people who did not share our political or religious views, but welcomed us at their table nonetheless. We were awestruck by the abject poverty of some places and awed by the largesse of others. As we drove across eleven states the radio sat silent for hours upon hours as we examined our thoughts and beliefs regarding our homeland, perused its difficult past, contemplated its complicated current situation, and voiced our hopes for its future. Our eye-opening food lover's tour to discover the *Secrets of the Southern Table* was one of the greatest gifts of my life and I am most grateful. Thank you Angie, for joining me on this odyssey, as well as for your incredible friendship. (And, you, too, Johnny Mosier for being one of best damn men I have ever met.) I love you both.

Tremendous gratitude to my basherte, my love and life partner, native-born Southerner via Westchester, Lisa Ekus. Your belief and support in me in this project as with all, both personally and professionally, has been without measure. Our wonderful journey started ten years ago, and I look forward to many more years to come. I would not be the person or cook I am today without the unconditional love and instruction of my sweet mama, Jenny B. Willis. Thank you, Mama, for instilling in me the love of food and cooking.

In nearly all the photos of my childhood my sister is right beside me, holding my hand. While she may no longer be seen in every photo, she is nonetheless always with me. Jona, I love you to the moon and back.

To my friends for their love, constant cheerleading, recipe testing, and tasting: Gena Berry, Regina Beyer, Tamie Cook, Deanna Hilton, Debi Loftis, Barbara Owen, Barb Pires, Jenni Ridall, and Gayle Skelton.

It was my endeavor to include as many voices and points of view as possible to demonstrate the richness and diversity of the Southern table. Many thanks to the many contributors and resources: the Atlanta Community Food Bank, Chef Norman Van Aken, Chef Jeremy Ashby of Azur, Chef Rafih Benjelloun of Imperial Fez, Chef Vishwesh Bhatt of SNACKBAR, Sheila Bowman of the Monterey Bay Aquarium's Seafood Watch, Chef Sean Brock of Husk, writer and producer Von Diaz, cookbook author and food writer Nathalie Dupree, Dr. Marcie Cohen Ferris, cookbook author and food writer John T. Edge, Chef Kelly English of Restaurant Iris, cookbook author Martha Foose, Georgia Organics, cookbook author and food writer Sandra Gutierrez, Dr. Jessica Harris, Chef Liz Hernandez of Arepa Mia, Chef Elizabeth Karmel, Chef Anthony Lamas of Serviche, cookbook author and food writer Rebecca Lang, Lodge Cast Iron and Mark Kelly, Chef Jiyeon Lee and Cody Taylor of Heirloom Barbecue, cookbook author and food writer Ronni Lundy, Chef Matt Neal of Neal's Deli (and those incredible biscuits!), cookbook author and food writer Nancie McDermott, soul food scholar Adrian E. Miller, Chef Irv Miller, Carrie Morris of Callie's Biscuits, Joyce Pinson of Friends Drift Inn Farm, cookbook author and food writer Kathleen Purvis, cookbook author and food writer John Taylor, Chef Anne Quatrano of Bacchanalia, Chef Drew Robinson of Jim 'N Nick's, Shepherd Craig Rogers, Chef Nico Romo of NICO, Chef Stephen Satterfield of Miller Union, Chef Chris Shepherd of Underbelly, Chef Jason Stanhope of FIG, Chef Frank Stitt, Chef Bill Smith of Crook's Corner, the Southern Foodways Alliance, cookbook author and food writer Nicole Taylor, Tuskegee University and Dr. Walter Hill, USA Rice, and Whole Foods Market with regional marketing director Cheryl Galway, who has been a tremendous supporter from the very beginning.

This book would not be possible without the kind and generous people who let me into their lives to tell their stories and those of their communities: Anson Mills with Glenn Roberts, Hal Hanvey, and Catherine Shopfer, Dave Bellanger of Clammer Dave's Sustainable Gourmet, the Davis and Woodford families of Bluewater Creek Farm, the wonderful and beautiful Natalie Chanin, Amy C. Evans and Sofia, Farmer's Daughter Preserves with April McGreger, Foggy Ridge Cider and Diane Flynt, Gilliard Farms with Mathew Raiford and Jovan Sage, Manchester Farms with Brittney and Matt Miller, Many Fold Farm with Ross and Rebecca Williams, Metro Atlanta Urban Farm with CEO Bobby L. Wilson, Muddy Pond Sorghum and the Guenther family, Newsom's Country Hams with Nancy Mahaffey, Joe Patti Seafood Market, Laura Patricia Ramirez of Tortillería y Taquería Ramírez, Richard Farms with Christian and Julie Richard, the Texas Vietnamese community, Robb Walsh, and lastly, White Oak Pastures and my dear friends, the Harris family.

Thanks to my agency—the Lisa Ekus Group with Sally Ekus, Jaimee Constantine, and Sara Pokorny. Thank you for your continuous efforts and unparalleled encouragement.

None of this would have been possible without Cynthia Morrow Kitchel seeing the possibilities of my dream. Thanks to the great team at HMH including Breanne Somner and Jessica Gilo for their valuable publicity and marketing support, the beautiful work of art director Rachel Newborn, and my editor, Stephanie Fletcher, for helping me shape these stories, craft my words, and make my dream a reality.

INDEX

Page numbers in *italics* indicate illustrations

Peppers. *See also* Chile(s);
  Jalapeño(s)
  in Chicken Chopped Salad,
    Latin Fried, 172–173
  in Chicken Stew, West
    African, with Collard
    Greens and Peanuts, 207–
    209, *208*
  chopping, 209
  in Chow Chow, 214
  in Romesco Sauce, Peanut,
    118–120, *119*
Pho Bin Trailer, Houston, Texas,
  82
Pickled
  Chow Chow, 214
  Onions, 91, 92
Pie(s)
  Chocolate Chess, 280, *281*
  French Pie Pastry, 282–283
  Pimento Cheese Tomato-
    Herb, 31–32, *33*
Pigs, heritage breeds of, 116
Pilaf, Winter Squash and Herb
  Rice, Stovetop, *62*, 63
Pimento Cheese Tomato-Herb
  Pie, 31–32, *33*
Pinson, Joyce, 212
Pluff mud (plough mud), 188
Pork. *See also* Bacon; Ham;
  Sausage
  brining, 164
  Carnitas Nachos, 133
  Chops, Cuban-Style, with
    Mojo Sauce, 143
  from heritage breeds, 116
  Ribs, Rainy-Day, *134*, 135, *136*
  Shoulder, Spicy North
    Carolina, 138–139
  Soup Beans with Chow Chow,
    Kentucky, 212–214, *213*
  Tenderloin, Char Siu,
    Mississippi-Style, 130–
    132, *131*
  tenderloin, removing silver
    skin, 132
Potato(es)
  in Catfish Mulldown, 203

in Cioppino, Gulf Coast, 94, *95*
Greek Crispy Lemon-Herb, 58
Oyster Stew with, Country-
  Style, 198, *199*
in Shrimp and Roasted Corn
  Chowder, *200*, 201–202
in Sugar Cake, Moravian,
  255–257, *256*
Yukon Gold and Butternut
  Squash Colcannon, 59
Pound Cake, Buttermilk, with
  Roasted Strawberries,
  290–291
Preserves
  Chow Chow, 214
  Farmer's Daughter Brand
    Preserves, 54, 230, 232–
    235
  as Southern tradition, 230,
    233
Pudding
  Mexican Chocolate, with
    Bourbon Cream, *284*,
    285–286
  Sweet Potato Bread, with
    Peanut Streusel, 287
Pumpkin Seeds (Pepitas), in
  Chicken Posole Soup,
  204–206, *205*
Purvis, Kathleen, 242

Q

Quail
  eggs, 149, 150
  farming, 147151
  hunting, 146, 149
  Stuffed Roast, with
    Mushrooms, 182–183
Quatrano, Anne, 182

R

Raiford, Althea, 11, 12
Raiford, Matthew, 8, *10*, 11–12, *13*
Ranch Dressing, Salsa Buttermilk,
  173
Reusing, Andrea, 233

Ribs
  Beef, Glazed BBQ, 128–129
  Pork, Rainy-Day, *134*, 135, *136*
Rice
  and Broccoli Bake, Cheesy,
    68, 69
  Chicken Bog, Ginger, 210–211
  Creole, Grillades Stew with,
    216, 217–219
  cultivation in Louisiana,
    46–51, 162
  in jambalaya, 49
  Jambalaya, Chicken and
    Andouille, Weeknight,
    162
  Paella, Chicken and
    Butterbean, 169–171, *170*
  Pilaf, Winter Squash and
    Herb, Stovetop, *62*, 63
  Waffles, Crispy, 251
Richard, Christian and Julie,
  49–50
Richard Rice Farms, 49
Riviana Foods, 49
Roberts, Glenn, 224, 227–228
Robinson, Drew, 174
Rogers, Craig, 141
Rolls, Sweet, Dulce de Leche
  Pecan, 246–248, *247*
Romesco Sauce, Peanut, 118–120,
  119
Romo, Nico, 186, 188, 191
Rose, Stephen, 295
Rub, Sweet Heat, 138
Rutledge, Sarah, 207

S

Sage, Jovan, 8, *10*, 11
Salad(s). *See also* Slaw
  Chicken Chopped, Latin Fried,
    172–173
  Chicken Larb with Georgia
    Peanuts, 158, *159*
Salad Dressing
  Feta-Buttermilk and Arugula,
    Roast Beets with, 23–25,
    24